New Approaches to Discourse and Business
Communication

New Approaches to Discourse and Business Communication

Edited by

Fernando Ramallo

Anxo M. Lorenzo Suárez

Xoán Paulo Rodríguez-Yáñez
Faculty of Philology and Translation, University of Vigo, Spain

and

Piotr Cap
Institute of English, University of Łódź and University of Economy in Bydgoszcz, Poland

palgrave
macmillan

First published 2009 by
PALGRAVE MACMILLAN

Palgrave Macmillan in the UK is an imprint of Macmillan Publishers Limited,
registered in England, company number 785998, of Houndmills, Basingstoke,
Hampshire RG21 6XS.

Palgrave Macmillan in the US is a division of St Martin's Press LLC,
175 Fifth Avenue, New York, NY 10010.

Palgrave Macmillan is the global academic imprint of the above companies
and has companies and representatives throughout the world.

Palgrave® and Macmillan® are registered trademarks in the United States,
the United Kingdom, Europe and other countries.

ISBN-13: 978-1-4039-4736-9 hardback

This book is printed on paper suitable for recycling and made from fully
managed and sustained forest sources. Logging, pulping and manufacturing
processes are expected to conform to the environmental regulations of the
country of origin.

A catalogue record for this book is available from the British Library.

A catalog record for this book is available from the Library of Congress.

10   9   8   7   6   5   4   3   2   1
18   17   16   15   14   13   12   11   10   09

Printed and bound in Great Britain by
CPI Antony Rowe, Chippenham and Eastbourne

Contents

v

List of Tables, Figures and Images

Tables

Figures

Images

Acknowledgements

The editors would like to thank Eloi Gestido de la Torre for his help with the index. We are also grateful to Melanie Blair and Priyanka Pathak of Palgrave Macmillan for their encouragement and support.

Notes on the Contributors

Fabienne Alvarez is an Assistant Professor of Business and Management at the University of Antilles and Guyane in Guadeloupe. Her research interests and publications relate to the behavioural impacts of managerial innovation and change processes, critical discourse analysis, organization and human resources management in small companies. Her recent publications include: 'L'interaction chercheur–sujets organisationnels: du discours au sens' (2007, with Fabienne Oriot, *Sciences du Management*); 'Production de discours managérial et changement organisationnel' (2006, *Revue Entreprise et Histoire*); and 'A New Paradigm for Qualitative Investigations: towards an Integrative Model for Evoking Change' (2004, with Christopher Ann Easley, *The Organizational Development Journal*).

Leila Barbara is Full Professor of Linguistics in the Pontifical Catholic University of São Paulo (PUC-SP) and is senior researcher of the Brazilian council of CNPq (The National Scientific and Technological Research Council). Her research interests are mainly discourse analysis of language at work in Brazil and Portuguese grammar, based on systemic functional theory and making use of corpus linguistics tools.

Tony Berber Sardinha received his PhD from the University of Liverpool and he is Professor of Applied Linguistics at the Pontifical Catholic University of São Paulo (PUC-SP). His main interests are corpus linguistics, systemic functional linguistics, discourse analysis, metaphor, translation, computer programming and language teaching.

Paul Bick is a PhD candidate in cultural anthropology at the University of Illinois at Chicago. His research interests include language and capitalism, political ecology, and alternative resistance in the postcolony. His recent publications include 'Swoosh Identity: Recontextualizations in Haiti and Romania' (2007, with Sorina Chiper, *Visual Communication*).

Sonia Bittencourt Silveira is Associate Professor at the Federal University at Juiz de Fora (Minas Gerais), with an MA in letters and linguistics

(1976), PhD in letters and linguistics (1998) and postdoctoral studies in discursive psychology (2007). She has researched in recent years in applied linguistics, with an emphasis on identity and social interaction, categorization procedures and positioning.

Attila Bruni is a researcher at the Department of Sociology and Social Research of the Faculty of Sociology of Trento University, where he teaches sociology of technological phenomena.

His last book in English is *Gender and Entrepreneurship: an Ethnographic Approach* (2005, with Silvia Gherardi and Barbara Poggio).

Marcel Burger teaches in the field of discourse analysis and communication and media at the Faculty of Arts of the University of Lausanne and at the Institute of Journalism and Communication of the University of Neuchâtel. His main research interests include the construction of identity in media and political discourse. Besides several papers in French and English, he has published *Les Manifestes. Paroles de combat. De Marx à Breton* (2002). He is also a contributor and the editor of *L'analyse linguistique des discours des médias. Entre sciences du langage et sciences de la communication* (2008), *Argumentation et communication dans les médias* (2005) and *Tourist Communication. Discursive Approaches to Identity and Otherness* (2004).

Piotr Cap is Full Professor and Head of the Department of Pragmatics at the University of Łódź. He has published books and papers in the fields of linguistic pragmatics, political linguistics, language of the media and business communication. A Fulbright Fellow at the University of California, Berkeley and Boston University, he has been invited to lecture at several American and European universities.

Paulo Cortes Gago is Associate Professor at the Federal University at Juiz de Fora (Minas Gerais), with an MA in applied linguistics (1997) and a PhD in letters and linguistics (2002). He teaches undergraduate courses in linguistics and Portuguese language, and his research focuses on language and social interaction with a special interest in institutional discourse. In recent years, he has dedicated his work to mediation interaction and third-party intervention in conflict situations in judicial and parajudicial settings.

Norman Fairclough is Emeritus Professor at Lancaster University, and an Emeritus Fellow at the Lancaster Institute for Advanced Studies.

His most recent books are *Analysing Discourse: Textual Analysis for Social Research* (2003) and *Language and Globalization* (2006).

José Roberto Gomes da Silva is Associate Professor in the Business School at the Pontifical Catholic University of Rio de Janeiro. A former consultant for IBM, he is currently involved with human resource management for different Brazilian organizations. He is author of 'Communication and the reconstruction of identities in the context of organizational change in Brazil' (2004) and co-author of 'Organizational change and the meaning of time' (2007, with Ursula Wetzel, *Brazilian Administration Review*).

Carlos A.M. Gouveia holds a PhD in applied linguistics and he is an Assistant Professor at the Department of English (Faculty of Letters, University of Lisbon) and a researcher at ILTEC, Instituto de Linguística Teórica e Computacional (Theoretical and Computational Linguistics Institute). His research areas are discourse analysis, critical discourse analysis and systemic functional grammar. His published work includes several articles and some books in these areas, both in Portuguese and in English.

Călin Gurău is Associate Professor in Marketing at GSCM–Montpellier Business School. His research interests are focused on high-technology marketing, international marketing and business communications. He has published more than 40 articles in academic peer-reviewed journals such as *Journal of Consumer Marketing*, *International Marketing Review*, *Journal of Marketing Communications* and *Journal of Communication Management*.

U-maporn Kardkarnklai is Lecturer of Intercultural Business Communication at Srinakharinwirot University in Bangkok. She has conducted research on Thai and Japanese discourse in business communication. Her special interests include workplace business communication, teaching of business English, and Thai–English translation. She is currently conducting needs analysis research on workplace oral communication of Thai graduates and students in the business English for international communication programme.

Maria do Carmo Leite de Oliveira is a Professor in the Department of Language Studies at the Catholic University at Rio de Janeiro. Since 1980, she has provided consulting services in organizational communication as part of interdisciplinary teams including specialists in business administration. She is co-editor (2005, with Barbara Hemais and Britt-Louise Gunnarson) of a volume on *Communication, Culture and Interaction in Organizational Contexts* (*Comunicação, cultura e interação em contextos organizacionais*), and co-author of 'Identity and personal/institutional relations: people and tragedy in a health customer service' (2006, *Discourse and Identity*).

Anxo M. Lorenzo Suárez has a PhD in Hispanic Linguistics from the Universitat Autònoma de Barcelona. He is Associate Professor of Galician Studies at the University of Vigo where he teaches and supervises research projects in Galician sociolinguistics, language policy and planning, and contact languages. He is co-editor of *Discourse and Enterprise* (2005) and author of several works about Galician sociolinguistics, language contact phenomena and language policy and planning.

Laura Lucia Parolin is post-doc at Milano-Bicocca University where she teaches information and communication technology. She has a PhD in information systems and organization from Trento University. She has research interests in practice base studies and is currently working on knowledge and organizational network topics. Her recent publications include: 'Design industria e artigianato nel settore legno ed arredo: un network di lavoro della conoscenza' (2008); 'Workplace studies. Tecnologia e interazione sociale nei contesti di lavoro' (2008, *Studi Organizzativi*); and 'Knowing in a system of fragmented knowledge' (2007, with Attila Bruni and Silvia Gherardi, *Mind, Culture and Activity*).

Yvonne McLaren-Hankin is a Lecturer in French at Heriot-Watt University in Edinburgh, where she teaches and supervises research projects in the areas of translating and interpreting, translation studies, text linguistics and pragmatics. She obtained her PhD in 2000 for her thesis entitled 'The discourse of company advertising in France and the United Kingdom: a contrastive textology', and has continued research since then on various aspects of business communication, focusing most notably on linguistic, textual and pragmatic features of business genres in English and French.

Fernando Ramallo is Lecturer of Linguistics at the University of Vigo. His main areas of interest include sociolinguistic methods and fieldwork, language planning and language policy, minority languages, media discourse and business discourse. His publications include 'The strategic discourse of multilevel marketing as a base for its reproduction' (2004, with Lourdes Juncal) and 'Business discourse in Spain' (2009, with Estrella Montolío Durán). He is co-editor of *Discourse and Enterprise* (2005) and founder and co-editor of the journals *Estudios de Sociolingüística* (2000–6, University of Vigo) and *Sociolinguistic Studies* (from 2007, Equinox).

Xoán Paulo Rodríguez-Yáñez teaches linguistics at the University of Vigo. He was co-organizer of the First and the Second International Symposium on Bilingualism (Vigo, 1997 and 2002), and co-editor of the proceedings volumes and of the book *Bilingualism and Education*, 2005. He is co-editor of *Discourse and Enterprise* (2005) and founder and co-editor of the journals *Estudios de Sociolingüística* (2000–6, University of Vigo) and *Sociolinguistic Studies* (from 2007, Equinox).

Beverly A. Sauer, PhD, is Professor of Management Communication at Georgetown's McDonough School of Business. Previously, she was Professor of Management in the Carey Business School of Johns Hopkins University and Associate Professor of English and Rhetoric at Carnegie Mellon University. Her book, *The Rhetoric of Risk: Technical Documentation in Hazardous Environments* (2003), was awarded the prize for best book in scientific and technical communication from the National Council of Teachers of English. Her research investigates the multimodal dimensions of risk communication in difficult cross-cultural and institutional contexts and her current project focuses on risk communication in South African coal mines.

Mauro T. B. Shobie has a PhD and MA in applied linguistics from the Pontifical Catholic University of São Paulo (PUC-SP), specialized in marketing administration and graduated in electronics engineering. Besides his professional work as a technical translator, he currently conducts research in the areas of business language and evaluation in language within the framework of systemic functional linguistics.

Dorien Van De Mieroop is a Lecturer at Lessius University College in Antwerp. Her research focuses mainly on identity construction, both in institutional interaction and in narratives of personal experience, and she has written a number of articles on this topic (e.g. in

Discourse and Society, Discourse Studies, Journal of Pragmatics, Pragmatics and *Research on Language and Social Interaction*). She is also interested in business communication, about which she has published mainly in Dutch, but also in English (e.g. in the *Journal of Business and Technical Communication*).

1
Discourse and Business Communication: an Introduction

Piotr Cap
University of Łódź and University of Economy in Bydgoszcz

Even a brief look at the contemporary publishing market in the broadly demarcated field of humanities and social sciences leads to the following question: what is it about discourse and business communication that makes it such a popular field of investigation? Is it the institutions, organizations, which give business discourse some common social relevance and thus grasp the attention of scientists working in different disciplines? Or is it, as Grant and Iedema (2005) or Braecke et al. (2006) would say, the very *discourse*, a medium which, once used in an institutional or commercial setting, starts manifesting some special and uniquely interesting features worth noting in their own right?

While looking for the definitive answer (if ever possible) would entail a massive ethnographic survey among the researchers – a project which, to the best of my knowledge, has never been attempted – a more inviting alternative is to take these questions as prompts for explaining the generic complexity and methodological heterogeneity of business discourse. Defining business discourse, its hallmarks, domains, methodologies as well as types of data investigated, is a necessary prerequisite for specifying what kind of input can be expected from a volume such as this one, and what the apparent constraints are on providing a genuinely fresh contribution to the field, which has already been extensively explored.

The scene of business discourse: analytic advantages and hazards[1]

Business discourse has its roots in the LSP (language for specific purposes) studies (Johns, 1986) and even though the last two decades have seen its detachment from the applied, prescriptive tradition (Louhiala-Salminen, 2002; Bargiela-Chiappini et al., 2007), the amount and diversity of research that has accumulated lead to understanding business discourse in necessarily broad terms. Bargiela-Chiappini et al.'s (2007: 3) definition essentializes this perception: 'Business discourse is *all about* how people communicate using *talk or writing* in *commercial organizations* in order *to get their work done*' [italics mine]. Such a broad view of the field, shared indeed by most analysts as well as captured in the aims and scope of the most influential in-field periodicals (*Business Communication Quarterly*, *Journal of Business Communication*, etc.) has its advantages and disadvantages – both affecting any further additions to the existing literature. On the one hand, it promotes interdisciplinary and inter-generic dialogue, contributing to the explanatory power of the particular studies within their area of investigation. It produces an incentive to compare and contrast different genres and domains (negotiations, mediations, business meetings, professional presentations, (news) interviews, document design, business–customer communication, etc.), from a perspective that involves both oral and written modes of communication. Also, it delivers a stimulus to look at a vast array of different 'business' organizations, from industry, manufacturers and services, through broadcasting and the media, to schools and hospitals – as long as the analyst deems all of them commercial enterprises. Assuming the commercial denominator, the analyst overrides the rather unclear, and in my view unnecessary, distinction between 'business and the professions' (Boden, 1994). Lastly, the 'all-in' approach is advantageous when it comes to analysing the power factor underlying the ways in which business people 'get their work done'. Here, the explanatory power of studies profits substantially from the combination of methods utilized by a number of pragmatics-related schools which consider (business) discourse a social action, an action situated within a broad context of power inequalities, an action reflecting the discourse reality just as much as being constitutive of a new reality, finally, an action aimed at accomplishing the maximum of real-life benefits, at the lowest (social) cost possible. Indeed, many studies in business discourse (Tannen, 1995; Holmes, 2000; Yeung, 2004; Vine, 2004, to name but a few) are, methodologically, blends of various forms of critical scholarship, most notably critical linguistics (CL; pioneered by Fowler 1979), systemic functional linguistics (SFL; works following the agenda set out in Halliday, 1985) and, most recently, critical discourse analysis (CDA; see e.g. Fairclough, 1995; Wodak and Chilton, 2005). Of course, research in power relations quite naturally invites numerous grounds of comparison (across genres, across organization types, across modes of communication), thus subsuming all the analytic stimuli and research avenues discussed above. Altogether then, we arrive at an immense body of theory as well as countless possibilities of linking multiple models/methods with multiple fields of application. This, as I said before, clearly enhances the explanatory power of individual studies within their area of investigation. One can think of, say, an analysis of Burger King's written job advertisements which is at the same time qualitative from the critical standpoint and quantitative-qualitative according to the document design tradition, which is formally structural and in this sense self-contained but at the same time (indirectly) informed by contrastive research in similar ads placed by McDonald's or Wendy's, which draws upon comparison of all the many ways, involving both written and spoken modes of communication, in which the company promotes its image as a reliable and attractive employer.

The question remains: to what extent is such a study representative of the genre it addresses and the methods it utilizes? This concern leads to another, more general one. Rich in theoretical and empirical input as such analyses are at the level of each particular domain of investigation, do they really contribute to crystallization of the concept of business discourse, so it could yield an organized agenda for further research? Paradoxically, the prevailing 'all-in' approach is opening up new and exciting possibilities of study, while at the same time constraining its scientific validity. Take an example that brings together research data, genre analysis and the intercultural perspective. In the contemporary world of business organizations, communication often occurs across national borders between people who do not share the same culture. This causes many business discourse analysts working on a generic description of a specific form of business communication (for instance, the business meeting; see e.g. Yamada, 1990, 2002) to collect data from different organizations based in different countries (and cultures), in order to work out a conceptual compromise on the definition, scope and characteristics of the genre (Sarangi and Roberts, 1999). Unfortunately, results are often disappointing because access to some of these organizations can be more difficult than to others, let alone confidentiality constraints on publishing the data, which differ not only across organization types, but also across countries (Bargiela-Chiappini et al., 2003; Spencer-Oatey and Franklin, 2009). In response to such limitations, researchers frequently complement their studies with simulated data (i.e. collected from 'participants' in a 'business setting', who receive instructions to play a specific role; see e.g. Planken, 2002), but then, again, there is no guarantee that the simulated data mirror the authentic material that could not be accessed. In this sense, the use of simulated data can produce a mismatch between analytic expectations and the actual-time and -place functions of a business discourse, the kind of flaw anticipated (indirectly) as early as 1988 by scholars working in the applied tradition (Williams, 1988).[2]

The problems that affect crystallization of the core concept of business discourse, as a prerequisite for defining its research agenda, lie also in the understandable disproportion between the (vast) amount of literature devoted to genres and sub-genres no longer promising a great deal in terms of characterizing or even typifying the principal field (i.e. 'business discourse'), and a much smaller coverage of those genres or other-than-generic factors which indeed make such a promise – for, apparently, many years to come. Consider the extensive research on negotiation, originally management-based and normative (e.g. Putnam and Jones, 1982; Donohue and Diez, 1985), and later essentially language-based (e.g. Firth, 1995; Ehlich and Wagner, 1995). The focus of these works is primarily on the spoken mode of communication and analytic tools are applied and advocated accordingly, with a clear preference for conversation analysis (Firth, 1995). On the other hand, research in negotiations has yet to fully accommodate the rapidly growing importance of (mostly written) electronic communication – e-mail in particular (Louhiala-Salminen et al., 2005) – which goes a long way towards essentializing the major characteristics of the genre not only for today, but, conceivably, for the future as well. From this point, there is only a step to accept that the concept of 'business discourse' in general is likely to be viewed decreasingly through its genre-based typology and increasingly through its principal method of communication, which will continue to demonstrate some stable and universal characteristics (structural efficiency, prevalence of content over form, flexibility with speed/frequency/place of interaction) – regardless of the genre. Yet, as of today, there does not seem to be enough literature that could warrant a fast way of defining business discourse along these lines and, indeed, it is the highly dynamic process of technological change that takes a lot of 'blame' for obstructing a clear vision of our research agenda.

Does all this mean that we are currently unable to capture and highlight any regularities in business discourse that could successfully stand the test of time, thus indicating ways in which research methods could be systematized for the benefit of future studies? There seem to be some optimistic prospects, after all.

Towards organizing business discourse studies: representation and interaction

Bargiela-Chiappini et al. (2007: 3) see the scope of business discourse studies as a vast area of research aimed at 'telling us how people in business organizations achieve their *organizational* and *personal* goals using language' [italics mine]. While it is difficult to say from the subsequent argument whether such has been the intention of the authors, this postulate invites two levels from which business discourse could be looked at. One is the global conceptual level, which involves *representation* of the organization, i.e. all the many mutually coherent ways in which the organization builds up its image and identity whereby it is recognized and distinguished from the market competition. Studying these ways can range from an analysis of advertising leaflets and brochures, to fully fledged mediatized communication, such as press releases or broadcast business speeches in which the speaker is the mouthpiece of the organization – all of which have been exemplified in the present book. The other level is inherently *interactional*, involving ways in which members of the organization accomplish smaller-size (personal) goals, such as promoting one's point of view, managing their floor in a business meeting, or (most notably in the case of managers) instructing other members on a course of action. Although we shall see that the two levels and, thus, two lines of research seem to attract different methods (a much-promising factor in terms of defining the division of analytic labour), they still feed into each other in a manner that warrants an extensive coverage of the field. The interactional line starts with the very tiniest discourse chunks responsible for enacting micro- and personal goals, and ends where the speaker's or writer's act of communication constitutes both a 'personal move' and a recognizable contribution to the construal of the organization as a whole (viz. conflict-softening strategies pursued in a company by its Thai and Japanese members, as described in Kardkarnklai's chapter in this collection). The representation line takes it from there, extending the scope of analysis towards the description of complex, interdependent, cognitive–pragmatic strategies by means of which the organization enacts its image and identity.

The proposed distinction is not merely a result of pondering upon the contents of Bargiela-Chiappini et al.'s postulate, but, more importantly, a tentative attempt to respond typologically as well as methodologically, to the evolution of business discourse studies observed over the last decade or so (one might want to look at Candlin and Gotti (2004), Gouveia et al. (2004), Trosborg and Jorgensen (2005), etc. as attempts to balance the two research trends on a general plane, but there are further publications which take up individual issues from either a 'representational' or 'interactional' standpoint – just compare Iedema et al. (2003) with Nickerson (2000)). The important thing is that, as has been mentioned before, the commitment to one of the two lines of research means, essentially, a commitment to a specific set of apparatuses of analysis. Thus we have, for instance, cognitive linguistics, frame semantics, critical approaches (informed by political research) or cognitive pragmatics as viable handles on the issues of representation, and discourse analysis, conversation analysis, corpus linguistics and societal pragmatics as instruments to account for the interactional phenomena. And although the above breakdown involves inevitable simplifications, it may be sketching some potentially useful ways in which to organize research in business discourse according to its focus and level of analysis.

Organization of the volume and the contributions

That said, we can move to the structure of this collection and an overview of the chapters. There are, first, eight chapters which deal with issues of general representation, followed eventually by five contributions whose focus is on various kinds of interaction within the organization. In between, however, there are two chapters (Kardkarnklai; Gago and Silveira) which bind together the two groups of texts, by offering insights into interactional strategies and behaviours as important in the context of the organization's global image. Altogether, the chapters draw upon an extensive spectrum of genres and, generally, ways of 'doing' business discourse (business letters, political addresses, academic tests, advertising, online communication, intercultural negotiations, job interviews, press releases, computer-mediated communication, etc.) in different countries and cultures, studying both oral and written aspects of communication, in the light of the multiple models and theories as outlined in the previous section.

The first two chapters, by Norman Fairclough and Carlos Gouveia respectively, demonstrate the most general focus, discussing issues of organizational identity and culture in the broad contexts of political economy and developments in theories of social change. Close already in their methodological fit, they show further similarities on empirical grounds, addressing and analysing fragments of texts related to e-culture in business settings. A distinctive characteristic of Fairclough's chapter is his proposal for a refined version of transdisciplinary dialogue between research in political economy and the strategic (as opposed to ideological and rhetorical) critique of discourse. On the other hand, Gouveia's approach is more from the side of the discourse itself, and leads to the question of how the growing hybridization of discourses, genres and styles (encouraged by e-culture and, specifically, computer-mediated communication) influences the perception of discourse as a facet of social change as well as of social and institutional identity.

The remaining contributions in the 'representation' part are a bit less preoccupied with methodological *disputes* (though they still describe and opt for preferred methods) and their theoretical underpinnings, and more focused on either specific genres or organization types. Mauro Sobhie places his critical lens on advertising brochures and analyses them in terms of four stages of company–customer interaction: presentation of the brochure, presentation of product or service, legitimization, and request for contact. In his argument, he not only provides adequate evidence for the organization's image being construed through a continual feed of updates, but also points to SFL and some later, more cognitively oriented approaches, as feasible groundworks to account for this dynamic process.

The theme of 'advertising' is continued by Paul Bick, yet his chapter offers an interesting and apparently provocative change of perspective. Exploring the issue of the corporate identity of McDonald's, Bick concentrates on attempts, by *Adbusters* magazine, at deconstructing this identity in a series of negative advertising strategies. His particular interest is in the existing 'community of ideology' that unites McDonald's and its customers, and the organized, discourse-dependent, strategic ways in which to 'extract' the customer from this community.

The next three chapters, by Dorien Van de Mieroop, Yvonne McLaren-Hankin and Călin Gurău, and Marcel Burger, are all examples of data-driven search for methods that would suit the macro analysis of representation of the organization in the most systematic manner possible. In addition, the latter two show common interest in (the ways of researching) mediatized business communication. Van de Mieroop, who works with a corpus of 40 business speeches enacting a company's institutional identity, opts for an eclectic, intrinsically complementary, qualitative–quantitative approach which uses frame and cognitive semantics and pragmatics as initiators of analysis, accompanied by corpus methods which play the role of verification tools. This analytic stance is apparently shared by McLaren-Hankin and Gurău, who analyse ways in which reputation of a pharmaceutical company is created, first, through the company's own press releases, and second, through independent articles appearing in the British national press. The naturally varying representations and points of view are, McLaren-Hankin and Gurău claim, best captured within the complex methodology of frames and patterns of cognition, which, however, will still need interpretive complementation from more formalized approaches. While there is no denial of such a conviction in Burger's chapter on the French-language television debates, this contribution comes in an even more evident contact with McLaren-Hankin and Gurău's text in its follow-up on a twofold role of the media in general. In Burger's view, the media have to be responsible for the construction of institutional identity, simply because they are anchored in the public sphere. But at the same time, they are economically constrained enterprises, which often causes them to reshape, reformulate or, at worst, distort information so it constitutes the most efficient way to 'do business' – a cynical but accurate conclusion, yet hardly facilitating the job of the analyst.

The objectivity factor raised in Burger is further addressed by Piotr Cap, whose contribution on persuasive properties of legal language constitutes, in a sense, a *meta-theoretical coda* to the section on (researching) representation. His main question, informed by cognitive and pragmatic research, is the following: is there a link between a type of business discourse being investigated as well as the degree of expert knowledge that the discourse analyst has about it, and the methods that are employed in analysis? Using both his own and other analysts' work on a wide range of legal texts, Cap shows that there is indeed a link: legal discourses invite a combination of deductive and inductive approaches, which are adopted depending on the analyst's 'closeness' to each individual type under investigation.

As has been indicated earlier, in between the 'representation part' and the 'interaction part', there are two chapters, by U-maporn Kardkarnklai and Gago and Silveira, which show most explicitly how the two lines of research feed into each other, thus ensuring an extensive coverage of the field. Incidentally, both chapters arise from organizational settings which are potentially conflictual and in this sense they point to conflict studies as contributing 'upwards' to global issues of identity and image of the organization, and, at the same time, 'downwards' to the understanding of how conflicts are managed and resolved at the level of personal goals and aspirations of the organization members. All-importantly, both chapters make it clear that conflict management within an organization is equally crucial to the personal well-being of the members, and, in the longer run, to the reputation of the organization as a whole. Kardkarnklai illustrates this view in cross-cultural analysis of Thai–Japanese interactions in an international company, while Gago and Silveira look at *conflict talk* occurring in a public mediation institution in Brazil.

Next, and finally, come five chapters whose primary focus is on various forms of interaction between the organization members. Presenting the case study of a Brazilian company in the energy sector, Maria do Carmo Leite de Oliveira and José Roberto Gomes da Silva explore the model of so-called 'participative management', which involves recognition of the many discursive and behavioural ways in which members of the organization contribute to the 'collective construction of meaning' at different levels of interaction (employee vs management, employee vs employee, general meetings). The issue of intra-company relationships, reflected in as well as constructed through, discourse, is further investigated by Fabienne Alvarez. This time, however, the problem is tackled in a much heated context of organizational change. Looking at social consequences of a major company merger in the French health-care industry, Alvarez investigates strategies that could be used to legitimate and implement the change, thus winning support of clinicians towards the new arrangements. Some common themes, such as organizational and technological innovation, resound in the contribution by Attila Bruni and Laura Lucia Parolin, who discuss the role and potential benefits of teleconsulting in working out a medical diagnosis. They conclude that in order for any medical practitioner to make the most of this technique, he or she must be equipped with not merely professional knowledge, but also specific discursive skills. Lastly, there are two chapters which both deal with minimal units of interaction, yet of a different semiotic nature. Leila Barbara and Tony Berber Sardinha analyse the functionality of language 'chunks' in business meetings, studying such forms as collocations, lexical bundles and other recurrent lexical choices. The focus is on how fixed sequences of words contribute to role assignment and topic sequencing, which count among the most important of the meeting (discourse) procedures. Closing the entire volume is the chapter by Beverly Sauer, which enriches the material and keeps the reader's attention by offering a refreshingly visual perspective. Preoccupied with issues of power and race differences in a South African mining workplace, Sauer studies the gestures used by an Afrikaans-speaking trainer in pre-training interviews to disambiguate his ideas regarding the assignment of 'separate work-spaces' to workers, management and trainers. Combining an interest in spoken/written and visual modes of communication, and presenting an adequate body of data reflecting these apparently disparate but actually complementary modes, Sauer's contribution is a clear voice in favour of extending the semiotic scope of business discourse studies.

Notes

1. While accepting the fact that, unlike *business discourse, business communication* might once imply a pedagogical or vocational focus (Swales, 2000), I use the two terms interchangeably and without any applied orientation.
2. In 1988 Marian Williams published an article reporting on the relationship between the language used by native speakers of English in business meetings and the language taught by business English textbooks at that time for use in meetings. She analysed the language used in three meetings by a total of 12 native speakers of English and then compared this with the language taught for meetings in 30 English textbooks. *She found that there was almost no correspondence between the meetings and the textbooks and that the speakers' use of language was far more complex than the way in which it was represented for the student* (after Bargiela-Chiappini et al., 2007: 9, italics mine).

References

Bargiela-Chiappini, F., A.M. Bulow-Moller, C. Nickerson, G. Poncini and Y. Zhu (2003) 'Five perspectives on intercultural business communication', *Business Communication Quarterly*, 66 (3), 73–96.

Bargiela-Chiappini, F., C. Nickerson and B. Planken (2007) *Business Discourse* (Basingstoke, UK: Palgrave Macmillan).

Boden, D. (1994) *The Business of Talk: Organizations in Action* (Cambridge, UK: Polity).

Braecke, Ch., G. Jacobs, K. Pelsmaekers and T. van Hout (eds) (2006) *Lodz Papers in Pragmatics*, 2 (Special Issue on Discourse in Organizations).

Candlin, C.N. and M. Gotti (eds) (2004) *Intercultural Aspects of Specialized Communication* (Bern: Peter Lang).

Donohue, W.A. and M.E. Diez (1985) 'Directive use in negotiation interaction', *Communication Monographs*, 52, 305–18.

Ehlich, K. and J. Wagner (eds) (1995) *The Discourse of International Negotiations* (Berlin: Mouton de Gruyter).

Fairclough, N. (1995) *Critical Discourse Analysis: the Critical Study of Language* (London: Longman).

Firth, A. (ed.) (1995) *The Discourse of Negotiation: Studies of Language in the Workplace* (London: Pergamon).

Fowler, R. (1979) *Language and Control* (London: Routledge).

Grant, D. and R. Iedema (2005) 'Discourse analysis and the study of organizations', *Text*, 25 (1), 37–66.

Gouveia, C.A.M., C. Silvestre and L. Azuaga (eds) (2004) *Discourse, Communication and the Enterprise* (Lisbon: University of Lisbon Center for English Studies).

Halliday, M.A.K. (1985) *Spoken and Written Language* (Oxford: Oxford University Press).

Holmes, J. (2000) 'Women at work: Analysing women's talk in New Zealand workplaces', *Australian Review of Applied Linguistics*, 22 (2), 1–17.

Iedema, R., P. Degeling, J. Braithwaite and L. White (2003) 'It's an interesting conversation I'm hearing: the doctor as manager', *Organizations Studies*, 25 (1), 15–33.

Johns, T. (1986) 'Micro-concord: a language learner's research tool', *System*, 14 (2), 151–62.

Louhiala-Salminen, L. (2002) 'The fly's perspective: Discourse in the daily routine of a business manager', *English for Specific Purposes*, 21, 211–31.

Louhiala-Salminen, L., M.L. Charles and A. Kankaanranta (2005) 'English as a lingua franca in Nordic corporate mergers: Two case companies', *English for Specific Purposes*, 24 (4), 401–21.

Nickerson, C. (2000) *Playing the Corporate Language Game. An Investigation of the Genres and Discourse Strategies in English Used by Dutch Writers Working in Multinational Corporations* (Amsterdam: Rodopi).

Planken, B. (2002) *Face and Identity Management in Negotiation* (UB Nijmegen).

Putnam, L.L. and T.S. Jones (1982) 'The role of communication in bargaining', *Human Communication Research*, 8 (3), 262–80.

Sarangi, S. and C. Roberts (eds) (1999) *Talk, Work and Institutional Order. Discourse in Medical, Mediation and Management Settings* (Berlin: Mouton de Gruyter).

Spencer-Oatey, H. and P. Franklin (2009) *Intercultural Interaction: a Multidisciplinary Approach to Intercultural Communication* (Basingstoke, UK: Palgrave Macmillan).

Swales, J. (2000) 'Languages for Specific Purposes', *Annual Review of Applied Linguistics*, 20, 59–76.

Tannen, D. (1995) *Talking from 9 to 5: Women and Men at Work* (New York: Quill).

Trosborg, A. and P.E. Flyvholm Jorgensen (eds) (2005) *Business Discourse. Texts and Contexts* (Bern: Peter Lang).

Vine, B. (2004) *Getting Things Done at Work: the Discourse of Power in Workplace Interaction* (Amsterdam: Benjamins).

Williams, M. (1988) 'Language taught for meetings and language used in meetings: Is there anything in common?', *Applied Linguistics*, 9 (1), 45–58.

Wodak, R. and P. Chilton (eds) (2005) *A New Agenda in (Critical) Discourse Analysis: Theory, Methodology and Interdisciplinarity* (Amsterdam: Benjamins).

Yamada, H. (1990) 'Topic management and turn distributions in business meetings: American versus Japanese strategies', *Text*, 10, 271–95.

Yamada, H. (2002) *Different Games, Different Rules: Why Americans and Japanese Misunderstand Each Other* (Oxford: Oxford University Press).

Yeung, H.W.C. (2004) *Chinese Capitalism in a Global Era: Towards Hybrid Capitalism* (London: Routledge).

2

Critical Discourse Analysis and Change in Management Discourse and Ideology: a Transdisciplinary Approach to Strategic Critique

Norman Fairclough
Lancaster University, United Kingdom

2.1 Introduction

My objective in this contribution is to develop a particular approach to interdisciplinary research involving critical discourse analysis (henceforth CDA) on the one hand and other disciplinary areas and theories on the other, which I call 'transdisciplinary'. A transdisciplinary approach brings into focus ways in which theories, methodologies, disciplines, paradigms, traditions, etc. might be enhanced and developed through dialogue with others in interdisciplinary research – 'how a dialogue between two disciplines or frameworks may lead to a development of both through a process of each internally appropriating the logic of the other as a resource for its own development' (Chiapello and Fairclough, 2002). I shall refer to the transdisciplinary dialogue between CDA and the New Sociology of Capitalism initiated in the Chiapello and Fairclough paper, but I shall extend it by linking it with the dialogue between CDA and a particular version of political economy initiated in Jessop (2002).

My purpose in doing so is to argue on the one hand that changes in management and organization are productively researched from the perspective of strategies in Jessop's sense and strategic critique, and on the other hand that transdisciplinary dialogue between this version of political economy and CDA points the latter in the direction of a strategic (as opposed to both ideological and rhetorical) critique of discourse and of texts which better enables it to enhance and develop the discourse analytical element which is already present in Jessop's critique of political economy.

This is not a matter of eclectically grafting categories of one theory or method onto another, it is a matter of using the logic of another disciplinary area or theory as a resource for thinking in the development of the categories of one's own theory and methodology. For instance, categories such as 'strategy' (specifically, 'discursive strategy' – Wodak, 2001) and 'genre' already exist within CDA, it is a matter of drawing upon theorizations of strategy in work such as Jessop's in extending one's thinking about, theorization of, and methodological operationalization of such categories. I shall concretize the argument with some analysis of extracts from the same book which was used for illustrative purposes in Chiapello and Fairclough (2002) – a management 'guru' text by Rosabeth Moss Kanter (Kanter, 2001).

2.2   Discourse in social research on change

My particular area of concern both in this chapter and in my recent research more generally is with discourse as an element or 'moment' of processes of social change, how discourse figures within such processes in relation to other elements or moments, and what constitutive or performative effects discourse may have, under what conditions, upon these other (non-discursive) elements or moments. This broad concern with discourse as a facet of social change is present in a great deal of contemporary social research. In attempting to open up transdisciplinary dialogue between CDA and such research one is therefore usually in the position of continuing a dialogue which is already going on. There are of course many theories and methods which can be subsumed under 'discourse analysis', and even 'critical discourse analysis'.

The interest of the particular version of CDA I now work with in transdisciplinary dialogue is on the one hand in convincing colleagues in other areas and fields that it is better equipped to help them enrich the discourse analytical aspect of their research than other versions of (C)DA, and on the other hand to continuously develop its capacity to contribute to social research through rethinking its theoretical categories and methodologies in transdisciplinary dialogue with others.

Let me frame the more focused attention to the New Sociology of Capitalism and Jessop's political economy below with some rather summary comments from the perspective of my version of CDA on the strengths and limitations of the ways in which this and some other work in social research addresses discourse. Bourdieu and Wacquant, in a series of popular and politically oriented interventions (2001), have presented neo-liberalism as a political project or strategy oriented to removing obstacles to the full implementation of the new 'global economy'. Neo-liberal discourse is a significant resource in the pursuit of this strategy – they point to the 'performative power' of the 'new planetary vulgate', its power to 'bring into being the very realities it describes', its power at the same time to make a contingent set of policy choices appear to be a matter of inexorable and irreversible world change.

This work is remarkable in highlighting the absolute importance of discourse and language in the transformations of 'globalization' and the new capitalism, but its impact is somewhat lessened because they do not have the analytical resources to show *how* the slippage between description and creation ('bringing into being') is pervasively effected in contemporary policy and other texts, or *how* the contingent is textually construed as necessary. Their account of the 'new planetary vulgate' goes no further than a list of keywords.

Jessop (2002) presents CDA as one of a number of central theoretical elements out of which he has developed his own version of political economy. More recently he has begun to use the term 'cultural political economy', partly to capture the theoretical and methodological integration of discourse. One can get a sense of how discourse figures in cultural political economy from his discussion of crisis. He views structural change in moments of crisis as mediated by hegemonic struggle between strategies which have a partly semiotic character – discourses which project imaginaries for a new 'fix' in the co-regulation of regimes of accumulation and political regimes. The development, dissemination and instantiation/materialization of strategies are partly semiotic processes.

This explicit dialogue with CDA on the part of a major theorist of the state is a significant advance for transdisciplinary research. But as in much social theory, discourse in the abstract sense (or what I call below 'semiosis', signification as a moment of the social in a general sense) is reduced to particular discourses, i.e. to merely matters of representation. Yet discourse in the abstract sense subsumes processes of acting, relating and identifying as well as processes of representing, and therefore other categories are needed in addition to 'discourses' – certainly 'genres' (ways of acting and relating), and I would suggest 'styles' (ways of being, identities), and possibly others. These categories are essential for accounts of social change. For example, the success of the strategies and associated discourses Jessop refers to depends upon the powers of dissemination and recontextualization of social agents, which semiotically includes powers with respect to genres, powers for instance with respect to genres of media and mediation such as those of advertising, as well as with respect to styles.

Another extremely fruitful dialogue between discourse analysis and political economy is to be found in Harvey's work (especially Harvey, 1996). Harvey's main contribution is to elaborate the dialectics of discourse – the dialectical relations between discourse and other elements or moments of the social. I draw upon this elaboration in the brief presentation below of a (dialectical–relational) version of CDA. It is striking by contrast that in a recent study of the 'new imperialism' (i.e. US imperialism) – which is admittedly a series of lectures directed at a non-specialist audience – Harvey says nothing about discourse or the dialectics of discourse, but does discuss the 'rhetoric' of the new imperialism. I am sure that Harvey would recognize a difference between discourse and rhetoric, and there is a distinction drawn between them in Jessop's book. But it is noteworthy that it often seems somewhat arbitrary whether semiosis is addressed as discourse or as rhetoric in social research, as if these were one and the same thing. I shall differentiate them below.

Boltanski and Chiapello (1999) argue, on the basis on a comparative analysis of corpora of management studies texts from the 1960s and 1990s, that the historical transformations of capitalism entail changes in 'the spirit of capitalism', the ideology which justifies people's commitment to it. The spirit of capitalism both legitimizes and constrains the process of accumulation. It indicates (a) what is 'stimulating' (liberating, etc.) about capitalism; (b) what forms of security it offers, (c) what is just or fair about it. A new spirit of capitalism began to emerge with the recent transformations of capitalism in the 1980s, developing through a selective appropriation of elements of the 1960s–1970s critique of its predecessor, specifically the critique of bureaucracy and hierarchy. The 'fairness' dimension of the spirit of capitalism is explicated through the category of 'justificatory regime' (*cité* in French).

Justificatory regimes can be specified in terms of (a) a principle of equivalence or 'general standard' according to which all relevant actions, things and persons can be evaluated; (b) a state of greatness – the 'great one' embodies the regime's values, the 'small one' lacks them; (c) a format of investment, linking greatness to sacrifice, (d) a paradigmatic test which best reveals a person's greatness. Several justificatory regimes coexist in a spirit of capitalism, and the new spirit of capitalism includes a new 'Project-oriented' justificatory regime appropriate to organization in terms of networks (in which activity is structured around short-term projects involving shifting networks) which is combined especially with the pre-existing 'inspirational' regime. The Project-oriented regime's equivalency principle includes project initiation and networking, its state of smallness includes reliance on roots, rigidity, inability to get involved, its state of greatness includes adaptability, flexibility, sincerity in face-to-face interaction, capacity to generate enthusiasm, its format of investment is readiness to sacrifice one's private life and long-term plans for the company, its paradigmatic test is ability to move from project to project.

Although the Boltanski and Chiapello study is based upon analysis of bodies of texts, it is mainly a limited form of thematic analysis centred upon identifying pre-established categories (including the justificatory regimes). It is thus typical of much social research in having rich textual data from which it derives rather limited research results. One objective of Chiapello and Fairclough (2002) was to explore how a transdiscipinary dialogue between CDA and the New Sociology of Capitalism might help the latter to enrich its analysis of the processes and change it is concerned with in the textual materials in its research base. We approached this by conceptualizing a 'spirit of capitalism' in CDA terms as an order of discourse, whose justificatory regimes are *Discourses* (with a big 'd'), realized as articulations of discourses (with a small 'd'), and dialectically enacted in 'action models' (e.g. tests) which are in part genres, and inculcated the styles of the 'great' and 'small' ones.

In these various cases, then, transdisciplinarity is a matter of developing a dialogue which already exists between discourse and text analysis and other forms of analysis with a view to enhancing analysis of discourse and text as a facet of social analysis, but also with a view to theoretically and methodologically enhancing CDA.

2.3   Critical discourse analysis

To proceed with the main concerns of the chapter, I need to give a brief and partial account of the version of CDA which I am currently working with. In the interests of space I simply give a summary of a number of its key features (see Chouliaraki and Fairclough, 1999; Fairclough, 2003; Fairclough et al., 2004). Note that point 10 incorporates Jessop's perspective on strategy.

1. Discourse in the abstract sense (using 'semiosis' instead avoids the common confusion between different senses of 'discourse', see

Fairclough et al., 2004) is an element of all social processes, though social processes are not simply discourse.

2. The relationship between abstract social structures and concrete social events is mediated by social practices, relatively stabilized forms of social activity.

3. Each has a semiotic element: languages (social structures), orders of discourse (social practices), texts broadly understood (social events).

4. Social practices are constituted as articulations of dialectically related elements (or 'moments') including semiosis. These are different (and they cannot for instance all be reduced to semiosis as some versions of discourse theory claim), but not discrete: in Harvey's dialectical terminology, semiosis internalizes and is internalized in other elements (Harvey, 1996).

5. Semiosis figures in three main ways in social practices: discourses (ways of representing), genres (ways of (inter)acting), styles (ways of being – identities).

6. Social practices are articulated into networks which constitute social fields, institutions and organizations. Orders of discourse are more exactly the semiotic facet of such networks.

7. An order of discourse is a social structuring of semiotic difference, which can be seen to be constituted as a relatively stable articulation of discourses, genres and styles.

8. Social change includes change in social structures, social practices and social events.

9. Change in social practices affects how elements are articulated together in practices, how practices are articulated together in networks, and how discourses, genres and styles are articulated together in orders of discourse.

10. A crisis in a state, social field or organization opens up hegemonic struggle between the strategies for change of different groups of social agents. Differences between strategies are partly discursive – narratives, imaginaries (projective discourses) for new 'fixes', etc.

11. In the implementation of a strategy for change which becomes hegemonic, there is a dialectic through which new discourses may be enacted as new ways of (inter)acting including genres, inculcated as new ways of being including styles, as well as materialized in for example new ways of structuring space. This operates through a dissemination across structural and scalar boundaries which 'recontextualizes' new discourses.

12. One aim of CDA is strategic (as well as ideological and rhetorical) critique – critique of how discourse figures in the development, dissemination and implementation of strategies for change.
13. CDA claims that analysis of social processes and change is productively carried down into detailed textual analysis. More detailed (including linguistic) analysis of texts is connected to broader social analysis by way of interdiscursive analysis of shifting articulations of genres, discourses, styles in texts.

2.4   Forms of critique

In point 12 above I referred to the contrast between strategic, ideological and rhetorical critique. These are all forms of 'negative critique' as opposed to 'positive critique' (the normative specification of more socially just, equitable, sustainable, etc. alternatives). The distinction between them can be formulated as follows:

- *Ideological critique*: critique of how a system of social relations is sustained through representations of a social order which are in contradiction with its realities.
- *Rhetorical critique*: critique of the subordination of considerations of truth and sound argumentation to the will to persuade.
- *Strategic critique*: critique of how discourse figures in the development, promotion and dissemination of the strategies for social change of particular groups of social agents, and in hegemonic struggle between strategies, and in the implementation of successful strategies.

As I shall show below, these forms of critique are not strictly alternatives in that the same text can be subjected to all three, but depending on one's research objectives one or other of them may be given primacy – and I shall be arguing here for the primacy of strategic critique – which determines not the presence or absence of the different forms of critique in analysis so much as the *relationship* between them.

I shall now concretize the issues raised above through analysis of extracts from Rosabeth Moss Kanter's book *Evolve! Succeeding in the Digital Culture of Tomorrow* (Kanter, 2001). I shall begin with an overall description of the book and then move to the particular extracts in focus.

The book is based upon an extensive body of research, yet it is not a research monograph. The relationship between the book and the research it is based upon is implied by Kanter's statement that 'The result of all this work is reflected in the lessons of this book.' It is in a broad sense a pedagogical book, directed at conveying 'lessons' about what Kanter calls 'e-culture' to a readership which is envisaged as mainly executives and managers. E-culture is explained as follows:

> The World Wide Web is both the stimulus for a new organizational culture (making it necessary) and a facilitator of that same culture (making it possible). I call that new way of working e-culture. E-culture defines the human side of the global information era, the heart and soul of the New Economy. People and organizations everywhere must evolve to embrace this business culture of tomorrow.

And the book is said to consist of:

> insider stories and lessons about effectiveness drawn from organizations at all stages of Net change. It describes role models and best practices: how life is lived and work gets done in companies that lead the pack. It tells cautionary tales; why change is fumbled or resisted in those that lag behind. And it includes practical conclusions that readers can use to ensure personal and business success in their own ventures and workplaces.

Part One ('Searching, Searching: the Challenge of Change'), comprising the first three chapters, develops the argument that

> e-culture derives from basic principles of community: shared identity, sharing of knowledge, and mutual contributions. Online, community is a metaphor. Offline, the spirit of community is required to implement the changes that the Internet makes possible ... the Web's hidden secret: that it provokes a shift towards more collaborative work relationships, ones that resemble open, inclusive communities more than they resemble secretive, hierarchical administrative bureaucracies.

Part Two defines 'the essence of e-effectiveness' and 'best practices in implementing e-culture principles', with chapters on 'strategy development as improvisational theatre', 'nurturing networks of partners', 'reconstructing the organisation as a community' (with 'flatter hierarchies, more fluid boundaries, more team oriented, and emphasis on process over structure'), and 'winning the battle to attract and retain the best talent'. Part Three is 'a practical guide to change', with chapters

on 'overcoming the common barriers and successfully implementing systemic change – a step-by-step practical roadmap', 'leadership
for change' (this is the chapter, Chapter 9, which I shall analyse
extracts from), and a final chapter which asks 'are we on the verge
of the next stage of social evolution – a great leap forward to shared
consciousness?'

The main extract from Chapter 9 which I shall analyse comes from
the beginning of the chapter. I have numbered the paragraphs:

Chapter 9: Leadership for Change: New Challenges and Enduring
Skills

'We must find the radicals, the true revolutionaries, and support them.'
Louis V. Gerstner, Jr., Chairman and CEO, IBM

To live with e-culture is to live with change. Not just isolated,
one-time, occasional changes, but ongoing, continuous, ubiquitous,
never-finished change. Change as a condition of existence... [1]

Wait a minute. Haven't we heard this before? Of course we have.
Calls to 'embrace change or else' have been issued for decades, well
before the World Wide Web was a gleam in its creators' eyes. And
leaders responded to that call for action long before the advent of
a New Economy. So some lessons of the past are still relevant. But
what is different today is the pace, depth, and scope of change, and
how many people must get involved in coping with it. Change moves
faster, and so do the reactions to change, as viral marketing spreads
the good news but e-organizers and Web protestors create bad news
just as quickly. The reach of change is broader and deeper: to bigger audiences in more places at greater distances, and into the inner
workings of long-taken-for-granted institutions and daily routines.
Internet-enabled change has the potential to reshape nearly every
aspect of life, all at once. [2]

Each aspect of change by itself might be manageable, but together
they can seem overwhelming. So the skills to deal with change can't
be casual afterthoughts, they must be well understood parts of everyone's repertoire. More people, at more levels in more organizations,
must learn to master change and lead it. More of us must play leadership roles, whether we are invited to the task or appoint ourselves.
Thus, the lessons to be learned from successful leaders featured in this
book can be a survival guide for the Internet Age. [3]

(section omitted)

With resistance to change possible even under benign circumstances, leaders must be even more skilful at handling the human

side of change when the environment is turbulent and the impact of change revolutionary. The skills of New Economy leaders are similar to those of Old Economy leaders, but the pace and complexity is much more demanding, and the audiences for every act are much bigger. E-culture requires leaders who are especially adept at leaping over barriers and converting resistance to commitment. The new challenges of the Internet Age increase the need for leaders who are masters of change. Like webmasters who guide the images that appear on-screen, changemasters guide the activities that occur behind the screen. More people, in more walks of life, must add 'changemaster' to their skill set. [4]

Seven classic skills are involved in innovation and change: tuning into the environment, kaleidoscopic thinking, an inspiring vision, coalition building, nurturing a working team, persisting through difficulties, and spreading credit and recognition. These are more than discrete skills; they reflect a perspective, a style, that is basic to e-culture. [5]

Skill 1. Sensing Needs and Opportunities: Tuning into the Environment

Innovation begins with someone being smart enough to sense a new need. Of course, being 'smart enough' comes from focusing time and attention on things going on in the environment around you that send signals that it's time for change. Changemasters are adept at anticipating the need for change as well as leading it. They sense new ideas or appetites emerging on the horizon – sometimes because they feel hungry themselves. The concept of eBay came from the desire of Pierre Omidyar's girlfriend to swap Pez dispensers, and the idea for Worldroom.com, a Hong Kong startup, came from journalists who needed a way to download files and get local information on the road. [6]

2.5 Strategic critique

As I have indicated, Jessop views structural change in moments of crisis as mediated by hegemonic struggle between strategies which have a partly semiotic character – discourses which project imaginaries for a new 'fix' in the co-regulation of regimes of accumulation and political regimes. The development, dissemination and instantiation/ materialization of strategies are partly semiotic processes. From a strategic perspective, Kanter's book is a sample from just one facet of just one element, that of dissemination, in a chain of strategic action (which is also a chain or network of genres) which includes the emergence, dissemination and instantiation/materialization of what has become a hegemonic strategy for a new political-economic regulative fix. Kanter herself points to the wider strategic frame in construing e-culture as the new organizational culture of the 'global information era' and the 'New Economy'. Strategically, we can broadly situate it within the neo-liberal project. The processes of recontextualization involved in dissemination are of course far from straightforward: such texts may have little effect on organizations – they may be dutifully read then ignored, resisted or appropriated in all sorts of ways. Recontextualization is not a simple matter of spread, or flow, or colonization; on the contrary, it is a colonization/appropriation dialectic. But such texts do cumulatively contribute to institutional and material change, even if the process is highly uneven and complex. The object of research is ultimately the whole chain of strategic action, but my concern here is only with how the perspective of strategy affects analysis of texts of this type – with strategic critique of such texts.[1]

This implies the primacy of strategic critique, yet Boltanski and Chiapello give primacy to ideological critique – they approach their corpus of texts not primarily with a view to the strategic action that is going on but primarily with a view to detecting the new spirit of capitalism as a presence, an ideology. Their approach is relatively static, oriented to a contrast between old and new structures in their ideological aspect, rather than primarily dynamic, oriented to strategies which are directed at the work of restructuring.

The primacy of strategic critique entails privileging a dynamic view of text as 'texturing', as productive process, as one form of productive action within a larger strategic project. This means giving primacy to action over representation and identification, to genres over discourses and styles. But this is in no sense action/genre *rather than* representation/discourses, or *rather than* identification/styles. These are analytically distinct but dialectically interconnected in action – it is a matter of one's way into this dialectic, giving primacy to action/genre but recognizing the imbrication of representation/discourses and identification/styles within action/genre.

Some approaches to CDA, especially Wodak's, give salience to textual strategies, for example the strategies of legitimation which van Leeuwen and Wodak have written about. These are not to be confused with the hegemonic strategies Jessop talks about, but deploying 'strategy' as a category at different levels of analysis helps integrate textual analysis into strategic analysis in Jessop's sense.

The blurb describes the book as a 'blueprint' and 'guide', which identifies reasonably accurately the primary action and genre: this is primarily pedagogical action and interaction, and the genre is primarily a pedagogical genre oriented to an actional sequence which in principle (not necessarily always in practice) moves from transmitting knowledge to acquiring knowledge to applying knowledge – from teaching to learning to doing.

'Primarily' indicates that the generic profile of a text can be complex – a mixing of genres, genres embedded within genres, etc.

The pedagogical action and genre in this case are a mixture of informing/describing, prescribing, persuading, legitimizing. This implies that strategic critique does not preclude rhetorical and ideological critique – persuading entails rhetoric and describing, prescribing and legitimizing entail ideology. Strategy, rhetoric and ideology are analytically distinct but dialectically interconnected in action, and strategic critique is a particular way of organizing the three types of critique which gives primacy to strategy but recognizes the imbrication of rhetoric and ideology within strategy.

So summing up: when we get to analysis of text we give primacy to strategy and to action/genre, but also trace the imbrication within them of rhetoric and ideology, and of representation/discourses and identification/styles.

Let us begin at the beginning of the chapter, though leaving aside the title and quotation: 'To live with e-culture is to live with change. Not just isolated, one-time, occasional changes, but ongoing, continuous, ubiquitous, never-finished change. Change as a condition of existence...' The opening sentence is a descriptive statement, a statement of fact, a categorically epistemically modalized *realis* statement, an identification with a relational process, an act of informing, telling, defining. The semantic relationship of the other two sentences to this one is a relationship of elaboration (Fairclough, 2003). The opening strategic move is a definition which equates living with e-culture and living with change. This is a pedagogical move, a pedagogical act, which immediately sets up certain expectations and recognitions with respect to genre. But strategy is at once imbricated with ideology and with rhetoric. The mode of elaboration is dramatic (the three dots marking incompletion are actually in the text) and persuasive and of rhetorical import. And ideology enters the frame with the representation of 'change' as an abstract, nominalized process without agents – an entity whose existence and factuality are presupposed – which itself is ascribed agentive powers as the text unfolds ('Internet-enabled change has the potential to reshape nearly every aspect of life'), but then contradictorily change is represented as a process that has to be and can be 'mastered'. Ideological critique centres both on this internal contradiction and on the contradiction between these representations of change and the actual process of change (which we can access only in the form of other representations, other discourses, of change which are more 'practically adequate' (Sayer, 2000). These comments on ideology also indicate how genre is imbricated with discourses, strategic action with particular representations. And if we focus on the modality of the initial statement we can see how action is imbricated with identification, genre with style: the modality is epistemic and categorical, a strong claim to truth, which implicates the identity of one who knows, the teacher, the expert, the 'guru' in this case, and the complementary identity of one who does not know, the learner, the manager in a practical organizational context.

Let us proceed. There is now a brief shift of genre: 'Wait a minute. Haven't we heard this before? Of course we have.' This is a simulated dialogue between reader and writer, and one marker of the associated shift in social relations, and so in identities and style, is the inclusive 'we' attributed to both 'voices' in the dialogue, as well as the shift in grammatical mood (from declarative to imperative and interrogative) and speech acts (command and question). The genre shift shows the imbrication of rhetoric in strategy: this brief levelling of the ground between teacher and learner may be persuasive through showing that the 'guru' is after all in touch with common managerial experience. Thereafter there is a resumption of categorical descriptive statement.

There is an oscillation throughout the chapter between descriptive statement (illustrated above) and prescriptive statement, and correspondingly between epistemic and deontic modality. So in the next paragraph we find a prescriptive statement: 'the skills to deal with change can't be casual afterthoughts, they must be well understood parts of everyone's repertoire. More people, at more levels in more organizations, must learn to master change and lead it. More of us must play leadership roles, whether we are invited to the task or appoint ourselves.' At this point, one can see this oscillation as texturing a pervasive strategy in contemporary guru literature as well as policy texts, the 'TINA' ('there is no alternative') strategy: 'this is the way the world is, so this is what we must do'. The way of the world is characteristically represented in this strategy as an inevitable and unchangeable matter of fact, linked here to the representation of 'change' as a process without agents which is itself agentive; and the consequences that 'must' follow are represented as equally inexorable – organizations must change, and leaders must overcome resistance to change, to the point where: 'if they can't be converted, get them out of the way' (from later in the same chapter).

But as the chapter develops, so the import of this oscillation shifts. Compare paragraphs 3 and 4 on the one hand and 6 on the other – let us specifically take 'leaders must be even more skilful at handling the human side of change when the environment is turbulent and the impact of change revolutionary' from 4 and 'Changemasters are adept at anticipating the need for change as well as leading it' from 6. The former is prescriptive/deontic ('must be . . . skilful'), the latter descriptive/epistemic ('are adept'). One might ask: why? 'Changemasters' is a textured membership category, i.e. created in the process of the text ('. . . the need for people who are masters of change. Like webmasters who guide the images that appear on-screen, changemasters . . .' paragraph 4), yet it then figures in descriptive statements of fact, without any of the claimed substantial body of research evidence being adduced to support them. There is a slippage between prescription and description throughout the chapter. Such descriptions can be taken as implicit prescriptions, a strategy of construing objectives as actual states of affairs which is reminiscent of Bourdieu and Wacquant's analysis of neo-liberal discourse, their identification of the 'performative power' of the 'new planetary vulgate', its power to 'bring into being the very realities it describes'. This oscillation between description and prescription is of significance as part of the pedagogical action, the genre, the text from a strategic perspective, and simultaneously of rhetorical significance in persuading people that in conforming with prescriptions they are merely bringing themselves in line with the way things are, and of ideological significance in that it represents a level of mastery of change which is contradicted by reality.

The reality that is described and change as it is prescribed are cast in general terms as having a universal validity, but there is also a pervasive strategy for texturing a relationship between the universal and the particular which is illustrated in paragraph 6 – an oscillation between these universal descriptions and prescriptions and brief anecdotal examples about particular leaders and companies which generally presuppose an 'insider' knowledge of the leader and the company on the part of the reader. Most of the anecdotes are exemplary – about successful companies and leaders.

Boltanski and Chiapello characterize the new 'spirit of capitalism' as a new articulation of different justificatory regimes – especially the Project-oriented and Inspirational justificatory regimes. What a strategic critique of texts can add is insight into the articulatory process. Articulations, more generally relations, are textually created, 'textured'. Classification is a continuous process in the work of texturing, and it proceeds by constituting relations of equivalence and difference between elements, where new relations of equivalence are de-differentiations, the 'subversion' of relations of difference.

Let us begin with lists. Lists are a prominent characteristic of this pedagogical genre, and their pedagogical power is self-evident. Paragraph 5 includes a list:

> Seven classic skills are involved in innovation and change: tuning into the environment, kaleidoscopic thinking, an inspiring vision, coalition building, nurturing a working team, persisting through difficulties, and spreading credit and recognition. These are more than discrete skills; they reflect a perspective, a style, that is basic to e-culture.

The items of a list are put in relations of equivalence, and in this case one can see relations of equivalence which texture the articulatory relation which Boltanski and Chiapello identify between Project-oriented ('coalition building, nurturing a working team') and Inspirational ('an inspiring vision', 'kaleidoscopic thinking') justificatory regimes, which Chiapello and I identify as Discourses with a big 'd', which themselves are articulations of discourses with a small 'd' (e.g. 'coalition building' versus 'nurturing') – the list textures articulatory relations at both levels.

Throughout the chapter, however, the texturing of relations of equivalence co-occurs with the texturing of relations of difference, particularly dichotomous relations of difference between protagonists and antagonists, 'pacesetters' and 'laggards'. This is illustrated in another extract from the chapter, which contains a bullet-point list (a sequence of three dots (...) indicates points where I have omitted parts of the text to economize on space):

> Companies that are successful on the web operate differently from their laggard counterparts. On my global e-culture survey, those reporting that they are much better than their competitors in the use of the Internet tend to have flexible, empowering, collaborative organisations. The 'best' are more likely than the 'worst' to indicate, at statistically significant levels, that

- Departments collaborate (instead of sticking to themselves)
- Conflict is seen as creative (instead of disruptive)
- People can do anything not explicitly prohibited (instead of doing only what is explicitly permitted)
- Decisions are made by the people with the most knowledge (instead of the ones with the highest rank)

Pacesetters and laggards describe no difference in how hard they work...but they are very different in how collaboratively they work.

Working in e-culture mode requires organizations to be communities of purpose.... A community makes people feel like members, not just employees – members with privileges, but also responsibilities... Community means having things in common, a range of shared understandings transcend specific fields. Shared understandings permit relatively seamless processes, interchangeability among people, smooth formation of teams...and rapid transmission of information....

The greater integration that is integral to e-culture is different from the centralization of earlier eras. Integration must be accompanied by flexibility and empowerment in order to achieve fast response, creativity, and innovation through improvisation. Web success involves operating more like a community than a bureaucracy.

The dichotomous relation between 'pacesetters' and 'laggards' excludes intermediate cases and grey areas, though the archaic term 'laggard' perhaps mitigates censure with a degree of humour. The texturing of relations of difference is effected through a range of contrastive relational structures and expressions (e.g. 'x instead of y', 'x is different from y', 'more like x than y'), and is particularly clear in the bulleted list, where the contrasted terms realize an antithetical relation between the positively valued justificatory regimes (or Discourses) of the new 'spirit of capitalism' and negatively valued justificatory regimes (including the Industrial justificatory regime). Elements which are in similar positions in contrastive relations are thereby textured in relations of equivalence – e.g. 'integration' and 'community' on the one hand, 'centralization' and 'bureaucracy' on the other; and other elements are textured in relations of equivalence through additive parataxis (e.g. 'flexible, empowering, collaborative'). As in the previous case, the texturing of relations of equivalence between such elements is a texturing of relations of equivalence between different discourses.

2.6   Conclusions

The following brief and summary conclusions pull together and partly develop the discussion above.

Discourse analysis and textual analysis contribute to political economic critique in the Jessop vein through giving analytical specificity to its discourse moment, but conversely they derive their social import from being framed within such broader theories and research programmes. Giving primacy to strategic critique within CDA facilitates this.

Contemporary hegemonic strategies for economic, social and organizational reconstruction are legitimized by claims about 'the way the world is', supposedly immutable matters of fact which are however characteristically the effects of policies which could be changed. Once these claims are accepted, the logic often seems quite compelling. Strategic critique of texts can contribute to broader critique of strategies in this regard by showing how relationships between fact and policy, 'is' and 'must', are textured.

Change in organizations is represented as inevitable, given 'the way the world is', and as originated and effected by 'leaders', part of whose task is to overcome 'resistance'. There is a concession at one point that some 'leaders' leave 'blood everywhere', but the more catastrophic consequences of organizational change are generally skated over. Strategic critique of texts can show how these omissions are textually accomplished.

As I have mentioned, a pervasive strategy which Bourdieu and Wacquant have identified in neo-liberal discourse is what I have identified as a slippage between description and prescription, representing something one is trying to bring about as something which already exists. Bourdieu and Wacquant identify the issue, but they do not use forms of close textual analysis to show how these slippages work, which one can through strategic critique of texts.

A relationship is textured between universal claims and prescriptions and exemplary anecdotes about leaders and companies. This way of texturing the universal/particular relationship stands in contrast with the ways in which the relationship between universal blueprints and radically diverse contexts is experienced – as notoriously in the international imposition of the 'Washington consensus'. Advocacy of universal panaceas without analysis of differences of circumstances which may affect their appropriacy and impacts can be profoundly damaging.

Strategic critique of classificatory processes of texturing relations of equivalence and difference can show the articulatory processes in the articulations and disarticulations identified by Boltanski and Chiapello in the 'new spirit of capitalism'. It can also point to ideologically significant contradictions between textured relations and real relations – for example between textured relations of equivalence and real contradictions in 'leadership', between textured dichotomies such as 'pacesetters'/ 'laggards' and more complex realities.

Recent research on organizational discourse has emphasized organizing as a process in opposition to an overemphasis on organizations as structured entities, and organizing as a discursive process tied to the constitutive potentials of discourse and, concretely, texts. What I would add is that since it is also a strategic process involving contestation between strategies to achieve hegemonic status, strategic critique of texts has a claim to primacy.

Note

1. The new 'organizational culture' which Kanter describes/prescribes (I shall come to the oscillation between these shortly) can be seen as a facet of a new order of governance – including a model for 'leadership' which extends beyond business organizations into public management and government. The power and generality of such models are evident for instance in the context I am currently working in, Romania, where there is a substantial investment in training for 'leadership' in the context of 'transition' to capitalism (and more specifically preparation for EU membership).

References

Boltanski, L. and E. Chiapello (1999) *Le nouvel esprit du capitalisme* (Paris: Gallimard).

Bourdieu, P. and L. Wacquant (2001) 'New-liberal speak: Notes on the new planetary vulgate', *Radical Philosophy* 105, 2–5.

Chiapello, E. and N. Fairclough (2002) 'Understanding the new management ideology: a transdisciplinary contribution from critical discourse analysis and the new sociology of capitalism', *Discourse and Society* 13 (2), 185–208.

Chouliaraki, L. and N. Fairclough (1999) *Discourse in Late Modernity* (Edinburgh: Edinburgh University Press).

Fairclough N. (2003) *Analyzing Discourse: Textual Analysis for Social Research* (London: Routledge).

Fairclough, N., B. Jessop and A. Sayer (2004) 'Critical realism and semiosis' in J. Joseph and J.M. Roberts (eds) *Realism Discourse and Deconstruction* (London: Routledge).

Harvey, D. (1996) *Justice, Nature and the Geography of Difference* (Oxford: Blackwell).

Jessop, B. (2002) *The Future of the Capitalist State* (London: Polity Press).

Kanter, R. M. (2001) *Evolve! Succeeding in the Digital Culture of Tomorrow* (Harvard: Harvard Business School Press).

Sayer, A. (2000) *Realism and Social Science* (London: Sage).

Wodak, R. (2001) 'The discourse–historical approach' in R. Wodak and M. Meyer (eds) *Methods in Critical Discourse Analysis* (London: Sage), 63–94.

3

On the Globalization of Consumer-Oriented Practices and Attitudes in the Internet[1]

Carlos A. M. Gouveia
University of Lisbon

3.1 Introduction

The objective of this chapter is to discuss some issues related to what has been identified as shifting relationships in discursive practices across different orders of discourse (see, for instance, Fairclough, 1992, 2004) and networks of different social practices. It will focus particularly on the Internet, aiming to show that the gradual commodification that is taking place in the Internet as a public space is changing the nature of public interaction but also provoking changes in the practices and attitudes of individuals.

Dealing with aspects related to the hybridization of discourses, genres and styles encouraged by a consumer-oriented Internet that makes it possible for advertising practices and 'discourses' to colonize computer-mediated communication (CMC) at different levels, we will examine how CMC technologies have taken up and motivated some of the transformations towards the new capitalism referred to by Fairclough (2004, p. 103) as the ' "restructuring" of relations among the economic, political and social domains'.

The first section of the work, 'Discourse, globalization and the flow of discourse', deals with aspects related with the frameworks for the study: Halliday's theory of grammatical description, systemic functional grammar (Halliday, 1994) and Fairclough's theory and method of critical discourse analysis (Fairclough, 1992, 1995). The second section, 'The Internet and the commodification of discourse', draws briefly on different authors who have worked on the concept of commodification at different levels, and focuses on different aspects of social life for the purpose of relating that concept with the Internet. It thus aims at a characterization of the Internet as a possible domain of commodification processes, enabling the formation of consumer-oriented practices and attitudes. The third section, 'Websites as new forms of social interaction', is a text-based analysis of five websites from different institutions, aiming at demonstrating that despite the differences in the social roles played by those institutions, the way they present themselves in the Internet, or rather, the way they present themselves as commodities, is quite similar.

I will finally conclude with a short systematization of the analysis in its relation to the aspects dealt with in the previous parts of the chapter.

3.2   Discourse, globalization and the flow of discourse

Systemic functional grammar (SFG) is a socially oriented theory of grammatical description that considers language to be a semiotic system structured in terms of strata, whose main purpose is the production of meaning by socially and culturally situated speakers (see Halliday, 1994, 2004). That is, SFG is functional and semantic in its orientation, aiming at explaining grammatical categories as the realization of semantic patterns, the instantiation of a meaning potential. It therefore describes languages in functional terms with the aim of providing 'a general grammar for purposes of text analysis and interpretation. It is therefore a grammar which provides a basic lingua franca for text analysts working in a wide range of differing contexts' (Martin et al., 1997, p. 2).

Considering linguistic systems to be the simultaneous expression of three functions of language – ideational, interpersonal and textual – SFG sees texts in their relation with contexts as the realization of field, tenor and mode of discourse. These three dimensions work together as variables for the register of texts and encode lexicogrammatical meanings that can be traced back to the three functions of language.

Once again, as Martin et al. (1997, p. 3) put it, SFG 'provides you with tools for understanding why a text is the way it is (...). It presents the difference between (...) variations as a choice about what is functional in a particular context (...).' Furthermore, SFG helps you understand why discourses are the way they are, how they get instantiated via the interrelationship between lexicogrammar (text), the context of situation (register), and the context of culture (genre).

For the purpose of this study, discourse will be taken to signify the whole process of meaning production through verbal interaction, a social practice that helps to constitute the domains, objects, activities and practices of what is being talked about. As Sarangi and Coulthard (2000, p. xxi) put it, 'discourse is best understood as a system of the possibility of Knowledge – enabling us, and at the same time constraining us, to do things'. It is through discourse that individuals 'occupy certain "subject positions" in both senses of the term: they produce discourse as well as being products of their own discourses'. This notion of discourse, which owes its formulation to Foucault (1971, 1980), has been further developed by critical discourse analysts, now being generally accepted that discourses are constitutive of social identities and relations. From Foucault and his work on discourse, Fairclough (1992, pp. 68ff) also adapts the concept of order of discourse to refer to configurations of discourse practices that work at three different but interdependent levels: situational, institutional and societal. As configurations of discourse practices, orders of discourse are open to transformation, to processes of restructuring thus referred to by Fairclough (2004, p. 105):

> The restructuring of orders of discourse is a matter of shifting relations, i.e. changes in networking, between the discourse elements of different (networks of) social practices. A prime example is the way in which the language of management has colonised public institutions and organisations such as universities, though I need to add at once that this process is a colonization/appropriation dialectic, i.e. not only a matter of the entry of discourses into new domains, but the diverse ways in which they are received, appropriated, recontextualized in different locales, and the ultimately unpredictable outcomes of this process.

How these processes work at the level of the relation of the individual with other individuals and institutions is a matter of another restructuring process involving global aspects of the world economy and the relationship between societies and cultures (Luke, 2002, p. 107):

> We can describe the impacts of globalization in terms of the variably regulated and unregulated, systematic and chaotic, organized and disorganized, intentional and accidental flows of bodies, capital, and discourse across what historically were constrained and regulated geographic, geopolitical, and cultural borders and boundaries. The

result is that many of the constants of postwar social formation – systems of government and regulation, economic exchange, and even place and displacement – have been disrupted, or, in instances, are morphing into different formations.

Globalization is transforming the world, affecting almost every detail of our daily lives, and should not be merely thought of as something that is remote from the life of the individual, for as Giddens (1999, p. 12) has put it, 'It is an "in here" phenomenon too, influencing intimate and personal aspects of our lives.' For the purpose of this study, globalization must be looked at alongside another concurrent trend influencing the lives of individuals, that is, the objectification and digitalization of culture, whereby the new technologies serve as an instrument not only for globalization but also for the attribution of specific values, labels and categorizations to processes and products thus globalized.

In his listing of the factors that have had an effect on the globalization of communications at the end of the twentieth century – the increased exploitation of cable systems and satellites, and the processing, storing and digitalization of the use of information – Thompson (1995, p. 161) stresses the strong importance of the last one. Lehtonen (2001, pp. 80–1), on the other hand, getting back to the aspects referred to by Thompson, but quoting also Morley and Robins (1995), connects these aspects of globalization to processes of commodification. In his words, 'Mediatization, commodification and globalisation speed each other up', but the changes 'they have generated is advanced by a process fresher than them, the digitalization of culture'.

Commodification, here understood as referring to those processes through which social relations are reduced to an exchange relation and to the transformation of symbolic forms into merchandise, has always been present in media culture and in CMC in particular. As a social process of a discursive nature, it has been addressed by critical discourse analysts and social theorists in different ways, perspectives and concerns (see, for instance, Fairclough, 1993; Chouliaraki and Fairclough, 1999; Wernicke, 1991). Capitalism has been structuring the whole of society around the production and distribution of commodities, via a social process where everything can be sold, everything can be transformed into a commodity and referred to in reason of its exchange value. This process of commodification affects not only the value of what is turned into a commodity – reduction of use value in favour of exchange value – but also the nature of social relations, which have thus become primarily exchange relations. Rather than citizens, speakers or subject beings, individuals have become consumers or exchangers of commodities. At the same time they become themselves objects of consumption and, as such, also objects for promotion (on the relationship of promotion and the commodification of individuals see, for instance, Fairclough, 1993).

3.3   The Internet and the commodification of discourse

It is an assumed fact that CMC in general, and the Internet in particular, has the capacity to change the way individuals interact with each other, while at the same time increasing access to information in ways never seen before. But, on the other hand, as Dahlberg (2001) has put it, what we are watching is the taking over and control of cyberspace by major corporations who are consumer-orienting the Internet, thus helping to transform the way individuals interact with it:

> The rapid commercialization of cyberspace and increasing control of Internet infrastructure and content by major corporate players (...) is leading towards a consumer-oriented cyberspace that promises to either marginalize online public discourse or incorporate it within privatized and individualized forms of interaction: online commerce, entertainment, and business communication. It is becoming more and more difficult for non-commercial sites to compete for the attention of online participants.

The aspect referred to by Dahlberg is a rather important aspect of the commodification of the Internet but it is far from being the only one. The fundamental thread here is, in fact, the colonization of other social and discursive practices in the Internet by consumer-oriented practices characterizing online commerce, entertainment, and business communication, in a similar process to that affecting other spheres of social life. What we are witnessing in the Internet is the growing importance of certain colonizing discourses, which are expanding their functions across different institutions, different genres and different orders of discourse. These are, according to certain authors (Habermas, 1989; Chouliaraki and Fairclough, 1999), discourses that have a particular status in late capitalist society and which expand systemically beyond shifting boundaries.

Playing an important role in CMC, multimodality, for instance, understood as the use of diverse but simultaneous modes for the production of meaning, ends up serving this purpose of boundary shifting in the production of discourse. As Kress and Van Leeuwen (1996, p. 39) have pointed out, 'the multi-modality of written texts has, by and large, been ignored, whether in educational contexts, in linguistic theorizing or in popular common sense. Today, in the age of "multimedia", it can suddenly be perceived again.' Even though it is not my intention to go into the discussion of multimodality, it is worth mentioning, following Kress and Van Leeuwen's conclusions, that each mode of expression or representation has a continuous history of contraction, expansion and movement from and into different areas and modes, that history being the result of the uses to which it is put. Also, the convergence and boundary crossing of modes of representation one witnesses on the Internet are part of that history, but also part of a more recent history of media mixing, for as Lehtonen (2001, p. 75) has stressed, 'multimodality and the mixing of media borders is characteristic above all to popular culture whereas high culture has traditionally been characterized by media purism'.

As said before, it is not in the scope of this chapter to discuss the role of multimodality (and of media mixing, for that matter) in the Internet. Nevertheless, one should bear in mind that the commodification of discourse one detects in the Internet, and particularly in the web pages analysed below, is not only a consequence of the aspects identified above, such as globalization and the objectification and digitalization of culture, but also a consequence of a continuous diversification of the available modes of representation throughout this modernity of ours.

3.4   Websites as new forms of social interaction

The texts under scrutiny here are the texts one gets to read when accessing the websites of five different institutions. That means that we will not be dealing with the entire contents of the websites of those institutions, but only with the text that constitutes the homepage of the website (the initial page in the whole set of web pages). The institutions were chosen on the basis of the differences between them and the roles they play in society, which presumably reflects itself on the way they construct their relationship with the individuals addressing them. The institutions, whose pages were accessed on Friday, 31 October 2003, and upon which the analysis was undertaken, are the following: the Terrence Higgins Trust (henceforth THT), a non-governmental organization for the fight against Aids, accessed at http://www.tht.org.uk; the British Army (henceforth BA), accessed at http://www.army.mod.uk; the Government of the United Kingdom (henceforth GUK), accessed at http://www.ukonline.gov.uk; Sainsbury's supermarket (henceforth SS), accessed at http://www.sainsburys.co.uk; and the University of Warwick (henceforth UW), accessed at http://www.warwick.ac.uk.

After a first glance at the five websites (see the Appendix), it is clear that they all share some characteristics, the most obvious being the fact that they all present texts where images (either photographs or cartoons/icons) and verbal language work together for the purpose of communication. Another common characteristic, deriving from the previous one, is the layout of the pages, as they all organize the information (both visual and verbal) in the same way, that is, following a structure that divides the screen into frames where different types of texts come together as a whole in reason of their frame-organization. From that organization the menus of the pages stand out (more clearly in some cases, less clearly in others) as a set of textual elements that help to structure the text of the entire website. In ideational terms, the menus meta-discursively define the field of discourse, thus working as concise representations of the world experiences of those institutions. The way those menus are textually organized serves the purpose of the representation (the production of ideational meanings). But they also encode attitudes and values which realize tenor of discourse, that is, they express interpersonal meanings. In fact, all the pages, with the exception of the one by Warwick University, make the point of having at least one item involving a direct interpellation of the reader: 'Get Involved', in the case of the THT; 'What's New', in the case of the BA; 'Your life' and 'Do it online', in the case of the GUK; and 'Go shopping', in the case of SS.

And even if Warwick University's page stands out as an example not conforming to the interpersonal principle detected in the menus of the other pages, one has to consider that it creates the same effect via the entire content of the page, which follows a generic structure of the kind *headlines* plus news text, more common in newspapers than in university websites. Notice from that matter the use of the hyperlink 'Other headlines', which presupposes the ideational construction of other parts of the page as headlines of news texts, while at the same time interactionally positioning the website surfer, the individual interacting with the institution, as a news reader.

This aspect of the interpersonal dimension of meaning in website designing is common not only to these pages but to all websites in the

Internet, considering that they all involve interaction with users. That is a fact. But the way this interaction is codified in discourse depends, or at least one is expecting it to depend, on the social nature of the institution. One should then expect to find some variation in register between these pages, since the relationship between the text and the context of situation is not the same in all of them, despite the permanence of the variable mode of register specific to this kind of CMC. It is in fact this variable of register, the mode, that explains many of the similarities referred to above. But that variable does not explain other similarities across the five pages such as: the advertising and promotional use of language and the commodification of discourse that constructs not only the pages themselves but also the institutions they reflect as commodities for consumption.

It is quite interesting to notice, in this respect, that there is almost no difference between 'Treat yourself to a cosy night in with comfort food, pampering and entertainment' in the website of Sainsbury's, and 'Have a look at the number of services now online' in the website of the Government online. There is in both cases a direct interpellation of the user for a concrete action having as final result a benefit for the reader. But if there are any doubts left concerning the similarities between the two pages, they are dismissed when we look at Sainsbury's and read 'See our Christmas to You aisle for weekly promotions', of which the line in the Government website seems to be a copy.

The differences detected between the pages are mainly differences of field of discourse, but even there some similarities can be detected. In fact, the subject matter of each of the websites, that is, the area of human experience that is being represented, is quite different in all of them; nevertheless, on looking closer at the words and structures used to encompass those experiential meanings, in relation to the long- and short-term goals of the texts, one cannot, once again, avoid noticing their similarity: 'Book a driving test' or 'Buy a TV licence', at GUK; 'Keep in touch', at WU; 'Campaign with us' or 'Fundraise for us', at THT; 'Stock up for Christmas', at SS; 'Army Careers Online', at BA.

These examples, whilst helping us to consider aspects that in some way stand in the transition between the field and the tenor expressed in the texts, also contribute to a better understanding of why they are so similar.

As a matter of fact, it is the tenor of discourse that explains the construction of the texts as they are, through their likeness. As it is known today, the Internet, or at least the discourse and designing in the Internet, cannot be separated from the promotional use of language, which works as a means of pressure towards the standardization of discourse practices and the social relationships enacted by and in the texts. I am referring, of course, to aspects of the technologization of discourse, as discussed by Fairclough (1996). These involve not only the one just referred to, the standardization of discourse practices (plus the standardization of the roles played by institutions and individuals when interacting together), but also 'the design and projection of context-free discourse techniques' and a 'strategically motivated simulation in discourse' (Fairclough, 1996, p. 73).

Concerning the object of this chapter, it can actually be said that it is the technologization of discourse that explains the fact that the individuals interacting with these different institutions are being constructed as clients by the institutions they are interacting with when surfing through their websites. It is not only a fact that in the Internet, and in computer networks in general, one is the client of some server, provider or remote host, or that the pages one gets to see are the client's pages as opposed to the server's pages, it is also a fact that while surfing, one is a client of all sorts of institutions – regardless of their social characteristics – who are the providers of information, goods or of themselves as commodities.

3.5 Conclusion

The comparative analysis of all these websites clearly shows that there is a promotional practice colonizing them, thus shading the differences one would expect to find between them. As Fairclough (1996, p. 74) has put it: 'The projection of (...) context-free techniques into a variety of institutional contexts contributes to a widespread effect of "colonization" of local institutional orders of discourse by a few culturally salient discourse types – advertising and managerial and marketing discourse (...).' But far from wishing to stress or discuss this fact, which seems to me beyond dispute, with this chapter I just wanted to stress the subjectification individuals may be subject to due to the technologization of discourse practices. I therefore focused particularly on the use of discourse techniques that are context-free, that is, that design and project different contexts in a similar way, thus constructing the interaction between their participants regularly through different orders of discourse. To conclude, the discourse produced by these different institutions forces the individual to occupy a certain subject position, that of a client, thus constraining their social identities.

Appendix

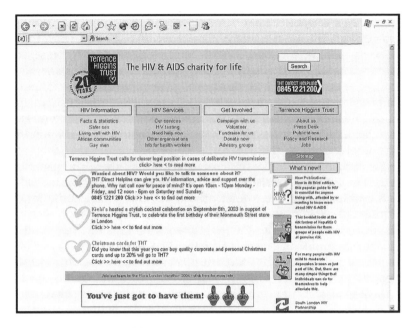

Plate 3.1   Home page of the Terrence Higgins Trust

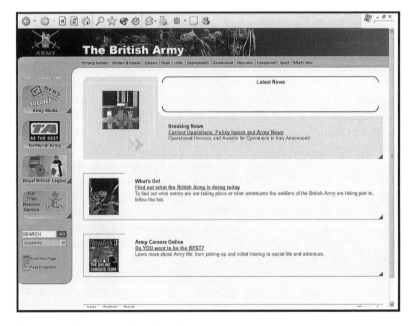

Plate 3.2   Home page of the British Army

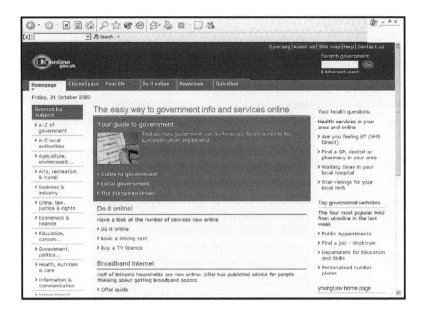

Plate 3.3   Home page of the government of the United Kingdom

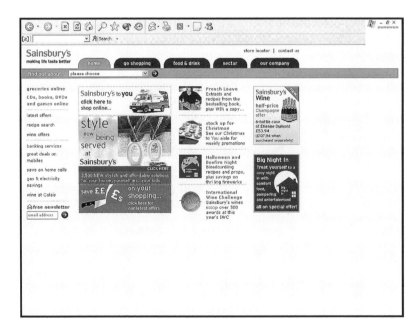

Plate 3.4   Home page of Sainsbury's supermarket

Plate 3.5   Home page of the University of Warwick

Note

1. I am indebted to my colleagues Luísa Azuaga and Paula Horta for reading and commenting on an earlier version of the manuscript.

References

Chouliaraki, L. and N. Fairclough (1999) *Discourse in Late Modernity: Rethinking Critical Discourse Analysis* (Edinburgh: Edinburgh University Press).

Dahlberg, L. (2001) 'Computer-mediated communication and the public sphere: a critical analysis', *Journal of Computer-Mediated Communication*, 7 (1), data accessed 30 January 2004.

Fairclough, N. (1992) *Discourse and Social Change* (Cambridge: Polity Press).

Fairclough, N. (1993) 'Critical discourse analysis and the marketization of public discourse: the universities', *Discourse and Society*, 4 (2), 133–68.

Fairclough, N. (1995) *Critical Discourse Analysis: the Critical Study of Language* (London: Longman).

Fairclough, N. (1996) 'Technologisation of discourse' in C. R. Caldas-Coulthard and M. Coulthard (eds) *Texts and Practices: Readings in Critical Discourse Analysis* (London: Routledge), 71–83.

Fairclough, N. (2004) 'Critical discourse analysis in researching language in the new capitalism: Overdetermination, transdisciplinarity and textual analysis' in L. Young and C. Harrison (eds) *Systemic Functional Linguistics and Critical Discourse Analysis* (London: Continuum), 103–22.

Foucault, M. (1971) *L'ordre du discours: Leçon inaugurale au Collège de France prononcée de 2 décembre 1970* (Paris: Gallimard).

Foucault, M. (1980) *Power/Knowledge: Selected Interviews and Other Writings, 1972–1977*, edited by C. Gordon (New York: Pantheon Books).

Giddens, A. (1999) *Runnaway World: How Globalisation is Reshaping our Lives* (London: Profile Books).

Habermas, J. (1989) *The Structural Transformation of the Public Sphere* (Cambridge: Polity Press).

Halliday, M. A. K. (1994) *An Introduction to Functional* Grammar, 2nd edn (London: Arnold).

Halliday, M. A. K. (2004) *An Introduction to Functional* Grammar, 3rd edn, revised by Christian M. I. M. Matthiessen (London: Arnold).

Kress, G. and T. van Leeuwen (1996) *Reading Images. The Grammar of Visual Design* (London: Routledge).

Lehtonen, M. (2001) 'On no man's land: Theses on intermediality'. *The Nordicom Review: Nordic Research on Media and Communication*, 22(1), 71–83.

Luke, A. (2002) 'Beyond science and ideology critique: Developments in critical discourse analysis', *Annual Review of Applied Linguistics*, 22, 96–110.

Martin, J. R., C. M. I. M. Matthiessen and C. Painter (1997) *Working with Functional Grammar* (London: Arnold).

Morley, D. and K. Robbins (1995) *Spaces of Identity. Global Media, Electronic Landscapes and Cultural Boundaries* (London: Routledge).

Sarangi, S. and M. Coulthard (2000) *Discourse and Social Life* (London: Longman).

Thompson, J. B. (1995) *The Media and Modernity. A Social Theory of the Media* (Cambridge: Polity Press).

Wernick, A. (1991) *Promotional Culture: Advertising, Ideology and Symbolic Expression* (London: Sage).

4
Stages in Business-to-Business Brochures

Mauro T.B. Sobhie
DIRECT Project/PUC-SP, Brazil

4.1 Introduction

Advertising materials have long been valuable objects of analysis for linguistics either as data for disclosing some feature of the language or for studies on the language of advertising itself. Contributing to this effort, we focus on the interaction between a company and its corporate customers in their advertising brochures describing the stages in which this interaction unfolds in these materials and the strategies used by the company to offer its products and services. The interest in this research arose from my professional involvement with these materials as a member of the technical and marketing community, and the resulting concerns about translation decisions and the adequacy of simply translating advertising materials for different markets versus creating them from scratch. In either case, when translating or creating brochures, the potential size of the business-to-business market in a globalized world can easily justify this research and make its findings valuable both for non-English-speaking companies intending to market their products to foreign marketplaces and global companies wanting to adapt their advertising materials to local cultures.

The theoretical background used in this research comprises Halliday's systemic-functional linguistics (hereinafter SFL), which sees language as a meaning-making resource used by people to fulfil certain purposes in specific situations within a social group, and the Register and Genre Theory (hereinafter R&GT) which, according to Eggins and Martin (1997), explains the meaning and function of variation between texts.

Additionally, the grammatical analysis was based on Thompson and Thetela's (1995) proposal of interpersonal systems.

When we say 'developing' or 'unfolding', we are talking about stages, in other words, what we are really looking for here are the stages of the interaction between the company and the customer. To identify these stages it is useful to know the job they do in the text. According to Martin (1985), the reason for genres to have stages 'is simply that we usually cannot make all the meanings we want to at once'; each stage contributes with one part of the overall meanings that must be made for the genre to accomplish its aim successfully. In the dynamic relationship between text and context, therefore, we will have configurations of meanings that will be recognized by a member of the community as elements fulfilling an identifiable social function. So, it is possible to devise two different approaches for identifying them. The first is to take the overall text and interpret it with our expert knowledge of the community where the text producer lives. The second one is to identify the most prominent grammatical features of the text, interpret each one separately based on the context of their use, and then categorize the meanings according to their social functions to finally identify the stages. To avoid *ex cathedra* statements that might arise from the analyst's previous professional experience and academic background, the analysis here is based on how to identify stages from the most relevant linguistic features in the corpus, which seems to be more consistent with Halliday's view (1994, p. xvii) that 'without a theory of wordings – that is, a grammar – there's no way of making explicit one's interpretation of the meaning of a text'.

The analysis was carried out on a corpus of 12 advertising brochures issued by a US company from the telecommunications sector. Starting from the physical features of the brochures to the roles enacted by the company in each composition element and the roles projected onto the discourse participants, manual and computer-based analyses have shown four distinct stages in which the company first presents the brochure, then highlights the products and their benefits, provides reasons showing why these benefits are important to the customers and invites them to contact the company. The results of these analyses were then interpreted in the light of the context to show how linguistic and non-linguistic resources are employed by the company to make offers backed by cultural and ideological values of the marketing and technical communities.

4.2   Theoretical background

A key aspect here is the creation of meanings from the friction between text and context (Halliday and Hasan, 1989, p. 47). Text is a form of exchange or, as defined by Ventola (1995, p. 4), 'is considered as an instance of contextually relevant and appropriate social behavior realized by the linguistic structures generated by the choices from the linguistic systems'. Context, *with the text*, 'goes beyond what is said and written: it includes other non-verbal goings-on – the total environment in which a text unfolds'. This environment also includes 'a set of previous texts, texts that are taken for granted as shared among those taking part' (Halliday and Hasan, 1989, p. 47). The use of the word 'friction' seems to imply in 'motion', which suggests that meanings are dynamically created as the text unfolds, in a dialectical relationship where 'the text creates the context as much as the context creates the text', or where context is continually modified as the text unfolds, therefore affecting the next meanings created.

In Eggins and Martin's (1997) model, social context comprises the social semiotic systems of register and genre. Register 'describes the immediate situational context in which the text was produced' (Eggins, 1994, p. 26) that relates the different uses of language in different situations. Genre is defined by Martin (1984, p. 25) as 'a staged, goal-oriented, purposeful activity in which speakers engage as members of our culture'. Genre explains relations between social processes, being a manner of 'using language to accomplish recognizable tasks within a culture, where texts of different genres are used to perform different tasks'. A genre can be recognized through the kinds of meanings coexisting in a typical pattern of this genre and also through the sequence of stages or steps in which this genre unfolds. Ventola (1995, p. 3) further describes stages' operation in genres, stating that 'the social functions of interactions are not readymade products. Rather they have to be negotiated and dynamically generated stage-by-stage' where 'each stage, or interaction element is functional and contributes to the achievement of the goals and purposes of the interactants'.

Additionally to register and genre, R&GT considers another layer of context (Martin, 1997, p. 7) referred to as ideology, which is focused on the distribution of discursive resources in a culture, and the divergent ways in which social subjects construe social occasions. As part of the context, therefore, ideology also modifies the meanings created in the text, or according to Martin (1992, p. 581) it may be seen as 'a system of coding orientations which makes meaning selectively available, depending on the subjects' class, gender, ethnicity and generation'.

Another feature of social context and language is their functional diversity, which is to say that they carry out different functions at a time. In SFL this functional diversity is modelled by the ideational, interpersonal and textual metafunctions. These metafunctions reflect on social context in the field (institutional practices, or what is going on), tenor (social relations) and mode (the role of language in the communication) and on language with linguistic resources related to representation, interaction and information flow aspects.

The interactional analysis herein was based on Thompson and Thetela's proposal of interpersonal systems, which describes 'a systematic set of choices for examining interaction' (1995, p. 105). The interactional function comprises the roles enacted by the writer and the reader, and the roles projected onto the participants involved in the language event. In this model, enacted roles are 'those which are performed by the act of speaking/writing itself', where 'choices chiefly (though not exclusively) within the mood element of the clause act to assign certain roles to the two people directly involved in the language event' (1995, p. 108), which for instance may act as a giver or demander of information by choosing declarative or interrogative clauses, respectively. Projected roles, on the other side, are those 'which are assigned by the speaker/writer by means of the overt labeling of the two participants involved in the language event' (1995, p. 108). They explain that 'this labeling may be done by the choice of terms used to address or name the two participants and by the roles ascribed to them in the processes referred to in the clause', so 'the person on whom the role is projected is simultaneously a participant in the language event and a participant in the clause' (1995, p. 108).

After this brief discussion of the linguistic theories involved in the research some contextual information is needed for text interpretation. Marketing oriented to the corporate market (b2b), comprises activities involved in the supply of goods and/or services to corporations, which in turn use them to produce their own goods and/or services to end-users or other companies. There are several differences between b2b and business-to-consumer, specially concerning the higher risk for a corporate buyer in case of a bad purchase decision, which may affect or even end a buyer's career. So, one of the objectives of the advertising material is

to give confidence to the buyer in relation to the products and the company, since the concerns about the negative consequences of

a bad purchase leads the individuals to make safe purchases, looking for products from renowned vendors in the market, contacting
the companies, requesting product demos and other precautions.
(Sherrington, 1993, p. 20)

Another characteristic of b2b is the complexity of the purchase process, which comprises several stages and involves many professionals
as described by Bonoma and Shapiro (1983, pp. 43–6), namely the initiator (who anticipates or establishes a problem that may be resolved by
the product or service purchased), the gateway (who controls information that enters the company or the access to it by the other members of
the purchase process), the influencer (who provides negative or positive
information for the purchase), the decisor (who ultimately decides what
will be bought) and the user (who will use the product or service).

In this market, the company under study is a worldwide high-tech
leader that provides products and services for telecommunication
companies such as operators, service providers and equipment manufacturers, which in turn offer their products and services to end-users
such as mobile phone subscribers and other corporate users. With this
purpose, it uses several communication channels, such as the company's
website, advertising in specialist magazines, participating in trade fairs
and seminars, arranging personal interviews with representatives, making product demos and mailing. From the several advertising materials
provided to the customers over these communication channels, the
brochures were chosen for this research because of their usefulness in
several steps of the purchase process and their extensive use of written
texts.

4.3   Methodology

Three research questions guiding this analysis of interaction are:

- How does interaction unfold over the brochures?
- How are the company and the customer shown in the interaction?
- How does the context affect the company's discourse?

To answer these questions, a corpus was collected with 12 brochures
from the wireless area of the company printed in the USA between
2000 and 2001. These brochures range from 6 to 12 pages printed on
high-quality paper with intensive use of complex layout features and
colourful figures. For the purposes of this analysis the brochures were

initially separated into three physical sections: front cover, internal pages and back cover.

1. *Front cover* – the first page of the brochures. In all 12 brochures, the front covers contain titles, one or more figures and optionally other elements as subtitles and slogans. All front covers also contain the company's logo and trademark at the bottom of the page.
2. *Internal pages* – pages enclosed between the front cover and the back cover. These pages use several resources such as titles and subtitles, frames, pull quotes and blurbs, one or more figures and other graphic elements such as tables, diagrams and slogans. Written content is arranged into columns and divided into blocks of paragraphs with titles. These pages contain organizational resources such as:

   - fonts in different sizes and colours
   - spacing between paragraphs and between paragraphs and titles
   - intensive use of attractive colours
   - use of markers to itemize sentences.

3. *Back cover* – the last page of the brochures. All 12 brochures carry a standard text on their back covers talking about the company's commitment to the customer, legal and administrative boilerplates, company's Internet address and telephone numbers for contacting the company's offices around the world. The company's logo and trademark are also included at the bottom of these pages.

An initial survey followed the identification of the physical features. The complexity found in the brochures and the extent of the research questions have dictated the need to perform further manual and computer-based analyses. A spreadsheet-based analysis has related the above composition elements (with special focus on titles and paragraph blocks) to mood (Eggins, 1994, p. 153). Then a computer-based analysis was performed with the Wordsmith Tools (Scott, 1999) application to find the most frequent projected roles by analysing the terms used to refer to the discourse's participants and the processes in which they are involved. Because of space limitations here, the methodology will be discussed in further detail in an upcoming article.

4.4 Results

As mentioned before, it was possible to identify the following inter-action stages in the brochures: (i) presentation of the brochure;

(ii) presentation of product/service; (iii) legitimization (as in Eggins and Martin, 1997, p. 246); and (iv) request for contact. These stages and the resources used to realize them are detailed below.

4.4.1 Presentation of the brochure

In this stage, the company ensures that its message will be acknowledged and accepted by a prospective buyer. This stage performs the phatic communion between the company and the customer on two different fronts, associating the brochure with the company and identifying the target customer of the brochure. It is mainly realized in the front and back covers, where the physical structure of the brochure itself places these covers as an initial stage of the interaction with the customer, thus encapsulating the message contained in the internal pages. In this stage the identification of the brochure and the customer may be accomplished by the following elements:

- *Company logo and trademark* – these elements act as a signature of the company. They are used at the bottom of the front and back covers. In 5 out of the 12 brochures the company also identifies itself by including its name in the title of the brochure, as shown in the example below:

  (1.) Optimize your wireless network with **Acme Telecoms** network optimization solutions

- *Visual identity* – the brochures follow a visual standard that may be associated with the company by its customers through typographical characteristics such as format and size, their use of colours and fonts.

On the customer side, the identification of the target audience may also be accomplished by the following elements:

- *Brochure titles* – identify – and select – the target audience of the brochures, since it is expected that the reader of these brochures is somehow interested in the product/service offered by the company. For the description of stages herein these titles are also considered a starting point for the next stage where the product/service is described.
- *Figures* – the front covers bring images recognizable by prospective customers such as the company's products and the end-users of the products and services.

Additional to these elements, the back covers of all brochures also contain information such as the code number and copyright of the document. This information shows that the brochures are inserted in a well-established legal and administrative environment, possibly increasing their credibility. Also, it is worthy to note that customer's acceptance may be improved by the whole semiotic spanning (Ventola, 1999) where the brochures are delivered to the customers, which may include talks with sales representatives in personal interviews, the company's logo in trade fair booths and other written texts on the company's Internet pages, which may reinforce the association between the brochures and the company and the customer.

4.4.2 Presentation of product/service

In this stage, the company gives salience to specific features of an offered product, product line and/or service, as well as other related services such as financing options and warranty, and the standard commitment of the company to the customer. Starting from brochure titles, this stage is mainly realized on the titles and subtitles of the pages and blocks, combining different linguistic resources used in imperative, interrogative and minor clauses with typographic features such as large bold fonts and spacing between the blocks of paragraphs to accomplish the purposes of this stage.

Minor clauses were the preferred choice for titles in the corpus. Using these clauses, the company increases the emphasis given to the message, as discussed by Rush (1998, p. 170). Also, similar to isolated words on a blackboard, the lack of a complete grammatical structure in these clauses leaves room for more non-realized meaning potential to be realized by the reader. For instance, it is possible to interpret these titles as offers as *do you want x?*, commands as *buy x!*, or information supplies, as *we are offering x* or *we are talking about x*, which can help to avoid a negative answer from the customer, as shown in the example below:

(2.) Network Planning and Design

In the above example it is possible to note that since grammatical words are left out of these clauses any offer may only be made in these clauses by their lexical words, which in the corpus usually refer to entities praised in the community such as the activities intended to improve a network.

Another frequent choice in the corpus was the use of imperative clauses, which are typical realizations of commands. In these commands, the expected response from the reader is the acceptance of the action requested in the command (Halliday, 1994, p. 69). However, there is an alternative response to the commands, the rejection, as discussed by Thompson and Thetela (1995, p. 115), which must be avoided by the text producer, for instance, by setting out the benefits for the customer of carrying out the action. Below are listed some of the various resources found in the corpus to mitigate commands and highlight benefits:

- Projecting to the customer the role of a person that performs positive actions on his/her environment:

    (3.) **Optimize** your wireless network with Acme Telecoms network optimization solutions

- Using adverbials that indicates an improvement in these positive actions:

    (4.) Plan and design networks **faster** with Wizard

- Using subordinate clauses of cause to justify the command:

    (5.) Use mobile screening at the point of service **to satisfy customers and reduce costs**

- Using adjectives to intensify the benefit:

    (6.) Make the **best** use of test engineering resources

With these resources, the company may reduce the possibility of a negative response from the customer and increase the chance that he/she accepts the role assigned to him/her in the interaction. By mitigating the commands, the speech role performed by the company will be something between making **suggestions** and **offers**.

The least frequent choice in the corpus, interrogative clauses are used to make offers in a non-congruent fashion, i.e. instead of acting as a demand for information (Eggins, 1994, p. 152), as shown in this example:

    (7.) Need help in meeting today's demands?

Some interrogative clauses put personal questions to the reader:

(8.) Frustrated that your planning tool will not be ready for the 3G build-out?

While the question in (8) might be considered a kind of invasion of privacy and a possible threat to the customer, it seems justifiable here because being concerned about his/her job makes a professional valued in this community. In this question, it is also possible to see the presence of the company's competitor, which is never explicitly referred to in the brochures (the word *competitors* is only used in the corpus as a reference to buyer's competitors), but indicated by a method or product less efficient or less desirable – a problem – in the company's discourse.

Analysing the three types of titles above, it is possible to note two aspects of this stage. The first is that when highlighting a feature of the product/service, the company prefers to do so by showing the benefits provided by these features rather than on the product/service itself, following today's marketing discourse ideology of 'focus on the consumer'. The second aspect is that the company seems to prefer clause moods that attract the reader's attention while using several resources to avoid a negative response from him/her.

4.4.3 Legitimization

In this stage, the company legitimates the claims of benefits made in the previous stage. It is realized by declarative clauses (and minor clauses from declarative clauses itemized to make reading easy), which are typical choices for supplying information. These clauses are grouped in blocks of paragraphs and carry most of the informational content of the brochures.

The company uses several resources to support the claims made in the previous stage. These resources fall into four categories: (a) promising improvement; (b) projecting roles; (c) providing reasons; and (d) providing evidence. It is worthy to note that in the corpus these resources are often combined in a single sentence and can be found in different sequences from one block to another.

(a) Promising improvements

The company anticipates needs and compares an existing situation and an ideal one. One manner to indicate this possible change is presenting a problem and proposing a solution, usually in the initial paragraphs of a block, as shown in the example below:

> (9.) Your mobile-phone customers want to use their phones any-where they go (...). Because you need to ensure the cover-age (...). Option xxx (...) lets you make indoor RF coverage measurements (...).

Here, legitimization has two aspects. The first aspect is that it requires that the reader identifies himself with the problem, i.e. the company must bring real problems to the buyer's attention. This implies that to be successful the company must use information provided by its customers or other professionals and from pre-existing texts in the community. The second aspect is the risk strategy undertaken by the company, which identifies its customer as a person in need. Although it may increase the chance of a negative response from the customer to the command, this strategy is again backed by the ideology of the market, which praises a professional who is aware of the problems faced by its company and their customers and who solves these problems.

An improvement may also be indicated by using future-oriented modals such as *will* and *can*, as shown below:

> (10.) Acme Telecoms **can** help you meet those demands by providing you with the solutions to develop (...)
> (11.) And, with a more efficient measurement and analysis process, you **will** require fewer drives and fewer technicians to maintain a site (...)

Thompson and Thetela (1995, p. 122) say that this modality may have two functions: (a) to invite the reader to accept the invitation to converge with the projected reader-in-the-text, who considers or possesses the product; and (b) to introduce conditionality since the ben-efits offered by the product will only be realized if the reader accepts the command implicit in the advertising. Therefore, modality may be used in advertising for realizing an interaction where the company promises benefits and the reader is obligated to buy in order to achieve the promised improvements for his/her own company. Additionally, an improvement may also be indicated by a material process such as *maximize, reduce* and *improve*, as:

> (12.) The platform's pre-defined architecture considerably **reduces** system design and planning times

The promise of improvement made with the material process often depicts the company and its products/services as active agents of change, working along with the second type of legitimization described below.

(b) Projecting roles

In this kind of legitimization, the company presents itself and its products/services as entities capable of providing the offered benefits. It is made by projecting roles onto these participants by ascription and naming. Because of its complexity this aspect of this stage will also be detailed in an upcoming article, but some examples are provided below for illustration purposes.

In the corpus, the role most frequently projected onto the company and its products/services is the role of someone who helps the customer, often in causative constructions, as follows:

(13.) Acme Telecoms can **help** you meet those demands (...)

Concerning the products and services, the preferred form to describe them is by the features and capabilities provided by them, such as:

(14.) Some key features of (product) are:
Accurate assessment of end-to-end performance
Standard voice quality measurements
Up to eight networks measured concurrently
Multiple technologies supported

When projecting roles using naming resources (Thompson and Thetela, 1995, p. 117), the company highlights specific features of the products/services by its choice of the terms used to refer to them and their modifiers (Halliday, 1994, p. 191), epithets and classifiers included in the nominal groups. For instance, products and services are often referred to as *solutions* and the employees that provide services as *experts*. On the other hand, the use of modifiers gives salience to characteristics such as quality, adequacy and easy use, such as *accurate, easy-to-use, built-in* and *next-generation*. By modifying these nominal groups the company projects onto products/services additional qualities related to customer needs that may be met, such as accuracy, efficiency, easy use and transport and 'up-to-dateness' in the rapid technological evolution of this industry.

(c)   Providing reasons

It relates the product/services to customer needs, being a resource that reinforces the claim made in the main clause, as follows:

> (15.) Our products support current and emerging formats, so that you can easily manage the constant change and expansion.
>
> (16.) By running data collection software for different technologies – GSM, CDMA and TDMA – on the system's laptop computer, you can do comparative studies (…)

(d)   Providing evidence

Another strategy used by the company to legitimate its claim is to provide concrete evidence to reinforce its offer, such as testimonies and specific promises instead of generic ones. For instance, in the example below the company assumes a concrete commitment stated in numerical terms (the test will take 150 milliseconds instead of 5 seconds) that can be easily verified on-site by the customer:

> (17.) For example, using the test set with the GSM mobile test application, a GSM phase-error measurement (typical 5-burst average), which takes 5 seconds to run on a previous-generation test set, now takes only 150 milliseconds

Testimonies are important instruments to create customer confidence. By transmitting to the customer a positive opinion on the company from well-known people from renowned companies in the market the company may improve the buyer's sense of safety about his/her own purchase as shown in the example below:

> (18.) 'By partnering with Acme, our customers benefit from access to leading-edge simulation and IC process technology enabling them to accelerate their aggressive product development and time-to-market objectives,' states Dr. John Lee, Executive Vice President and Chief Technical Officer at COMPANYCOM Incorporated.

Therefore, when legitimizing their claims the company make offers using declarative clauses in a non-congruent fashion and making associations with previous texts shared by the community such as recommendations and standards issued by standard committees and known problems. Additionally, it is possible to note references to values praised in the ideology of the community such as the image of its professionals and logical reasoning. All these resources may work together to increase the chance that a buyer will agree to identify him- or herself as a future owner of the product/service.

4.4.4   Request for contact

The stage realized mainly by imperative clauses included in paragraphs and sentences highlighted by typographical resources on the back cover:

> For more assistance with your test and measurement needs go to: (website)
> For the latest news, product and support information, and literature, visit our website at: (website) or call your local Acme sales representative.

We can see here another feature of the business-to-business advertising register, which does not use *Buy now!*, preferring instead to invite the customer to make contact, such as *'Let our experienced deployment experts help you implement networks on time and within budget.'* Here the company proposes a partnership with the customer, assuming the role of someone interested in providing help and improving purchase safety.

4.5   Final comments

From day-to-day experience we can see some similarities between the brochures analysed here and the newspapers. For instance, a newspaper reader passing by a kiosk might look for the newspaper he/she usually reads and be attracted by the headlines on the front page. Then, he/she could look for specific sections or news – identified by their titles. Finally, if this reader were really interested in some issue, then he/she could spend some time reading it; otherwise, he/she could just read the headlines and titles and go and do something else. (Of course, there are readers who read the newspaper from beginning to end, but this is not exactly what we could call a frequent behaviour.) Similarly, the readers of encyclopedias can also read only the entries they are interested in – again identified by their titles. Thus, we can imagine that these interaction stages are followed by millions and millions of people every day.

Another important feature characteristic of the brochures is the use of resources to make reading easier, such as the use of titles and paragraph blocks, and itemization of sentences. These resources may work on two fronts to make the material more attractive to the reader, making visualization easier and providing the reader with different entry points, that is, points from which he/she can start to read a brochure, as discussed by Allen et al. (2000), working at the brochure level similarly to the theme (Halliday, 1994, p. 37) in a clause. This characteristic is possibly related to the fact that the activity in which the brochures are involved (variable field) involves the transmission of a large amount of information. However, the community's ideology says time is money and stereotypes their professionals as busy people. These factors determine the use of a channel capable of transmitting large amounts of information while providing resources to make reading easy. Also, it is possible to imagine that efficiency in the transmission of information may help to provide the company with an image of efficiency.

Additional to the use of layout resources and a common physical structure (which makes it easy for the customers to find the information they need), we have another characteristic of the brochures that makes reading easy, the concentration of content in the legitimization stage. As we can see in the above description, legitimization is a more complex and resource-rich stage than the others, which use only titles and isolated clauses. Concentrating content may be considered a strategy to make reading easier. An example of how the purchase process might affect the interaction developed in the brochures is shown below:

- The company uses its position in the market to be accepted by the customer playing the role of gateway.
- The company presents its products/services and gives salience to some benefits offered by them. A buyer in the role of controller or influencer may rapidly know the whole contents of the brochure by only reading the titles and then recommends it or not to the decisor buyer.
- A decisor buyer may read more carefully the benefits proposed by the company and its arguments to prove them.

In the corpus it was also observed that the company makes a trade-off between proposing an offer and avoiding a negative response from the reader by a careful use of previous texts shared by the community, such as the company's image in the market, technical standards and publications, and even previous comments, suggestions and complaints from other customers. Also, using the strategies discussed herein the company may project a positive image to the buyer by projecting onto him/her roles positively valued in the community, such as a professional who makes rational and safe purchase decisions and is an active agent of improvement.

It seems interesting that another possible sequence of meanings may be found when we analyse the roles projected onto a company's discourse. In the corpus the company positions itself as a reliable partner who is aware of the problems faced by the buyers and who knows how to solve these problems. With this purpose, the company projects onto itself a positive image as a renowned and knowledgeable member of the technical community and a market leader. It also provides evidence of its knowledge of the market by offering benefits capable of solving these day-to-day problems and indicating the specific product and service features suitable for handling each of these problems. Overall, these strategies result in a higher chance that the request for contact made by the company is accepted by the buyer. It also seems worthy to note that the linguistic features used, and consequently the meanings created, to accomplish these functions are spread over the interaction stages and throughout the brochures, which may also reinforce the offer made by the company.

From the point of view of genre it seems to imply that it is possible that while accomplishing a local function for interaction in their respective stretches of text, meanings spread throughout the text can be taken together and interpreted by the reader as accomplishing a specific social purpose. In other words, it seems reasonable to suppose that the stages in which an interaction unfolds may be realized in a wave fashion instead of simply being snapped together as Lego blocks. In this vision, these choices would work similarly to the 'resonance in text' described by Thompson (1998, p. 29), who analysed 'choices which share the same potential resonance and which incrementally reinforce each other's effect'. This feature could explain the variation in the sequencing of stages usually found in advertising registers and the problems faced when identifying textual boundaries as discussed by Paltridge (1994), which seems to be an interesting issue to be exploited further. Finally, it seems useful to reanalyse the corpus in the light of recent developments in Appraisal Theory (Martin and White, 2005), focusing on issues such as the construal of attitudes and dialogism in texts.

This work provides some examples on how the use of layout and linguistic resources can be affected by context and ideology. Of course, it is not intended here to show an exhaustive analysis of this relationship, especially because of the huge amount of data that can be obtained from a small corpus. Besides, the relationship between text and context may assume myriads of subtle and intricate forms and, to be consistent with the theoretical foundation followed in this work, it must be considered that the interpretation of the data will depend on the relationship between the data and the previous knowledge of the researcher and is therefore always open to discussion.

References

Allen P., J. Bateson and J. Delin (2000) 'Genre and layout in multimodal documents: Towards an empirical account' in R. Power and D. Scott (eds) *Proceedings of the AAAI Fall Symposium on Using Layout for the Generation, Understanding, or Retrieval of Documents* (Menlo Park, Calif: AAAI Press), 27–34.

Bonoma, Th. and B. Shapiro (1983) *Segmenting the Industrial Market* (Lexington, Mass.: Lexington Books).

Eggins, S. (1994) *An Introduction to Systemic Functional Linguistics* (London: Pinter Publishers).

Eggins, S. and J.R. Martin (1997) 'Genres and registers of discourse' in T.A. van Dijk (ed.) *Discourse as Structure and Process* (London: Sage Publications), 230–56.

Halliday, M.A.K. (1994) *An Introduction to Functional Grammar* (London: Edward Arnold).

Halliday, M.A.K. and R. Hasan (1989) *Language, Context, and Text: Aspects of Language in a Social-Semiotic Perspective*, 2nd edn (Victoria: Deakin University Press).

Martin, J.R. (1984) 'Language, register and genre' in F. Christie (ed.) *Children Writing: Reader* (Geelong: Deakin University Press), 21–30.

Martin, J.R. (1985) 'Process and text: Two aspects of semiosis' in J.D. Benson and W.S. Greaves (eds) *Systemic Perspectives on Discourse* (Norwood, NJ: Ablex), 248–74.

Martin, J.R. (1992) *English Text: System and Structure* (Amsterdam: J. Benjamins).

Martin, J.R. (1997) 'Analysing genre. Functional parameters' in F. Christie and J.R. Martin (eds) *Genre and Institutions. Social Processes in the Workplace and School* (New York: Continuum), 3–39.

Martin, J.R. and P. White (2005) *The Language of Evaluation* (Basingstoke, Hants and New York: Palgrave Macmillan).

Paltridge, B. (1994) 'Genre analysis and the identification of textual boundaries', *Applied Linguistics*, 15 (3), 288–99.

Rush, S. (1998) 'The noun phrase in advertising English', *Journal of Pragmatics* 29, 155–71.

Scott, M.R. (1999) *Wordsmith Tools. Software for Text Analysis* (Oxford, UK: Oxford University Press).

Sherrington, P. (1993) 'What communicators must know about business market-
ing?' in C.H. Patti, S.W. Hartley and S.L. Kennedy (eds) *Business to Business
Advertising – a Marketing Management Approach* (Lincolnwood, Ill.: Business
Books).

Thompson, G. (1998) 'Resonance in text' in A. Sánchez-Macarro and R. Carter
(eds) *Linguistic Choices across Genres: Variation in Spoken and Written English*
(Amsterdam: John Benjamins), 29–63.

Thompson, G. and P. Thetela (1995) 'The sound of one hand clapping', *Text*, 15,
103–27.

Ventola, E. (1995) 'Generic and register qualities of texts and their realization',
in P.H. Fries and Michael Gregory (eds) *Discourse in Society: Systemic Functional
Perspectives* (Norwood, NJ: Ablex), 3–29.

Ventola, E. (1999) 'Semiotic spanning at conferences; cohesion and coherence in
and across conference papers and their discussions' in W. Bublitz, U. Lenk and
E. Ventola (eds) *Coherence in Spoken and Written Discourse. How to Create it and
how to Describe it* (Amsterdam: Benjamins), 101–25.

5

Toward Dialectic Discourse in Advertising: McDonald's, *Adbusters* and the Subvertising of Corporate American Culture

Paul Bick
University of Illinois at Chicago

Introduction

If we understand discourse as a vehicle for the co-construction of identity, and if corporations can be thought of as fully involved discursive agents, then individual consumers, as interactional participants in public corporate discourse, play a key role in co-construction of corporate identity. Likewise, this process contributes to the identity construction of consumers as well, as a consequence of their participation in it. Advertising, as an agent of identity construction, is a two-way street based on clearly defined scripts and well-understood roles. The role of the consumer in the traditional paradigm of corporate advertising discourse is to follow a carefully arranged trail of cues to arrive at a predetermined set of connotations (Pateman, 1990; Cook, 1992). To the extent that we arrive at this prearranged connotational location, and to the extent that we add the sponsoring corporation, its products *and ourselves* to the picture, an advertisement can be said to be successful regardless of whether or not we choose to buy the advertised product. If, for example, we come to understand, by repeated decodings of advertising messages, that a given oil company positions itself as 'the environmentally friendly energy producer', and we choose not to cognitively challenge this position, we support its construction by default. Advertisers control this discourse, but consumer compliance, though passive, is essential.

My intent here is to explore the ways alternative media, specifically *Adbusters* magazine, use the language, images and techniques of advertising to challenge consumers to question the corporate identities they have helped to create, in particular, that of the McDonald's Corporation. If advertising can be understood as an entirely public form of social co-practice, based on our competence in producing and decoding scripts, how might these scripts and their components be used by *Adbusters* to publicly 'dis-advertise' products and deconstruct the 'community of ideology' which unites McDonald's and its customers, while 'subvertising' its corporate identity? What role does the consumer play in this process and how do potentially shifting identities alter the traditional landscape of advertising?

5.1 Discourse

A discourse is not simply a unit of linguistic text, minimally two sentences or more in length, or even a related series of linguistic and visual items, but must be conceived of as a holistic 'unit of human action, interaction, communication and cognition' (de Beaugrande, 1997) and meaning within a given discourse is always jointly constructed by both speaker and listener (Goffman, 1959). Discourse is both (and often simultaneously) expressive and productive. As such, it is an enormously rich and complex human phenomenon – product and determiner of both the natural environment in which it occurs and the *entire human experience* of its participants. There is no such thing as simple discourse. The briefest exchange, or seemingly plain series of utterances, when viewed as integral, though inseparable, components (and products) of context cannot be meaningfully approached outside of that context. Any attempt to do so actually amounts to a contextual substitution; not simply a sterile removal from nature, but a replacement of natural context with an analytical context that necessarily and completely alters the data. As human interaction is by definition, *social*, discourse amounts to social practice or, more specifically, 'discourse *constitutes* the social' (Fairclough, 1992, p. 28). By extension therefore, if *the social* can be seen as part of what constitutes *the human*, then discourse must be approached as a living and dynamic social process by which we, as human beings, define ourselves and exercise our humanity. Even the most remote and isolated of hermits loudly performs discourse in part by his choosing to practise silence – *intention* itself can be viewed as a discursive act. As long as two or more human beings (hermits or not) walk the earth, there will be living, breathing data for discourse analysis.

Discourse is complex, non-static and governed by dialogic principles of heteroglossic continuum (Bahktin, 1981). Our looking at it changes its shape. The boundaries of discourse are difficult if not impossible to define. How then do we find a meaningful way to approach such an animal for analysis? Discourse must be approached from a perspective of analytical semiotics, from as many applicable angles as possible. Discourse analysis, as a field of study, encompasses a vast array of overlapping theoretical approaches and sub-approaches (critical discourse analysis, conversation analysis, narrative analysis, intertextual analysis, visual semiotics, design theory, social constructionism and cultural studies to name just a few), each with varying degrees of usefulness with respect to a given piece of discourse. Light cast from these various directions illuminates equally various aspects of discourse.

Whether or not certain data is chosen for analysis, or a specific theory is applied to a piece of data, is governed both by its relative applicability (theory to data) and, more interestingly, by the subjective interests and knowledge base of the analyst (Jaworski and Coupland, 1999, p. 36). For example, a career narrative analyst who is also a feminist is likely to look for ways to apply principles of NA and feminist ideology to any discourse data before considering other (perhaps more obvious) approaches. In this way, we as analysts bring our own set of passions and layers of text into the discourse. Ideally, to whatever extent a theoretical approach can be applied to a given discourse, it ought to be, bearing in mind that a diverse theoretical foundation benefits both the analysis and the specific theories used – by testing them anew against an ever-expanding universe of data.

Bearing in mind the above view of discourse, this work will attempt to draw from numerous discourse theories, including theories of critical discourse analysis (CDA) (Fairclough, 1995; Van Dijk, 1991; Dellinger, 1995), intertextual analysis within CDA (Fairclough, 1999), visual semiotic analysis (Saussure, 1959; Kress and van Leeuwen, 1996; Barthes, 1977), cultural studies (Lister and Wells, 2001), positioning (Davies and Harre, 1990), semantic script theory (Attardo and Raskin, 1991), and various theories of advertising as discourse, including Pateman (1990), Moriarty (1995), Cook (1992) and Barthes (1977), among others. CDA will provide the philosophical foundation of my analysis, by which I mean that all other theories will be presented under a 'critical' governing principle. The critical analysis of discourse has as its founding presupposition, the notion that all discourse is inherently social and inextricably tied to our beliefs, values and expectations as social beings. Within this framework, discourse represents a call to action in which texts are constructed by 'socially situated speakers and writers' who always have an ideological slant. Consequently, 'meanings come about through interaction between readers and receivers and linguistic features come about as a result of social processes, which are never arbitrary' (Dellinger, 1995). Or, as Fairclough (1995) has suggested, the critical analysis of discourse happens at the juncture of text, discourse practice and sociocultural practice.

The concept of intertextuality in part comprises the underlying essential structure of CDA. It is based on the notion that all writers and readers bring to a given discourse a subjective cumulative set of texts amassed from and shaped by previous discourse. The comprehension of discourse is made possible by the 'social resources' and 'experience' we draw upon from these texts in the process of decoding and interpretation. A given text, therefore, is defined and explained by its automatic cognitive contrast and comparison to related texts (Fairclough, 1999). An understanding of this dialogic interconnectedness of relevant texts is perhaps the most essential feature of CDA in that all of these component texts, taken together, comprise the ideological force – the social salience of discursive argument.

5.2 Discourse and identity

What is the relationship of discourse to identity? In one sense, our individual identities can be seen to derive from our participation in or adherence to a shared system of beliefs within the context of the wider society. Though we may be thought of as having multiple identities that we call upon as needed in context-specific scenarios (Goffman, 1959), identity, for purposes of this work, should be seen as an aspect of 'self' that is co-constructed within a 'community of ideology' (Fowler, 1991). There are a great many possible communities of ideology; at a minimum, such a community need only have two members, but 'advertisers and their customers' surely comprise such a community. The *fact of community* contributes to the identity construction of its individual members and in turn these individual members contribute via discourse to the larger community identity. Within these social structures, social interaction takes place and is manifested in the form of discourse. Unifying social attitudes are formed within these communities, which then provide frameworks for the decoding of discourse (Van Dijk, 1991; Dellinger, 1995). According to Dellinger (1995, p. 4): 'Each of these "group attitudes" can represent an array of ideologies which combine to create one's own personal ideology, which conforms to one's identity, goals, social position, values and resources.'

The relationship of ideology to identity is similar to that of discourse and identity in that ideology is both part and parcel of identity and part of the driving force behind it. Ideologies, therefore, are not simply '(...) arbitrary collections of social beliefs, but specific group schemata, organized by a number of categories that represent the identity, the social structure and position of the group' (van Dijk, 2004, p. 5). Ideology, identity and discourse are inextricably linked components of the self. They are constructs of the shifting self, or as Davies and Harre (1990, p. 3) put it,

> An individual emerges through the process of social interaction, not as a relatively fixed end product, but as one who is constituted and reconstituted through the various discursive practices in which they participate. Accordingly, who one is is always an open question with a shifting answer depending upon the positions made available within one's own and others' discursive practices....

I will argue that *with respect to these components* (ideology and the co-construction of identity), there is very little *functional* distinction to be made between the self of individuals, the community self and the corporate self. At all three levels of organization, the relationship between identity, ideology and discourse remain the same, interdependent and within fixed proximity to one another, which is to say, for our purposes here, corporate discourse 'behaves' like individual discourse. Like human beings, corporations rely (or attempt to rely) on variously mediated forms of discourse to co-construct desired public personas (identities), and do so out of not always apparent ideological frameworks. Advertisers manipulate and rely on a reader's ability to access a complex array of texts in order to establish an emotional connection with the reader. The extent to which co-construction is successful is largely determined by compliance (or at least non-resistance) of the readers, listeners, viewers – consumers involved in the dialogue. As invited agents of co-construction, consumers of corporate discourse are not bound to agree with the identity paradigm suggested by advertisers, however, our positioning within this structure predisposes us to do just that.

Also useful here are the related notions of 'indexical' and 'typification' extensions of reader position as developed by Davies and Harre (1990, pp. 6–7). By extension, I refer to the origins of a given position, or the 'account' of one's arrival at that position. In indexical positioning the meaning drawn from a 'position-imposed attribute' is derived from the entire index of our past experiences with that attribute. In this way, we know how a given positioning attribute should make us feel based on our cumulative feelings associated with this attribute in the past. A typification extension, on the other hand, develops as a reader derives the meaning of a position-imposed attribute from within a 'culturally well-established cluster of attributes'. In this model, position meaning is less a result of associated feelings than a recognition that the position-imposed attribute is part of a well-understood framework we have seen or been part of in the past. We come to recognize where an attribute places us in the bigger picture. In the corporation/consumer positioning framework, for example, consumers are often positioned with attributes of need (i.e. powerlessness, hunger, sexual desire, want of status, of wealth, friendship) and corporations position themselves as benign providers of fulfilment (power, satisfaction, beauty, popularity, happiness) and do so by drawing on the vast textual resources target consumers are presumed to possess (i.e. parenting text, American dream text, patriotism text). The embedded storyline these texts place us in as consumers of corporate discourse, can take many forms and position us in a variety of related ways, but one overarching position is given: the consumer is always responding to the discourse-initiating advances of the corporation. This positioning has explicit power implications. Advertisers always get in the first punch, so to speak, and get to set the rules and lay the groundwork for what follows. Consumers, as perennial responders, are always on the defensive, habitually locked in the position of having to evaluate, accept or reject these advances. We can choose to accept or reject these advances and their implications for identity construction just as we choose to buy or not buy a given product, but the discourse rules of advertising do not allow for an alteration of this fundamental positioning paradigm.

5.3   Corporate identity

Although corporate/consumer discourse can and does come in many forms, including such diverse vehicles as pay cheques, newsletters, policy statements and bookkeeping audits, to name just a few, we now narrow our focus to advertising discourse. We will further specify our inquiry to print advertising (as opposed to radio or television), but for now a general discussion of advertising will suffice. In order to explore the ways corporations use advertising to construct, in partnership with the vast universe of potential consumers, a positive public identity, we must first define, for our purposes here, the shape and nature of advertising. What is advertising? Or, more specifically, what is minimally required for a thing to be recognized as advertising by its targets?

At the most basic level, an advertisement is a sign, or unified construction of signs whose purpose is to sell products or services (and perhaps 'ideas'). More specifically (Pateman, 1990, p. 4):

> Individual advertisements are paradigmatically a means whereby the sale of particular products is promoted, and through the advertisement the...advertiser addresses...any actual reader or viewer as a potential consumer of the product in question.

By sign, I refer to Saussure's original two-part construction in which any word, sound or visual image is both a signifier (the sound, word or image itself) and a signified, the concept or meaning the signifier represents (Moriarty, 1995; Saussure, 1959). Pateman expands upon this basic description by suggesting that we are able to recognize advertising due to our fluency, in the identification of cultural scripts. With an understanding of a script as a 'structure that describes appropriate sequences of events in a particular context...a predetermined, stereotyped sequence of actions that defines a well-known situation' (Schank and Abelson, 1977, p. 41), we begin to see the world as being full of 'script-defined slots', and that we learn to use 'minimal and diverse cues to decide that something now occurring fills a slot in a script' (Pateman, 1990, p. 3). Advertising discourse then, tends to be found in predictable contexts (billboards, magazines, at regular intervals in television programming) and has a 'look', or semiotic organization, we have come to recognize as 'advertising'. 'Slots' are the equally predictable places we can expect to find an advertisement. Who, for example would look at the back cover of an American magazine and not expect to find an advertisement there?

Barthes expands on Saussure to illuminate the notion of signifier. Saussure's two-part sign is straightforward enough, but what exactly do we mean by 'concept or meaning' within a signifier? Bearing in mind our ability to recognize an image as advertising and our knowledge of its purpose, Barthes proceeds to break the notion of advertising signification into three parts: the linguistic message, the coded iconic message and the non-coded iconic message (1977). The linguistic message is the written or spoken linguistic text within an ad, including slogans, logos, company name references and longer text items. He then further divides the operation of the linguistic message into the 'denotational', what the words actually refer or point to, and the connotational, the sum of the images or associations the text inspires within the viewer/reader. Similarly, the coded iconic message is the connotational associations drawn from an image as simply the literal 'what we see' when we look at the image. According to Barthes (1977, pp. 38–9), all images are polysemous in that under the level of signifier, there exists a 'floating chain' of signifieds, from which the reader picks and chooses to construct meaning. Text functions in two possible ways (*anchorage* and *relay*) to help a reader navigate the floating chain to make the 'correct' choices. With anchorage, text guides the reader through these various signifieds, suggesting relevance for some and dismissing others. As anchorage, text teases out meaning from its image. In a relay system, text and image function in a more complementary fashion, one in which 'words, in the same way as the images, are fragments of a more general syntagm and the unity of the message is realized at a higher level, that of the story, the anecdote, the diegesis' (41). The meaning a reader finally attaches to an ad is often ultimately a combination of anchorage and relay, however, in fixed image advertising text usually functions more strongly in its capacity as anchor.

Fairclough has suggested that within CDA, the analysis of linguistic texts, both in terms of signifier (form) and signified (content) is essential to a fully realized comprehension of a sign. Underlying the various functional aspects of linguistic text is the foundational relationship of its form to its content. The shape (syntax) of a spoken or written utterance within a discourse may have broad implications for its ultimate comprehension. According to Fairclough (1999, p. 207), the components of a sign

(...) constitute a dialectical and hence inseparable unity in the sign so that one-sided attention to the signified is blind to the essential material side of meaning, and one-sided attention to the signifier (as in much of linguistics) is blind to the essential meaningfulness of forms.

Linguistic text, either as guide or complement, provides an entry point to image, but the enormous complexity of images, particularly photographic images, requires a multidimensional approach. Cultural studies and the science of visual semiotics take the analyst further into an image, beyond the initial impact to its often quiet yet powerfully suggestive underlying structure. Cultural studies has as its primary focus the 'forms and practices of culture (...) their relationships to social groups and the power relations between those groups as they are constructed and mediated by forms of culture', with a particular emphasis on the visual media (Lister and Wells, 2001). Methodologies of cultural studies include analysis of viewing context (what is it, where is it found), context of production, pictorial and photographic conventions, social conventions and semiotics. The point of these various approaches, these 'ways of looking', is that a visual advertisement contains an enormous wealth of potential meaning accessible at many levels. Producers of advertising are certainly aware of the complex and powerful layers of suggestive meaning in their work, and consumers are almost as certainly unaware of it. Responsibility for the interpretation of meaning in advertising rests squarely on the shoulders of the consumer. Advertisers merely suggest a possible interpretation and the consumer, almost without fail, confirms the suggestion. As Parkin (1971) put it: 'Advertisers get consumers to do their ideological dirty work for them, and keep their own hands clean. Of course, if consumers refused to play the game advertisers would have to change direction.'

Adbusters, an alternative bi-monthly journal, with a circulation of about 120,000 (as of 30 December 2003), is devoted to the proposition that consumers, their culture and their environment are being damaged by unchecked corporate greed, and that by taking a more active stance, particularly with respect to advertising and the relationship of the consumer to the corporation, people can change the behaviour of corporations. According to their mission statement:

> (...) want(s) a world in which the economy and ecology resonate in balance. We try to coax people from spectator to participant in this quest. We want people to get mad about corporate disinformation...and any industry that pollutes our physical and mental commons.

Adbusters is a slick, expensively produced, glossy magazine with a graphics-rich format, combining roughly equal parts photography, produced artwork and linguistic text. They neither sell space for, nor accept, advertising of any kind, although they regularly produce mock ads to fill slots where one would expect to find advertisements in mainstream magazines. These mock ads are designed to closely resemble 'real' ads in their close co-option of well-known corporate slogans, logos and techniques, but function to disadvertise, or 'subvertise' corporate culture, rather than promote it. These 'subverts' attempt to foreground aspects of corporate identity that are usually thought of as negative (damage to the environment, to public health, to the quality of life in poor countries, etc.) and are never emphasized by the corporations themselves. Although *Adbusters* targets many corporations, governments, societal trends and cultural icons, certain of these targets come up for scrutiny again and again. The McDonald's Corporation is one such target.

Consider the following subvertisement (see Figure 5.1), which appeared as the back cover of *Adbusters* 'Appetite' issue (Nov/Dec 2002, No. 44). Beginning from a cultural studies perspective, we first consider the viewing and production contexts for the image. Where is it with respect to both the physical and social environment? Immediately,

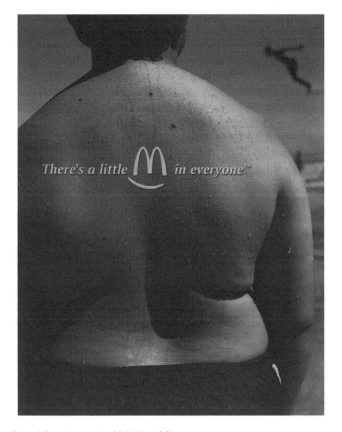

Figure 5.1   Advertisement of McDonald's

we recognize the back cover of a glossy magazine as a powerful script-defined advertising slot. This is a different – more visible, present, expensive and important position than a page inside the magazine. Experience tells us that only large, powerful corporations can afford to advertise in this high power position. So, to begin with, the image, whatever it is, occupies a high-visibility advertising slot in a glossy magazine. Based on what we intuitively know about advertising context, this image is either an advertisement or something designed to function like an advertisement.

What kind of magazine is this? Do we know that this is the back cover of *Adbusters*? If so, do we know what *Adbusters* is all about? If we are familiar with the magazine, we will have come to expect a mock ad in this slot and the time it takes us to process the image will be very short, due to our knowledge of the context in which the image was produced. Therefore, advertising text plays an important orienting role for the viewer from the onset. Expectations are intimately and importantly tied to the connotational choices we make in the decoding process. If a viewer knows *Adbusters*, he will not only expect a subversive text in this slot, but will likely be the type of person who wants to find fault with McDonald's, and knows intuitively where to take this information. If we have never seen *Adbusters*, and have no knowledge of the context of production, the image may be confusing, even indecipherable. What could McDonald's be *thinking*? What else is going on in this magazine? Obviously the subversive nature of the magazine as context is essential to the *proper* decoding of the image. Outside the context of this magazine, the image becomes confusing since it has the look and feel of a legitimate advertisement, but the image and the text do not 'match'. Furthermore, *magazine*, as a genre or setting for the image, even before one knows which magazine, will have a different impact on the viewer than other common types of mediation for advertising discourse, such as a television spot, movie clip, newspaper, poster or billboard would. Magazines come into our personal space. They can be held, contemplated, revisited, shared or simply glanced at. Unlike newspapers, they are not made to be read once quickly and thrown away, but are designed for repeated perusal by multiple readers (Lister and Wells, 2001).

Real McDonald's billboard ads using this identical slogan over more upbeat photographs (featuring culturally diverse groupings of children, children and the elderly, parent/child pairings – all back lit, smiling, healthy and happy looking) appeared along highways and on the sides of buses all over the country in 2001. As Lister and Wells (2001,

p. 66) describe it, 'billboards loom up to confront the spectator and then recede from their field of vision', as the viewer speeds past. The function of the billboard is simply to facilitate a quick, visceral connection with the potential customer, not to stimulate deep thought. Such ads seek to raise certain chains of positively connotational keywords into the consciousness of the viewer, such as McDonald's–wholesome–inclusive–satisfaction...for the purpose of eliciting an immediate or near immediate action (Pateman, 1990). These words answer to our hunger, our uncertainty, and sure knowledge that a McDonald's is nearby.

Where is the magazine located as we view it? Are we at home? At a newsstand? In the doctor's office? On a crowded subway? The subjective physical environment of any viewing will impact the decoding process to a greater or lesser extent. For example, a quick glance at the image while walking past a bookseller's window, might not distinguish it from any other McDonald's ad, and might result in its dismissal forever as more of the same. On the other hand, if the magazine has been on the viewer's coffee table for a month she may, from the comfort of her own couch, have considered the image carefully over time, consciously or subconsciously applying and reapplying various personal texts to its decoding, penetrating its various layers of meaning and their possible implications for herself, her family, her community. She may also come to develop a kind of relationship with its central character, feeling compassion, sadness, anger or disgust with him as her mood dictates. In either case, it is reasonable to assume that the more embedded an image is in our personal environment, the greater the level of intimacy we will come to have with it.

When confronted by a multi-modal (text over photo) image, a reader will look first to linguistic text for direction in how to proceed with decoding. In this case, a well-known marketing slogan, including a very familiar corporate logo, has been co-opted with every detail intact (including the trademark 'TM' symbol). The reader will immediately recognize the slogan/logo combination as belonging to the McDonald's Corporation. 'There is a little (logo) in everyone', appeared widely in McDonald's advertising during the period of the original *Adbusters* release date. Hence, the intertextual bond between this new item and most readers' vast experience with McDonald's advertising, logos and slogans is immediately established at the level of linguistic entry to the image. This discourse is *about* McDonald's and our subjective history with McDonald's prepares our expectations of what will come next. But while the text can be said to function at the most basic level as an anchoring device, providing entrée to the photograph, it is loaded with complex information as to how we, as readers and potential consumers, are to be positioned as we enter the image and with clues showing us how to proceed in its decoding.

Having had a life prior to its co-option by *Adbusters*, let us first look at the slogan in isolation, outside the context of its powerful photo, to explore the power inherent in its construction. At the level of basic denotation, the slogan is vague and ambiguous. It introduces McDonald's and establishes that there is a close relationship between McDonald's and 'everyone', but what exactly is that relationship? The empty, subjectless, 'existential there', contracted to 'there's', sets up the phrase as a gentle yet undeniable statement of fact. The contraction is a prelude to a coming acknowledgement of simple truth. The contracted form has less force and authority than the uncontracted, 'there is', which might suggest that the following true information is not so well known, or may not be recognized as truth by everyone, thus a bit more force is required. 'There's', however, is homey, inoffensive and inclusive. It suggests, there is no need to argue, we all *know* its true.

The NP and the head of the VP are thus joined in a quiet, nearly empty, yet suggestive way. This indicates that the coming object will carry whatever force and power the phrase has, but not so much power, we will see, as to separate it from the locative which anchors its meaning to the reader.

The adjective phrase 'a little' further softens the coming truth. 'A little' is a vague and relative quantifying adjective descripter. It can point to something tiny or something enormous, depending on context and the intertextual framework of the viewer, but is less vague in the softer and more focused sense, 'not too much'. 'There's a little', therefore, introduces the coming object in the gentlest possible way, but with a confidence born of truth.

'In everyone' is a prepositional phrase which locates the object in space. The phrase ties the object to every single human being. As opposed to 'with', 'by', 'on', 'at' or 'near', 'in' suggests an unbreakable bond. Here the referents have something akin to a meronymous relationship. The object is inside us, part of us, like an organ or an ethnic heritage. 'Everyone' (as opposed to 'every person' or 'all of us') encompasses the entire pool of potential customers while denying their individuality. We as individuals have no choice in the matter. It is a matter of simple inescapable truth that the 'object' is ingrained in the very fibre of humanity.

And what exactly is the object that resides within us? Why not just spell out the word McDonald's rather than use this particular logo? Interestingly, the logo is the only clue in the entire image that directly links the image to McDonald's, but it does so in an immediate and undeniable and connotatively complex way. The logo is part of, yet looms above the text, much like McDonald's is included within, yet stands apart from, the wider culture. The logo is much larger and far brighter and of a sunny yellow colour which contrasts with the bland surrounding text, although the logo is embedded within the text, implying both distinction and inclusion simultaneously. Only the largest and most ubiquitous of corporations can afford to leave out their corporate name or the names of the products they wish to sell, relying instead on near universal logo recognition. What Pateman calls the 'absent product' or 'default recognition' process that serves to remind the viewer of McDonald's colossal market saturation, further positions the restaurant as benignly omnipotent in relation to those it serves. The logo is a purely graphic image, a pair of golden arches with a child's crooked smile beneath it, that functions in this context as a syntactic unit of linguistic text; not as the capital 'M' (for 'McDonald's') it resembles, but as the entirety of our associated meanings for McDonald's. The coded iconography of the logo is more powerful and carries more connotational force than a linguistic spelling out of the company name ever could.

The logo links connotatively to the entirety of what we 'know' about McDonald's as framed by our expectations of McDonald's perceived purpose in presenting this material: to promote McDonald's culture (as manifested in its products) as a force for unity and inclusion throughout the world. In fact, our processing of the entire image draws from and contributes to the collective meaning we attach to this logo. In spite of its small size, the logo strikes at the heart, both literally and figuratively, of the ad (not coincidentally, it lies directly over the heart of the character in the photograph). The corporate identity of McDonald's, as they have systematically taught it to us over the years, is entirely encapsulated within this logo.

The enormity of our *positive* experience of McDonald's – positive, because as consumers of advertising we tacitly agree to process this data on the data producer's terms – is stored intertextually within our memories and can be accessed, called into play, with the turn of a key. The logo, of course, is that key. Perhaps more often than we would like to admit, McDonald's uses this key to access our memories and take them out for some exercise. Without regularly using the key, McDonald's runs the risk of losing us, losing our affection, our patronage. They cannot afford to allow their carefully constructed identity cues to become rusty, lest we forget our scripted role in the co-construction of corporate identity, our identity as consumers with respect to that corporation, and the purchasing of corporate product that goes hand in hand with these interlocking identities. This slogan, with its embedded logo, functions to remind us of our ultimate powerlessness and dependence on this truth so much greater than ourselves. It beckons us not to resist, but to embrace this happy and contented community of ideology that we already belong to – that we have always belonged to, whether we like it or not.

Up to this point we have examined, in isolation, the slogan as linguistic text, along with its embedded logo, as socially situated discourse. As a consequence of its having been lifted, in its entirety by the creators of *Adbusters*, from McDonald's advertising I find it useful to examine the slogan not as it appears in *Adbusters*, but out of context, as it was written, and as it is used by McDonald's. As anchoring text in billboard advertising, the slogan identified images of inclusion, diversity, happiness, etc. The images were not designed to elicit deep thought, but to reinforce established positions and suggest a simple, familiar, comfortable solution to any need (hunger) a viewer might have. Counter to our tried and true expectations, *Adbusters* places this familiar slogan/logo script in opposition to the photo script it anchors. This 'script opposition' produces an ideologically divergent cognitive collision within the viewer, which challenges us to re-evaluate the age-old identity paradigm we share with McDonald's (Attardo and Raskin, 1991). The photo is not only unexpected, but stimulates connotatively opposite and highly salient associations. The result is a not necessarily humorous, but highly ironic realization on the part of the viewer. The oppositional juxtaposition of the logo and the photo spins off an accumulating variety of related connotative juxtapositions, for example wholesome/unwholesome, inclusion/exclusion, happiness/sadness, satisfaction/longing, life/death. Each of these negatives has a corresponding positive which describes an established component of McDonald's identity framework. This must be, the viewer concludes, what advertising would look like if corporations chose to market the unseemly 'other' identities we always knew were there but never really think about. This juxtaposition plays on the seemingly reasonable suggestion that most consumers are by now quite aware that America, as a nation, is disproportionately obese and that McDonald's food, relative to other food sources, is fatty and nutritionally shallow. We might not consciously consider these alternative positions (consumer as obese, McDonald's as obesity producing) very often or at all, but this is not bombshell information. Most of us are aware of it to a greater or lesser degree. What is novel here is *Adbusters'* use of common identity frames to bring these subversive 'truths' together.

The role of the photograph in this script opposition is profound and moving. The image is almost completely dominated by the extreme foregrounding of an adolescent boy's naked back. The photograph is marked by and salient because of the child's obvious obesity, which renders him 'non-standard', and thus significant in the eyes of the viewer. The salience of obesity is further emphasized by a variety of compositional and design features. For example, the boy's shirtlessness lends a naked intimacy to the image and dramatic lighting emphasizes rolling folds of fat and skin. Even the child's moles look suspicious and unhealthy. The close proximity of the viewer to the subject, and our spatial orientation beneath him physically elevate this child to a larger than life enormity that all adult viewers must gaze up at. Cropping too, which excludes most of the child's head and his lower body (unnecessary features for building an obesity theme), leave us with a wet, rolling billboard (not accidentally) upon which the anchoring message can be displayed. The photograph, we may theorize, is *about* obesity, and we turn to the text for verification of this theory. The text indeed validates this theory and simultaneously connects 'obesity' to McDonald's and 'everyone'. The text, in this instance, firmly anchors the image to its significance and the image clarifies an inherent ambiguity in the text. 'In', the image informs us, is to be taken literally to mean, 'physically *inside* by eating'. The child is reduced to a canvas on which the shame of McDonald's culpability and a quieter, darker identity can be written.

The centrality of the child's obesity to *Adbusters'* message can be tested by simply substituting the obese child with a prototype standard boy, skinny, smiling, active (perhaps the boy on the diving board?). The result would not only de-signify *Adbusters'* message, but would convert the image from 'subvertisement', seeking to 'unbrand' McDonald's, back into exactly the kind of advertisement McDonald's uses to brand-promote itself.

From a Barthian point of view, the photograph denotes an overweight boy in a swimming suit, near a pool on a sunny day watching another swimmer dive from a diving board. On a very basic level, this is all the image 'means'. We must bear in mind of course that the apparent 'truth' of this denotation is subject to appropriate textual references and other subjective context variables. For example, if this image were to be viewed in a remote African or Indian village, the denotative meaning might not be at all clear and the slogan/logo text would only complicate matters. Without an 'appropriate' denotative interpretation, the intended connotative interpretation is out of the question. We must assume, therefore, that the intended meaning of the 'subvert' is only decodable in its target social context – North American and European, middle-class, moderately affluent, socially conscious consumers. The connotative meaning 'superimposed' on the denotative is heightened and focused by a variety of design techniques which reveal significance in reinforcing layers.

Consider, for example, the artist's framing choices. The overall frame is so tight around the primary subject, that it feels claustrophobic and suffocating. The boy's back almost completely fills the frame in much the same way billboards fill our field of vision along many stretches of highway. The child's enormity cannot be ignored. We cannot look past it or walk around it. It demands salience from the viewer. The image is, however, weighted in an off-balance way to the left, reminding us of the lack of balance in this boy's life, while allowing a sliver of the life beyond him to creep in from the right. The boy looks away from us, there is no visual 'direct address', but our close proximity to the subject closes the social distance and pulls us into the image. Is this boy someone we know? Is it our child? Is it me? Although the image and its private drama are offered up to the viewer as 'items of information, objects of contemplation, impersonally, as though they were specimens in a display case' (Kress and van Leeuwen, 1996, p. 124), our proximity to the boy results in an undeniable intimacy.

Within this central frame, a smaller frame is nestled within the top right corner of the image bounded by the boy's right shoulder. After taking in the overwhelming presence of the central character (the boy), the eye moves to this second frame, a frame within a frame, and begins to process the smaller, softer, yet highly significant image it contains (the diver). Here, Kress and van Leeuwen's notion of partitioning an image into left (given), right (new), top (ideal), bottom (real) comes neatly into play. The new, ideal information in this second frame – an apparently healthy-proportioned child diving, about to take flight from a high dive, sharply contrasts with the 'given', 'reality' of our central character. The boy stands in his colossal obesity, anchored to the earth like a mountain, while the diver soars above against a cloudless sky. Below the diver, the suggestion of other divers, running along a boardwalk en route to soaring, and a stretch of shade-dappled water, jewelled like a Caribbean cove.

The signification of this softly focused background represents a kind of paradise denied, a place of life and vitality the boy has no access to.

We see, from the safety of unobserved voyeurism, that the boy stands apparently slack-jawed, arms at his sides, head cocked slightly to the right, clearly focused on the diver before him. His stance and posture signify longing and respect for the world of the living. Here, the slogan/logo comes back into play, worn as a kind of tattoo, a permanent insignia across the boy's back, at perfect optical centre, one-third the way down from the top of the image. The boy's back is yet a third framing device, a billboard of skin, wet with tears, reminding us again that this sad exclusion, this limbo state outside of life, is not an accident of nature, but a real consequence of this child's (and our) relationship to McDonald's.

5.4 Dialectic

Just as 'normal' advertising calls upon the consumer to complete the identity picture it has partially constructed, *Adbusters* provides simple, 'factual' clues pointing the viewer toward a predetermined conclusion which lies at the junction of text and image: McDonald's is part of who we are, obesity is also part of who we are – is there a connection to be drawn? Text, image and icon (logo) work in a tightly knit unit to construct an undeniably powerful and unexpected signification, which derives a significant amount of its force from its co-option of an existing frame.

McDonald's is a uniquely American phenomenon and there are more than 30,000 McDonald's locations in the world (Schlosser, 2001). As probably the most ubiquitous symbol of American culture, there can be no denying that McDonald's is part of every American's identity and a deeply ingrained part of the larger American identity throughout the world. Here again we see that corporate, individual and community identities are inextricably tied together and interdependent. The corporate/consumer bond suggested by the slogan and logo is cast in a whole new light. Corporate and consumer identities are dialectically linked: a changing perspective on one necessitates a new perspective on the other.

Advertising lies at the heart of this co-constructional identity dialectic, and *Adbusters* co-opts the tools and techniques of advertising to call into question the fixed nature of advertising's identity-constructing paradigm. Are the positioning and the role structures in advertising, by definition, fixed? If not, how does the consumer assume the role of discourse initiator? How do we, as consumers, take an active role in the co-construction of our own identities with respect to corporations?

By questioning corporate/consumer identity structures with mock ads, calls to action, narratives, etc., *Adbusters* suggests that a failure to actively participate in corporate discourse relegates us to the sidelines not unlike our boy by the pool in the subvertisement just analysed. The underlying ideology in the re-formation of consumer identity suggested by *Adbusters* is quite clear: corporate/consumer discourse ought to be seen as a dialectic in which advertisers and their customers converse toward truth as equals in the process of supply and demand. *Adbusters* seeks to challenge consumers to educate themselves and to look at the whole corporation rather than the corporate 'face' they have always been accustomed to gazing upon in advertising. Within this emerging paradigm, consumers are responsible for their acquiescence, their positioning and their identities, both as individuals and as citizens of the American and world communities.

5.5   Considerations for future research

This work is a beginning attempt to look at ways mock advertising is employed by *Adbusters* toward the 'unbranding' of American culture. In addition to mock ads, *Adbusters* employs a variety of other techniques, including text as image, critical graphic design, accidental interventions, direct calls to action, co-option (and reanalysis) of corporate iconography, and 'traditional' journalism, all designed to work together toward the construction of an ongoing series of new corporate narratives. This work continually suggests that the inextricable link between corporations and consumers represents a dialectic of unfixed and potentially shifting identities in which consumers have the power to alter the traditional landscape of corporate/consumer discourse. My aim, as this project unfolds, is to use theories and techniques of CDA, explorations of intertextuality and visual semiotics among other methods, to explore the ways *Adbusters* and other alternative media attempt to construct new paradigms.

References

Attardo, S. and V. Raskin (1991) 'Script theory revis(it)ed: Joke similarity and joke representation model', *Humor*, 4(3), 293–347.
Bakhtin, M.M. (1981) *The Dialogic Imagination* (Austin: University of Texas).
Barthes, R. (1977) *Image Music Text* (New York: Hill and Wang).

Beaugrande de, R. (1997) *New Foundations for a Science of Text and Discourse* (Greenwich, Conn.: Ablex).

Cook, G. (1992) *The Discourse of Advertising* (London: Routledge).

Davies, B. and D. Harre (1990) *Positioning: the Discursive Production of Selves*. http://www.massey.ac.nz/~alock/position/position.htm

Dellinger, B. (1995) *Critical Discourse Analysis*. http://users.utu.fi/bredelli/cda.html

Fairclough, N. (1992) *Discourse and Social Change* (Cambridge, UK: Polity Press).

Fairclough, N. (1995) *Critical Discourse Analysis* (London: Longman).

Fairclough, N. (1999) 'Linguistic and intertextual analysis within discourse analysis' in A. Jaworski and N. Coupland (eds) *The Discourse Reader* (London: Routledge), 183–211.

Fowler, R. (1991) *Language in the News: Discourse and Ideology in the Press* (London and New York: Routledge).

Goffman, E. (1959) *The Presentation of Self in Everyday Life* (New York: Doubleday Anchor).

Jaworski, A. and N. Coupland (eds) (1999) *The Discourse Reader* (London: Routledge).

Kress, G. and T. Van Leeuwen (1996) *Reading Images, the Grammar of Visual Design* (New York: Routledge).

Lister, M. and L. Wells (2001) 'Seeing beyond belief: Cultural studies as an approach to analyzing the visual' in T. Van Leeuwen and C. Jewitt (eds) *Handbook of Visual Analysis* (London: Sage), 61–91.

Moriarty, S. (1995) *Visual Semiotics and the Production of Meaning in Advertising*. http://spot.colorado.edu/~moriarts/vissemiotics.html

Parkin, F. (1971) *Class, Inequality and Political Order* (London: MacGibbon and Kee).

Pateman, T. (1990) 'How is understanding an advertisement possible?' http://www.selectedworks.co.uk/advertisement.html

Saussure, F. de (1959) *Course in General Linguistics* (New York: McGraw-Hill).

Schank, R. and R. Abelson (1977) *Scripts, Plans, Goals and Understanding* (Hillsdale, NJ: Lawrence Erlbaum Associates).

Schlosser, E. (2001) *Fast Food Nation: the Dark Side of the All-American Meal* (New York: HarperCollins).

Van Dijk, T. (1991) 'Racism and the press' in R. Miles (ed.) *Critical Studies in Racism and Migration* (New York: Routledge).

Van Dijk, T. (2004) 'Discourse, knowledge and ideology' in M. Pütz, J. Neff and T. A. van Dijk (eds) *Communicating Ideologies. Multidisciplinary Perspectives on Language, Discourse and Social Practice* (Frankfurt/Main: Peter Lang), 5–38.

6
The *Unofficial* Goals of Business Speeches

Dorien Van De Mieroop
Lessius University College/KU Leuven, Belgium

6.1 Introduction

As Fairclough argues, every 'social practice' involves the construction of identity (Fairclough, 2000, p. 168). In this case, in the 'social practice' of professional speeches the construction of an institutional and professional identity is prominently present, which characterizes a context as institutional (Drew and Heritage, 1992, p. 25). The institutional identity construction in speeches can be defined as follows: the speaker is the mouthpiece of the organization he represents (Lammers, 2000) and the company image is the focus of identity construction; by the term 'professional identity' we understand that the speaker is constructing his own identity and is presenting himself as an expert (Dyer and Keller-Cohen, 2000). This work focuses on the construction of the company image and thus the professional identity construction is left out of consideration here.

In the theoretical background, I sketch how discourse analysts study identity construction by scrutinizing relevant passages in a limited number of cases. The conclusions almost never transcend the local use of strategies to this aim, which is also not the goal of these studies. Although these analyses are very valuable, the question arises whether there is no need for generalizable results, an issue which is quite similar to the debate on conversation analysis. Generalizable conclusions are usually obtained through quantitative analysis, which results in a discussion that revolves around the question whether the quantitative or the qualitative method is the best way to set out analyses. This contribution aims to address the issue of complementarity of these two methodologies, focusing here on the possibilities of quantitative research for the study of identity. For that reason, I draw on other quantitative research traditions to elicit useful methods to obtain an efficient way of quantitatively analysing my corpus. This method is described at length and the results for the distribution of the institutional identity construction are given. Some conclusions can be drawn already, while other hypotheses are formulated and linked to points for further research.

6.2   Theoretical background

The study of identity construction situates itself within the larger framework of discourse analysis. This framework is rather diverse in character, since there is no 'single coherent theory' in the field (Schiffrin et al., 2001, p. 5). In identity-oriented research, most studies focus on a limited number of text fragments, in which the locally constructed identity is analysed (e.g. Schiffrin, 1996; De Fina, 2000). These analyses are very valuable because in the close scrutiny of text fragments the exact strategies, discursive construction and mitigation techniques of identity are revealed. I set out my own analyses by using these techniques, which resulted in case studies of speeches (Van De Mieroop, 2002, 2003).

However, this type of text analysis never discusses larger corpora and it never results in generalizable conclusions, which is of course not the goal of these studies either. These observations are quite similar to the topics in the discussion on the generalizability of conversation analytical results (cf. Cappella, 1990 versus Jacobs, 1990 and Pomerantz, 1990). It is not my aim here to take part in that debate; on the contrary, I believe that it is more useful to try reconciling the differences of opinion. Therefore, I will attempt to analyse identity construction that goes beyond the scope of a few cases. My entire corpus of 40 speeches will be the focus of this work and I will study identity construction by incorporating quantitative analyses in my research. This idea is of course not very new, not even in identity-oriented discourse analysis: Schiffrin and De Fina also used quantitative analyses as a support in their qualitative research on identity (De Fina, 1995; Schiffrin, 2002). However, in these contributions the scope still remained limited to two cases and the quantitative data received a rather marginal role in the analysis and were not mentioned in the theoretical discussion. So methodologically, the quantitative aspect received very limited attention. Although she is not extensively concretizing her ideas, Holmes argues in favour of the incorporation of quantitative research in the study of identity:

> As Schiffrin says, identities are situated both globally and locally (...).
> Both quantitative survey research and qualitative discourse analysis
> can contribute in exploring the ways this is achieved, the ways
> in which gender identity and gender relations are constructed in
> interaction. (Holmes, 1997, p. 217)

Indeed, contrasting these two methodologies can provide a picture of identity construction that is more complete. Researchers from all kinds of different angles stated the same complementarity of quantitative and qualitative analyses (Biber et al., 1998, p. 131; Schegloff, 1993, p. 114).

In this work, I focus on the way this quantitative analysis is carried out for my corpus. For this goal, I draw upon several research traditions to support my analyses and to make sure that the measurements are made in a professional way. Therefore, it is interesting to base myself on quantitative research fields such as the variationist sociolinguistic approach and corpus linguistics in the tradition of Biber. But before I go into these traditions, I will first check whether my corpus qualifies for quantitative analyses. For this matter, I base myself on an influential paper by Schegloff (1993) which is very critical of quantitative research. He suggests that there are three criteria a corpus should meet, before measurements can be carried out. The first is that the denominator should be an 'environment of possible "relevant" occurrence' (Schegloff, 1993, p. 103) in which the numerator can occur. For example, in conversation laughter always needs to be triggered and therefore, laughter cannot be measured by the minute. The focus of my analyses is pronouns per number of words in a speech. Since every sentence has to have a subject, the occurrence of these pronouns measured per word gives a good idea of how many sentences are focused on identity construction in my corpus, and thus this gives a general image of the entire speech. The second criterion is that of the numerator: here, Schegloff stresses that the class of the numerator should be very similar. This is an important remark, and quantitative analyses often lose their value by neglecting this criterion, as for instance De Fina remarks (De Fina, 1995). It is indeed often a complicated matter to ensure a consistent group of numerators and it regularly requires meticulous preliminary qualitative analysis of the possible numerators in the corpus to guarantee the validity of the class. Also in this case, it is necessary to subcategorize the relevant pronouns before they can be measured. For this matter, I will base myself on sociolinguistic analyses, which I will discuss more in depth later. The last criterion is that of the need for a coherent universe as a basis for the analysis. Schegloff illustrates this point with the interview, stating that there is a 'need to discriminate different types of interview speech-exchange systems' (Schegloff, 1993, p. 113), according to the different types of interviews, e.g. survey, employment, language assessment interview. In my corpus, variation was minimized to a maximum: the setting was analogous, the soliloquy character of the speeches was respected in all cases, the structure of the seminar days was similar et cetera. So I believe my 'universe' for analysis is as coherent as possible in a natural setting.

Now that my corpus is 'qualified for quantitative treatment' (Schegloff, 1993, p. 115), I base myself on the precision of sociolinguistic studies to subcategorize the class of the numerator. This tradition is highly based on the work of Labov, who measured how and to what extent elements such as race, age, gender, profession and style influenced linguistic elements, such as the use of the passive (Weiner and Labov, 1983) or the variation in the pronunciation of '*r*' (Labov, 1972). Holmes also worked in this tradition and for instance her research on the pragmatic particle '*you know*' required careful analysis, based on intonational patterns, of the different functions of this particle before quantitative analysis was carried out (Holmes, 1986). This way of handling data is very inspiring, since it shows that substantial reflection preceded the measurements.

On the other hand, the corpus linguistic angle is also relevant, since the corpus under discussion here is rather large for the identity-oriented research question that is addressed in this work. In corpus linguistics, there has been a long tradition of quantitative analyses that started with Chafe's studies of the features of spoken versus written language (Chafe, 1982, 1986). Biber further explored these issues by researching the variation between spoken and written language in different genres, which resulted in his 'multifeature/multidimension' (Biber, 1985, p. 340) analysis of syntactic and lexical features. Much of Biber's studies are based on the automatic analysis of features such as pronouns, passives, hedges and modality by means of specialized computer programs and the results are statistically grounded. In another work (Biber and Finegan, 1989), the distribution of stance markers is analysed in 500 texts. From all these features, Biber and Finegan draw six categories by applying mathematical cluster analysis to the quantitative data. In the same type of research on stance, Watson also uses this method and provides an accurate definition of this type of analysis in linguistic settings:

> Cluster analysis, as the term implies, plots each text against others in relation to the distribution of the features under study. As previously stated, a cluster analysis groups together those texts which are maximally similar in terms of this space, thus reflecting similarity in their overall use of stance features. (Watson, 1999, p. 225)

The corpus linguistic tradition uses very elaborate methods in their search for variation or stance markers. The extent to which their automatic methods and statistical underpinnings are useful for identity-oriented research, is discussed in the following sections.

6.3   Research questions

As discussed above, the identity construction in an institutional context is many-sided. In this contribution the focus lies on the institutional identity construction and the goal is to measure its occurrence quantitatively. On the basis of the diverse linguistic traditions discussed in the theoretical framework, I combine insights from different angles in quantitative analyses in order to find an efficient method for this type of research in the setting of my corpus. In addition, I address some of the methodological issues that are raised by using quantitative analyses for identity-oriented research.

6.4   Method

6.4.1   Description of the corpus

In the course of 2001 and 2002, I gathered my data by attending business seminars. Each seminar consisted of several speeches by different speakers with an identical task, namely giving an informative presentation. The themes of these seminar days were rather technical, such as the handling of water sediment, pathogenic organisms or soil sanitation. Usually in the morning the speeches covered a theoretical or governmental angle, while in the afternoon case studies from companies were presented. This means that there is a certain amount of variation in my corpus, since the speakers had different backgrounds: there were people from the civil service, from universities and from companies. In all, I attended eight business seminars during which I videotaped

40 speeches, which is a relatively large number for discourse analytical studies. All the speeches were given in Dutch by Belgian speakers.

6.4.2   In search of a class of numerators

In his work *Media Discourse*, Fairclough states that the best way to set out identity-oriented research is by asking oneself the following questions: 'What are the participants (voices) in the text, and how are they constructed? – What relationships are set up between participants (...)' (Fairclough, 1995, p. 203).

These 'voices' are the social agents in an interaction and in the specific setting of my corpus, five different participants can be discerned, who can all be given a specific role in the speech and whose identity can be constructed by the speaker. The first and most obvious 'voice' is that of the speaker, who is always present in the setting. But in the content of the speech, the speaker may seem to be absent. For instance, this is the case when a speaker is purely giving information, without any personal comment on the content. Of course, when the speaker adds his own comment, he will start playing a role in the speech and he will show how he feels about the subject, thus assuming a specific position. This social positioning reveals the speaker's goals towards his own identity construction and this can be an interesting element that has to be taken into account. The second 'voice' is that of the passive audience, which excludes the preceding and the upcoming speakers. Usually, the audience does not play any role in the presentation of the speaker, but when it does, it has a very specific and quite pronounced function. When the speaker gives the audience a voice in his own speech, then this is a very marked way of positioning oneself socially. The third social agents are the other speakers, with whom the speaker can go into 'anticipating' or 'lagging' interaction. This is usually quite telling on the part of the speaker's own identity construction, since the speaker will often use these references to show that he is part of the in-crowd, that he knows the field and the persons who work in it very well. However, sometimes speakers criticize their colleagues' opinion, and thus, it is very hard to map this kind of social positioning. On top of that, these references to other speakers are quite rare. The fourth 'voice' is that of the organizers of the seminar day. Usually, the speakers briefly thank them for their effort. Sometimes, speakers go a step further and start discussing certain point of views of the organizers. Since this is only rarely the case and also because the role of the organizers is usually so minimal or implicit, the positioning of the speaker towards this role is not very important. The final 'voice' is that of the company or institution the speaker works for. Although this role is only present in the background, it can make an important contribution to the content of the speech. The presence of the company in the presentation is obviously an important element of image building, which is also a significant indication of the goals of the speaker.

In this work, I am of course concentrating on this last 'voice' and the way this identity construction of the company or the institution of the speaker is linguistically translated. Identity analyses focus on several linguistic elements like modality (Fairclough, 2000; Fairclough and Wodak, 1997), humour (Dyer and Keller-Cohen, 2000; Holmes and Stubbe, 2003), metaphors and passives (Chilton and Schäffner, 1997). All these studies have one feature in common that is relevant for all kinds of different angles of identity construction, and that element is the use of pronouns. In many studies, this feature is the focus of the analyses, with which other elements can be combined (Lammers, 2000, 2001) and the absence of which is also an important identity marker (Timor and Landau, 1998). In short, to summarize in Fairclough's words: 'Pronouns (as always) are worth noting (…)' (Fairclough, 1995, p. 145).

Institutional identity construction is reflected in the use of the we-pronoun and this will also be the feature that will be analysed quantitatively. But before we can start measuring its distribution, certain demands have to be met as to the exact referents of this pronoun.

6.4.3   Different categories in the class of numerators

In the literature it has been shown that pronouns are an excellent feature to be measured quantitatively (Alber et al., 2002; Suleiman et al., 2002), but as is shown in certain analyses of the we-pronoun, its referents can be vague and thus ambiguous, which renders quantitative data invalid for comparison (cf. De Fina, 1995). Pronouns are indexical markers of context, and thus local contextual analysis has to identify the different referents, which is the basis for a subcategorization of these we-forms. The category that has an 'institutional' meaning then qualifies for the quantitative analyses.

For this subcategorization I base myself on the classes of we-forms that Lammers proposes (Lammers, 2001). He suggests that there are five different groups of referents for the we-form. The first one is the institutional we-form, in which the referent is the organization or institution the speaker represents. The second is the interactional we-form, with which both the speaker and the other participants in the interaction are being referred to. The third category is that of the vague we-form, in which the exact reference is unclear. Lammers argues that in the type of interaction he studies, which is that of conversations between clients and employees of the social services, this we-form states a generally accepted opinion and thus has the function of an argument. This type of meaning is not regularly generated in my corpus, and the reason for this can be found in the monological character of my corpus. Since there is no interaction, the speaker cannot react to the audience's ideas. However, a very vague and general meaning of the we-form is present in my corpus, so in this respect this category is relevant here as well, although without this special function. The fourth type of we-form is that of the indefinite we, a form that is replaceable in a very specific way: this type of 'we + verb' can always be substituted by 'there is/are'. The final category is that of the we in quotes. All these types of we-forms occur in my corpus and in Table 6.1, an example of all the categories is given.

Categories 3, 4 and 5 are quite special cases: 3 has no definite referents, 4 does not have the real meaning of the personal pronoun we and the referents of 5 always switch according to the agent who is being quoted. Only the categories 1 and 2 have fixed referents and so they could have an identity constructional function.

Since the categories proposed by Lammers are intended for a truly interactional corpus, there are some minor changes and different referents for my corpus of speeches. The institutional category typically has the referent Lammers proposes, namely the company or the institution of the speakers. However, in certain cases the speaker refers by a similar type of we-form to a group of experts of whom he is a part. The same kinds of references are made as in the typical institutional referent, because by means of this form, the speaker is talking about an action that is not necessarily executed by himself, but instead by a group he represents. An example of this type of we-form referring to a group of experts can be seen here:

En ook polio kregen <u>we</u> onder controle. Dit is een euh een krant die in Los Angeles uitkwam op 12 april 1955 en het was voorpaginanieuws, wereldnieuws, dat het poliovaccin, waar een heel grote studie in de Verenigde Staten mee gebeurd was, dat dat bleek te werken, 80 tot 90 % effectief. (speech 19, p. 2)

And <u>we</u> managed to get polio under control. This is a, er, newspaper that was published in Los Angeles on 12 April 1955 and it was front page news, world news, that the polio vaccine, on which a huge study was executed in the United States, that that proved to be working, 80% to 90% efficient.

Table 6.1 The five categories according to Lammers (2001) and examples from my corpus

Category	Example
1. Institutional	Zeer kort euh, wil ik toch even zeggen voor wat wij staan, wat onze kern, wat onze core businesses zijn. (speech 17, p. 1)
	In short, er, I just want to say what we are, what our core, what our core businesses are.
2. Interactional	Euh, we zullen straks zien dat dat dus verschillend is met de bevoegdheidsverdeling in ons land. (speech 15, p. 1)
	Er, we shall see later that that is different from the division of authority in our country.
3. Vague	Nu, hoever zijn we verwijderd van een in werking treden van het Kyoto-protocol? (speech 3, p. 2)
	Now, how far are we removed from the Kyoto Protocol to become effective?
4. Indefinite	We hebben die waterbodem, die historische laag, die donkerbruine laag, dat is eigenlijk de historische waterbodem van dat ecosysteem, en dan het actieve sediment of dus die sedimentlaag. (speech 8, p. 2)
	We have the bottom of the water, that historical layer, that dark brown layer, that actually is the historical bottom of that ecosystem, and then the active sediment or that sediment layer.
5. In quotes	Bijvoorbeeld een bedrijf kan zeggen: 'Tja, euh, in 't weekend werken wij niet, dan heb ik eigenlijk niks nodig (...)'. (speech 15, p. 4)
	For example, a company can say: 'Well, er, in the weekend, we don't work, I don't need anything then actually (...)'.

The referent of this we-form is clearly beyond the scope of the speaker, through his explanation it becomes clear that it is a rather old American study, of which a relatively young Belgian speaker cannot have been a part. This type of referent of the we-form is categorized separately and it receives a special marking so that it can be studied at a local level in the qualitative analysis. So these identity markers are not incorporated in the quantitative analyses because they do not reflect institutional identity construction. Moreover, this category is only marginally represented in my corpus and thus the use of quantitative analysis is very limited. I will come back to this point later in the discussion of the results.

Also concerning the second group, there is a remark for my corpus. On the one hand, these kinds of interactional references have a strictly structuralizing function in my corpus, and so their contribution to the

Table 6.2 The two relevant categories for my corpus

Category	Different types of we-forms
1. Institutional we	– reference to the company the speaker represents
2. Structuralizing we	– interactional (inclusive) we
	– *pluralis majestatis*

content of the speech is quite limited. On the other hand, there are similar types of structuralizing references that refer solely to the speaker. This technique can be referred to as the rhetorical *pluralis majestatis*, in which the speaker refers to himself by means of a plural pronoun, as in the following example:

> (. . .) gaan we seffes nog iets over zeggen (. . .). (speech 19, p. 1)
> *(. . .) we are going to say a bit more about that later (. . .).*

Also the we-forms of this type have a strictly structuralizing function. Therefore, I call the second group the structuralizing category, since in my corpus it has this function only. In summary, Table 6.2 shows the two types of we-forms that may be relevant for my corpus.

6.4.4 Different levels or 'frames' in speeches

The final question is whether both categories are relevant for an analysis of identity construction in my corpus. To answer this question, I would like to draw on Goffman's notion of frame analysis and related notions by Chafe, Fauconnier and Zupnik.

In his seminal work *Frame Analysis* (Goffman, 1974), Goffman introduces the notion of frames in the analysis of discourse. He suggests that these are different levels of discourse of which a participant has a lot of expectations, based on preliminary experiences. Since Goffman 'offered few explicit guides as to his research strategies' (Drew and Wootton, 1988, p. 2), it is easier to work with Collins' definition:

> Goffman's vision is that conversation is always part of a larger frame in interaction. Only if the larger frame is properly handled can the conversation take place; and just how that larger frame is set will determine what kind of conversation can proceed within it. Most of the time we don't notice this larger frame, because it is routine and can be taken for granted; that is why Goffman is at pains to pick out instances when it is not quite routine, and hence intrudes in the

form of 'byplay' and the like. (...) Goffman is saying that talk needs to be analysed 'from the outside in', with the larger frame setting the conditions for what can emerge within it. Now, what determines the larger frame, with which the analysis should begin? There are several layers here, which [making more explicit what Goffman refers to only in passing] we can call (1) the physical world, (2) the social ecology, and (3) the institutional setting. (Collins, 1988, p. 51)

Within this institutional setting, there are still several different layers, which Goffman refers to as 'frame spaces' or 'footing' (Goffman, 1979). Interaction can thus be divided in different levels, or different worlds, as Chafe puts it (Chafe, 1979, 1980). He illustrates this idea by showing how interviewees, who had to retell the story of a film they had seen, 'shift worlds' when the focus of their talk changes from the content of the film to the interview setting. From a cognitive point of view, Fauconnier introduces the notion of 'mental spaces' (Fauconnier, 1994) where a shift of spaces is constructed by means of 'space-builders'. Unfortunately these three interesting notions are not really concretized in any of these papers.

One exception is a paper by Zupnik, in which the term 'discourse space' (Zupnik, 1994) is based upon the ideas of Goffman, Chafe and Fauconnier. She argues that especially through pronoun analysis, one can see a shift from one discourse space to another. She applies this theory by analysing a panel discussion on the topic of the viewing of a controversial political movie. The basis of all these different concepts is quite similar, namely that there are several levels of discourse. When applying this theory to my corpus, it is quite obvious that there is a difference between a speaker's talk on his background, his daily activities and his colleagues at his firm as opposed to references to the setting of the speech, the seminar day or the other speakers. The first type of examples is part of the content frame of the speech, while the second type is linked to the context frame or speech-setting frame. Of course, the institutional identity construction situates itself on the level of the content frame of the presentations, building a 'self' outside of the speech. As Zupnik showed in her article (Zupnik, 1994), pronouns are excellent markers of these different frames, as is also the case in my corpus. The institutional we-form refers to a world beyond the specific setting of the speech and thus helps to construct identity in the 'real world', while the structuralizing we steers the presentation in the right direction. Thus for the study of identity construction, the institutional class is the subcategory that is relevant and thus qualifies for quantitative analysis.

6.4.5   The type of pronouns that are taken into account

One final remark concerns the type of pronouns that are counted: both personal and possessive pronouns serve the goal of identity construction, an opinion that is shared in the literature:

> Moreover, as Wilson acknowledges (1990, p. 58), reference to self or others can be achieved in discourse through the use of possessive pronouns, like 'my', 'mine', 'our', 'ours', 'your', etc; Therefore a taxonomy of items that can realize personal reference in English cannot be limited to personal pronouns but should include other types of pronouns. (De Fina, 1995, p. 386)

and

> We noted that the principal dimensions that determine possessive constructions are the same ones we identified for personal pronouns, i.e. those of control or power and distance or proximity. (Mühlhäusler and Harré, 1990, p. 226)

6.5   Results

The results of the quantitative analyses are shown in Figure 6.1, which shows the frequency of the institutional we-form in the numerator and the amount of words in the speech is the number in the denominator. The fraction is then normalized to the occurrence of we-forms per thousand words. This is the regular way of presenting data which are used for comparison (see for example Biber and Finegan, 1989, p. 98) and it is a reliable way of normalizing since the average amount of words in the speech is more than 4500. For instance, speech 11 has the highest frequency of institutional markers, since there were 173 occurrences of institutional identity markers. This speech contained 4372 words, and thus this result is normalized to almost 40 instances of institutional we-forms in every thousand words of the speech.

6.6   Methodological conclusions

In this part, I will draw some conclusions on the basis of these results. In these considerations, one easily bumps into the restrictions of this analysis. However, I also try to show how the quantitative measurements complete the type of findings from qualitative analyses. In the end, it is

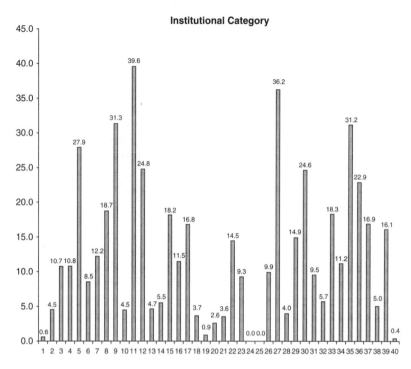

Figure 6.1   The results of the institutional category in 40 speeches

clear that the combination of different methodologies is indeed a very fruitful and also a highly necessary method.

As was discussed in section 6.4.3, there are some speeches in which the we-form refers to a group of experts of which the speaker is a part. Out of 40 speeches, there were only three in which this type of reference occurred. Speech number 19 had mixed references, while the institutional we-forms in speeches 24 and 25 were strictly referring to this group of experts. These are obviously cases that are very interesting to analyse at a more local level, thus by means of qualitative analysis. The comparison between speeches with institutional references and these speeches is an interesting angle, since the strategies and goals of these different identity constructions are probably quite diverse. This is a question that can only be answered by means of the scrutiny of text fragments. The presence of these markers is of course not reflected in the qualitative data since they could not be included in the measurements because of the criterion of similarity in the denominator. Because of its marginal frequency, the analysis of this type of identity construction is restricted to a qualitative study of the strategies and goals of the speaker. Although this presence is highly interesting, the fact that it cannot be included in quantitative analysis is a clear disadvantage of this methodology. On the other hand, because these measurements are applied to the entire corpus, the fact that another type of identity construction is present, is revealed. So this is actually also a plus point of quantitative analysis: because of the feasibility of large corpus studies, unexpected techniques are exposed and can be analysed further by means of other methodologies.

In addition, through these analyses another type of conclusion can be drawn, namely that it gives insight into 'the bigger picture' (Haakana, 2002, p. 228) of the corpus. From the qualitative analyses, the question emerged to what extent the same attention is paid to corporate image building in the 40 speeches. Of course, because of the time-consuming techniques of text scrutiny of a limited number of fragments, qualitative analyses are obviously restricted to case studies (cf. Schiffrin, 1996; De Fina, 2000). However, there was one hypothesis that came out of these analyses, namely that in most speeches, limited attention is given to identity construction. Most speakers seem to focus on the informative goal and neglect the way they present themselves or their company. From the quantitative study of the distribution of the institutional we-forms, there is an obvious conclusion which answers this question. The data clearly show that there are quite a lot of speeches of which the institutional identity construction is rather weakly present. In 13 out of 40 speeches, the speaker uses the institutional we-form five times or less per thousand words.

This finding is comparable to one of Biber and Finegan's conclusions on the analysis of 'stance'. In a way, the expression of 'stance' is quite similar to identity construction, since this also deals with the positioning of the speaker towards the subject of the speech: 'By stance we mean the lexical and grammatical expression of attitudes, feelings, judgments, or commitment concerning the propositional content of a message' (Biber and Finegan, 1989, p. 93). In their analysis of stance in a very large corpus of texts, Biber and Finegan came up with the following results:

> Cluster 2 ('Faceless stance'), marked by the relative absence of all affective and evidential stance features considered here, is by far the largest cluster identified in the present study. It has 326 texts (65%) of our corpus (...). There are also large majorities of prepared speeches

(86%) (...). This overall pattern indicates that such expression of stance (affective or evidential) is a 'marked' choice in English, and that the prevailing norm is to leave stance lexically and grammatically unmarked, thus putting the burden on addressees to infer a speaker's stance. (Biber and Finegan, 1989, p. 108)

So this result could be anticipated on the basis of the conclusions of Biber and Finegan.

However, this type of conclusion demands more research as to the reason why this frequency is divided as such. At this point, a shift in methodologies is required, as Lazaraton also states in her discussion of the two types of methods: 'In other words, quantitative discourse analysts seek to determine how often something happens, while why and how things happen are the focus of the qualitative discourse analysis' (Lazaraton, 2002, p. 33). So there could be two explanations for this high frequency of neutral speeches: on the one hand, the identity construction may be hidden in other linguistic elements. As was discussed above, there are quite a lot of strategies and linguistic features that support and construct identity. It may be the case that these speakers do not use pronouns as identity markers. On the other hand, it may simply be that the neutral variant of the speech is more frequent. In the setting of my corpus, I suppose that the speakers were asked to give an informative presentation and thus that the persuasive goal of building institutional identity is quite *unofficial*. The option of pursuing this goal is left open in the job with which the speakers were charged, so it is up to them whether they choose to build an institutional identity or not. To find an answer to this question, the matter has to be investigated more thoroughly. For this purpose, one has to start by scrutinizing relevant passages by means of qualitative analyses. However, this does not suffice to account for all the aspects of this issue. The question concerning the kind of task the speakers were given arises as well, since it influences the markedness of the choice of building identity. This type of issue can be addressed by using ethnographic techniques, which will have to be carried out retrospectively. By interviewing the organizers of the seminar days and some of the speakers, these voids in my data can be filled. By interviewing the speakers, another issue will be raised, namely to what extent their intended identity constructions are perceived as such by the audience. This matter is dealt with by a survey that was carried out during the seminar days, thus adding a completely different methodology to the preceding three types of methods.

The aim of researching the same matter from four different angles is indeed to fill in the gaps and to complete the picture. As such, a complete as possible analysis is provided of the identity construction in speeches. This method of combining different research techniques is called triangulation. This term is borrowed from sociological studies and can be described as follows: '(...) triangulation is similar to the common rule in journalism not to report anything that is ambiguous or controversial without at least two and preferably three sources to give it additional support' (Roth and Mehta, 2002, p. 153). By combining different angles, the credibility of the conclusions increases (Janesick, 1998, p. 119) since they are corroborated by data from other methodologies.

The quantitative analysis forms a very important angle in this combination of methods, since it gives information on the identity construction in the entire corpus. The choice of the numerator is seriously considered, the subcategorization is meticulously carried out so that the data are truly valuable. The type of conclusions that can be drawn at this point is limited to describing the distribution of a linguistic element as marker of institutional identity. But the measurements in this chapter are only the start of the quantitative project in this research. In the following section, I describe the complementing measurements and I explore some of the far-reaching possibilities of this type of research.

6.7 Points for further research

The results described here are of course limited to analysing the degree of institutionality in the speeches. However, as was discussed while discerning the different 'voices' in the setting of my corpus, there are two other participants that can play an important role in the social positioning of the speaker and thus in his identity construction. These two other categories also correspond to pronouns: the category of the speaker is reflected in the first person singular pronouns, while the group of the audience is shown through the analysis of the second person, both singular and plural. These pronouns obviously need a preliminary subcategorization as well before the measurements can be carried out, similar to the method described here. Once the identity-oriented markers are extracted from the corpus, the identity construction of the two other 'voices' can be measured as well. This results in three different dimensions of identity construction, which will give a more complete picture of the way identity is distributed in the entire corpus. So actually, every speech will receive data on three variables, namely institution, speaker and audience dimension. Inspired by the work of some corpus linguists (Biber and Finegan, 1989; Watson, 1999), mathematical cluster analysis can be applied to these results, which will group the 40 speeches in clusters of similarity. This would of course provide an overview of the way the identity-constructing pronoun markers are distributed among this rather large corpus, and it would supply me with an interesting starting point for a local, qualitative analysis of the exact strategies that are used to build this identity. In addition, other variables such as passives and the expression of uncertainty by means of modal verbs could be studied as well. These elements also contribute to the way identity is constructed, or on the contrary, responsibility avoided.

At the micro-level, quantitative analysis also provides further possibilities: for instance, the distribution of the identity-marking pronouns within the speeches is an intriguing matter as well. The qualitative case studies suggested that speakers tend to focus more on identity construction at the beginning of a speech. This was typically reflected in a company presentation in the introduction. To what extent this conclusion is applicable to the rest of my corpus, remained an unanswered question. Quantitative analysis within the speech may succeed in addressing this issue. Another opportunity of this type of methodology is applying a subcategorization that is even more radical than the one described above. By extracting from the relevant identity-constructing categories two intriguing types of identity construction, one could come to more content-oriented conclusions. As Dyer and Keller-Cohen suggest, the distinction between epistemic and agentive references is quite telling as to the strategies used in constructing identity:

> The agentive self is associated with action and the temporal progression of narrative, and the epistemic self with thoughts, feelings and beliefs. Such a template seems well suited to the construction of professional expertise, since the narrator is able to depict himself as the main protagonist in the narrative, controlling the action, and also explaining and justifying his actions through his epistemic self. (Dyer and Keller-Cohen, 2000, p. 294)

So if each category was studied in more depth by quantitatively distinguishing between these types, the combination of the three dimensions would give content information on the way identity is strategically constructed throughout the entire corpus. So I believe that quantitative analyses offer a lot of opportunities because their corpus can be quite extensive. I am also convinced that by researching different variables and combining these results, quantitative analyses can contribute to a more intrinsic study of identity-constructing strategies.

References

Alber, J., D. O'Connell and S. Kowal (2002) 'Personal perspective in TV news interviews', *Pragmatics*, 12 (3), 257–71.

Biber, D. (1985) 'Investigating macroscopic textual variation through multifeature/multidimensional analyses', *Linguistics*, 23 (2), 337–60.

Biber, D., S. Conrad and R. Reppen (1998) *Corpus Linguistics: Investigating Language Structure and Use* (Cambridge: Cambridge University Press).

Biber, D. and E. Finegan (1989) 'Styles of stance in English: Lexical and grammatical marking of evidentiality and affect', *Text*, 9 (1), 93–124.

Cappella, J.N. (1990) 'The method of proof by example in interaction analysis', *Communication Monographs*, 57, 236–42.

Chafe, W. (1979) 'The flow of thought and the flow of language' in T. Givón (ed.) *Syntax and Semantics*, Vol. 12: *Discourse and Syntax* (New York: Academic Press), 159–81.

Chafe, W. (1980) 'The deployment of consciousness in the production of narrative' in W. Chafe (ed.) *The Pear Stories, Cognitive, Cultural, and Linguistic Aspects of Narrative Production* (Norwood: Ablex), 9–50.

Chafe, W. (1982) 'Integration and involvement in speaking, writing and oral literature' in D. Tannen (ed.) *Spoken and Written Language: Exploring Orality and Literacy* (New Jersey: Ablex Publishing Corporation), 35–53.

Chafe, W. (1986) 'Evidentiality in English conversation and academic writing' in W. Chafe and J. Nichols (eds) *Evidentiality: the Linguistic Coding of Epistemology* (New Jersey: Ablex Publishing Corporation), 261–72.

Chilton, P. and C. Schäffner (1997) 'Discourse and politics' in T. Van Dijk (ed.) *Discourse as Social Interaction* (London: Sage), 206–30.

Collins, R. (1988) 'Theoretical continuities in Goffman's work' in P. Drew and A. Wootton (eds) *Erving Goffman. Exploring the Interaction Order* (Cambridge: Polity Press), 41–63.

De Fina, A. (1995) 'Pronominal choice, identity, and solidarity in political discourse', *Text*, 15 (3), 379–410.

De Fina, A. (2000) 'Orientation in immigrant narratives: the role of ethnicity in the identification of characters', *Discourse Studies*, 2 (2), 131–57.

Drew, P. and J. Heritage (1992) *Talk at Work. Interaction in Institutional Settings* (Cambridge: Cambridge University Press).

Drew, P. and A. Wootton (1988) 'Introduction' in P. Drew and A. Wootton (eds) *Erving Goffman. Exploring the Interaction Order* (Cambridge: Polity Press), 1–13.

Dyer, J. and D. Keller-Cohen (2000) 'The discursive construction of professional self through narratives of personal experience', *Discourse Studies*, 2 (3), 283–304.

Fairclough, N. (1995) *Media Discourse* (London: Edward Arnold).

Fairclough, N. (2000) 'Discourse, social theory, and social research: the discourse of welfare reform', *Journal of Sociolinguistics*, 4 (2), 163–95.

Fairclough, N. and R. Wodak (1997) 'Critical discourse analysis' in T. Van Dijk (ed.) *Discourse as Social Interaction* (London: Sage), 258–84.

Fauconnier, G. (1994) *Mental Spaces: Aspects of Meaning Construction in Natural Language* (Cambridge: Cambridge University Press).

Goffman, E. (1974) *Frame Analysis. An Essay on the Organization of Experience* (Boston: Northeastern University Press).

Goffman, E. (1979) 'Footing'. *Semiotica*, 25 (1/2), 1–29.

Haakana, M. (2002) 'Laughter in medical interaction: From quantification to analysis and back', *Journal of Sociolinguistics*, 6 (2), 207–35.

Holmes, J. (1986) 'Functions of "you know" in women's and men's speech', *Language in Society*, 15, 1–21.

Holmes, J. (1997) 'Women, language and identity', *Journal of Sociolinguistics*, 2 (1), 195–223.

Holmes, J. and M. Stubbe (2003) *Power and Politeness in the Workplace* (London: Longman).

Jacobs, S. (1990) 'On the especially nice fit between qualitative analysis and the known properties of conversation', *Communication Monographs*, 57, 243–9.

Janesick, V.J. (1998) *Stretching Exercises for Qualitative Researchers* (Thousand Oaks: Sage).

Labov, W. (1972) *Sociolinguistic Patterns* (Philadelphia: University of Pennsylvania Press).

Lammers, H. (2000) 'Het gebruik van we/wij in media-interviews', *Tijdschrift voor Taalbeheersing*, 22 (3), 200–19.

Lammers, H. (2001) 'Het gebruik van we/wij in medewerker-cliëntgesprekken bij de sociale dienst', *Tijdschrift voor Taalbeheersing*, 23 (3), 218–35.

Lazaraton, A. (2002) 'Quantitative and qualitative approaches to discourse analysis', *Annual Review of Applied Linguistics*, 22, 32–51.

Mühlhäusler, P. and R. Harré (1990) *Pronouns and People* (Oxford: Basil Blackwell).

Pomerantz, A. (1990) 'Conversation analytic claims', *Communication Monographs*, 57, 231–5.

Roth, W.D. and J.D. Mehta (2002) 'The Rashomon Effect, combining positivist and interpretivist approaches in the analysis of contested events', *Sociological Methods and Research*, 31 (2), 131–73.

Schegloff, E.A. (1993) 'Reflections on quantification in the study of conversation', *Research on Language and Social Interaction*, 26 (1), 99–128.

Schiffrin, D. (1996) 'Narrative as self-portrait: Sociolinguistic constructions of identity', *Language in Society*, 25, 167–203.

Schiffrin, D. (2002) 'Mother and friends in a Holocaust life story', *Language and Society*, 31, 309–53.

Schiffrin, D., D. Tannen and H. Hamilton (2001) *The Handbook of Discourse Analysis* (Malden: Blackwell).

Suleiman, C., D. O'Connell and S. Kowal (2002) '"If you and I, if we, in this later day, lose that sacred fire…": Perspectives in political interviews', *Journal of Psycholinguistic Research*, 31 (3), 269–88.

Timor, U. and R. Landau (1998) 'Discourse characteristics in the sociolect of repentant criminals', *Discourse and Society*, 9 (3), 363–86.

Van De Mieroop, D. (2002) '"Ik weet niet of ik niet al te veel tijd gesnoept heb": een analyse van corporate image-markeerders' in R. Haest, L. Van Waes and D. Caluwé (eds) *Communicatief bekeken: liber amicorum Stijn Verrept* (Mechelen: Kluwer), 181–7.

Van De Mieroop, D. (2003) 'De wisselwerking tussen eigen en institutionele iden-titeit' in L. Van Waes, P. Cuvelier, G. Jacobs and I. De Ridder (eds) *Studies in Taalbeheersing*, Vol. 1 (Assen: Van Gorcum), 330–42.

Watson, G. (1999) 'Evidentiality and affect: a quantitative approach', *Language and Literature*, 8 (3), 217–40.

Weiner, E.J. and W. Labov (1983) 'Constraints on the agentless passive', *Journal of Linguistics*, 19, 29–58.

Wilson, J. (1990) *Politically Speaking; the Pragmatic Analysis of Political Language* (Oxford: Blackwell).

Zupnik, Y.J. (1994) 'A pragmatic analysis of the use of person deixis in political discourse', *Journal of Pragmatics*, 21, 339–83.

7

Shaping the Corporate Reputation of PowderJect Pharmaceuticals plc: a Text-Based Analysis

Yvonne McLaren-Hankin
School of Management and Languages, Heriot Watt University, Edinburgh, UK

and

Călin Gurău
GSCM – Montpellier Business School, Montpellier, France

7.1 Introduction

A good reputation ranks among the most valuable assets of any company. It not only increases the value for shareholders, it also wins the loyalty of customers and consumers, maximizes the return on investments into communications, stimulates employee motivation, and provides protection in times of crisis.

The aim of this contribution is to analyse issues of image and reputation in relation to PowderJect Pharmaceuticals plc, a British biotechnology company specializing in the production of vaccines, through an investigation of various textual representations of the company. The focus will be twofold: firstly, the image and reputation which the company seeks to create for itself through press releases; and secondly the corporate reputation shaped by the British media through articles appearing in the press. Following scholars such as Fowler (e.g. 1991) and Simpson (1993), amongst others, this study is based on the view that there is no real version of reality, only varying representations, points of view or angles of telling, and that the resources of language may be used to privilege any one.

The media play a key role in the shaping of corporate image and reputation through their presentation of corporate news, where they inevitably 'frame' the message, emphasizing specific information or interpretations of events. According to Palenchar (2001), media frames involve the context, content, topic, coverage and package of news events, and as Gitlin (1980) notes, framing involves persistent patterns of cognition, interpretation and presentation, of selection, emphasis and exclusion, by which symbol-handlers organize discourse. Furthermore, as others (e.g. Davis, 1995; Tewksbury et al., 2000; Van Dijk, 1988) have suggested, the framing of a topic significantly affects the perception of that topic and the audience's reaction to it. Indeed Tewksbury et al. (2000) found that exposure to one single news article on a particular issue was influential enough to direct respondent comments on the issue several weeks later. Framing analysis thus looks at how the media create meaning out of an issue or event, define it for the public and direct discussion about it (Lane, 1998).

The context for the study of corporate image and reputation in this work is the British biotechnology sector. The communication environment of the biotechnology sector is very complex, being characterized by many conflicting views and highly sensitive topics (Gurău and McLaren, 2003). The controversial nature of biotechnology products and activities forces companies to structure their corporate communications in order to present favourably their competitive advantage and technological expertise, but at the same time to answer sensitive questions raised by the public, or acknowledge the specific risks of their entrepreneurial activity. Furthermore, in biotechnology, product innovation and development are an extremely lengthy and costly process – the full development of a new biotechnology product can take as long as six to eight years and it costs typically about £250 million (Gracie, 1998) – with the result that companies require high levels of investment, particularly in the early stages (Bank of England, 2001). However, the biotechnology sector is a high-risk sector, since outcomes are uncertain. Companies are therefore faced with a difficult situation: they are heavily dependent on investment, but for investors the level of risk is high. A successful communication strategy, which seeks to create a positive corporate image, is therefore crucially important for business development.

PowderJect has been chosen as the focus of this study for a further reason, which makes it an especially interesting company to investigate from the perspective of communication and image: in April 2002 the company gained public notoriety when it was involved in a so-called 'cash-for-contracts' row stemming from the fact that PowderJect's CEO, Paul Drayson, donated £100,000 to the Labour Party in the 12 months prior to the announcement that PowderJect was to be granted a

£32 million contract to supply the government with a vaccine against smallpox, without the contract having first gone through tendering. When this came to light, accusations abounded of 'sleaze', of preferential treatment being accorded by the government to key financial backers of the party, and of a lack of transparency over the affair. Both the government and PowderJect were on the receiving end of such allegations during press and media coverage which lasted several months. When the scandal broke, the treatment of the company by some parts of the press changed completely. This was a highly undesirable situation for the company since its image and reputation were dramatically affected – for the worse – with inevitable implications for its relations with investors.

7.2　Adopting a text-based approach to the study of corporate image and reputation

In this study corporate image and reputation will be examined through an analysis of texts – on the one hand, press releases issued by the company and, on the other, a series of media articles based on these press releases published in the UK. The aim will be to show how PowderJect Pharmaceuticals has been represented in texts issued to the public, including the community of investors, and how the media have 'framed' news about the company. The focus will be on the topics covered in the texts and the language used to present PowderJect. Relatively little research has adopted this type of approach to the study of corporate image and identity, although a considerable body of research in business and marketing has examined these issues from other perspectives.

Previous research into understanding the process of corporate image formation has concentrated both on the process of creating and projecting the corporate image by the organization, and on the process of reception of the corporate image amongst audience members (Kazoleas et al., 2001). This complicated process of producing, managing and receiving the organization's image has been recognized as a flexible, dynamic and multi-factored process, often subject to environmental factors that are outside the control of the organization and of the audience members. Research in this area which is oriented towards marketing, advertising and consumer behaviour has suggested that commercial organizations create images in order to foster increased sales. One of the main findings of consumer behaviour-oriented research is that multiple images are used by various segments of customers, and that these are variable and subject to constant change (Ackerman, 1988; Dowling,

1986; Garbett, 1988; Gray and Smeltzer, 1987; Knoll and Tankersley, 1991). On the other hand, business management research privileges the term 'corporate identity' and argues that this identity is primarily a form of social identification and association between the employees and the organization (Albert et al., 2000; Ashford and Mael, 1989; Carlivati, 1990; Kovach, 1985; Pratt and Foreman, 2000). Finally, public relations research has argued that image is created by the interaction between the organization and its audiences during a complex communication process (Alvesson, 1990; Fombrun and Shanley, 1990). One particular conceptualization of image formation is built on the cultural model of meaning, which acknowledges that meanings (images) are generated not only by multiple kinds of factors, but also through the intersection or struggle among these factors (Hall, 1986). This vision emphasizes the dynamic, flexible and conflictual nature of corporate image formation (Moffitt, 1994a, b; Williams and Moffitt, 1997).

Issues of language and text in relation to representations of a company and the projection of a company's image, on the other hand, appear not to have attracted much attention as yet. This point is made by Jacobs (1999a) who notes that '(...) until recently, the focus was on communication-*within*-organisations', while the 'capacity to communicate as an organization ... was strangely ignored ... (Taylor and Cooren, 1997)' (1999a, pp. 3–4). Since the main focus here is communication at the level of the company, in particular the ways in which PowderJect communicates its news to the world and projects an image of itself, and how that news and image are then communicated onwards (or not) by the press, this study will draw on work by scholars such as Rogers and Swales (1990) and Swales and Rogers (1995), who have analysed a number of corporate texts and investigated the link between corporate identity and linguistic and textual features. In their examination of the ethical code of a large US company, the Dana Corporation, Rogers and Swales (1990), for example, look at 'how corporations refer to themselves ... in the formal expression of their ethical philosophy and policies' (1990, p. 294). They find that the Dana Corporation's ethical code is characterized by the use of subjects (e.g. *we*) which refer in various ways to Dana, i.e. the company itself, its employees, or various sectors of those employees.

In his study of a corpus of 600 company press releases Jacobs (1999a, b) emphasizes the importance of what he calls the 'preformulated' nature, or 'tellability' of press releases; in other words, the writers of press releases design their texts in such a way that these texts can be copied in their entirety by journalists whose job it is to write articles reporting the news published in the press release. Thus in press releases, as Jacobs notes, 'self-referencing is almost exclusively realised in the third person, in particular through the use of the organisation's proper name' (1999b, p. 220). This means that journalists are not required to make any changes in terms of reference and point of view and, furthermore, that the press release looks 'objective': 'Third person self-reference makes press releases look disinterested and neutral rather than self-interested, promotional' (Jacobs, 1999b, p. 232). The aim of those who write company press releases is therefore to try to ensure, as far as is possible, that the news they wish to present is reproduced in the resulting press articles.

The issues of interest in this contribution are closely related to those examined by critical linguists such as Fairclough (e.g. 1989, 1992, 2000), Fowler (1991), Hodge and Kress (1993) and Trew (1979a, b), amongst others, in their work on language and ideology. Their interest is not in corporate communications but rather in how different points of view are put forward in texts and how the same events can be represented in quite different ways, notably by the media. To illustrate the link between linguistic choices and point of view, Simpson (1993) examines a number of newspaper reports on the same topic – a revolt led by former Prime Minister Ted Heath against the Conservative government in 1984 – looking in particular at reference forms and naming strategies. His analysis shows that the 'choice of one type of name over another can encode important information about the writer's attitude to the individual referred to in the text' (1993, p. 141) and that 'despite their shared topic, each text presents a different "angle of telling"' (1993, p. 140), a different representation of reality. Clearly opposing attitudes are in evidence: in some cases (e.g. the *Daily Mail*) events are presented negatively, while in others the stance adopted is more positive. In all cases the judgements made belong to what Hunston and Thompson (2000) call the 'good/bad-positive/negative parameter' (2000, p. 22), where evaluations of good and bad are dependent on the value system underlying the text.

Similarly, it will be shown in the following analysis that in many cases PowderJect's presentation of itself and its news in its press releases is often very different from the way in which it is framed in the media.

7.3 Data

The corpus of data used in this study consists of a selection of press releases issued by PowderJect Pharmaceuticals plc in 2000, 2001 and 2002, and articles based on these press releases which appeared in the

British media, specifically *BBC News Online, The Guardian, The Observer, The Independent, The Scotsman, The Financial Times,* and the associated website of *The Financial Times,* FT.com.

Company press releases are issued with a view to making public some news about the company (e.g. financial results, information about new collaborations, takeovers or mergers, or the results of tests or clinical trials or progress in research). This news is mainly of interest to existing and potential investors, although not exclusively; other groups, such as market analysts or competitors, will also have an interest in the news being announced. A key function of press releases is therefore to inform; however, press releases also seek to present the company in as favourable a light as possible. As Cook (1989) notes in a discussion about American politics, 'the point of a press release is not accuracy so much as showing the representative in a good light' (in Jacobs, 1999a, p. 45). Press releases can therefore be used by companies to shape their corporate image, to demonstrate how well they are doing and to persuade potential investors that the company is worth investing in, as well as reassuring existing investors that their choice is still a good one. This is particularly important in the British biotechnology sector because of the enormous financial costs of pursuing research in this area.

In contrast, media articles report news in accordance with the concerns, interests and needs of the readers. There is not the same concern with presenting the company favourably; on the contrary, reporting may be extremely critical. In the data selected for inclusion in the corpus a range of audiences and purposes are represented. Articles from *The Guardian, The Observer, The Independent* and *BBC News Online,* which are mainstream publications, have a relatively general orientation and cover a broad range of topics, although there are specialized sections (e.g. business and economy section), whereas *The Financial Times* and FT.com focus almost exclusively on economic and business matters and target a narrower audience of business people, the City and investors.

In the next section part of the findings of the analysis will be presented. It will be shown that texts from different sources frequently present the same events in quite different ways, with the result that several different images are projected of PowderJect.

7.4 Findings of the analysis

7.4.1 PowderJect's image and reputation before April 2002

PowderJect's communication strategy was relatively consistent between 2000 and 2002. In press releases issued in 2000 and 2001, which will be the focus of this section, the company projects a positive image of itself, seeking to demonstrate that it is making progress, that it has a promising future, and that it is worth investing in. Overall the media stance between 2000 and early 2002 is neutral. These tendencies will be discussed and exemplified in this section.

7.4.1.1   Example 1: July 2001

On 3 July 2001 Powderject published two press releases, one reporting on its acquisition of Swedish vaccine group SBL Vaccin ('PowderJect Acquires Sweden's Leading Vaccine Company'), the other presenting the company's preliminary results for the year ended 31 March 2001 ('Preliminary Results for the Year Ended 31 March 2001').

In the first of these press releases information is given about SBL and the acquisition itself. The news is presented in a very positive manner with considerable emphasis placed on SBL's assets and the benefits of the acquisition for PowderJect. This is illustrated by extracts (1) to (4):

(1)   PowderJect Pharmaceuticals plc (PowderJect; London: PJP) announced today that it has entered into an agreement with Active Biotech AB (Active; Stockholm: ACTI) to acquire its wholly-owned subsidiary SBL Vaccin AB (SBL), Sweden's leading vaccine company.

(2)   The acquisition also provides PowderJect with two key strategic assets: Strong sales and marketing infrastructure and a distribution collaboration with Aventis Pasteur.

(3)   This acquisition is another key step in PowderJect's strategy to become a major player in the global vaccines market.

(4)   SBL is a particularly strong vaccines brand in the Nordic region, and is the clear market leader in Sweden.

In these extracts there is clear evidence of the company's strategy of positive evaluation, including self-evaluation. Choices such as 'Sweden's leading vaccine company', 'two key strategic assets', 'strong sales and marketing infrastructure', 'another key step', 'a major player in the global vaccines market', 'a particularly strong vaccines brand', and 'the clear market leader in Sweden', for instance, work together to project a highly positive impression. Extracts (1) to (3) also show the use of third person self-reference forms by PowderJect, which is wholly in accordance with the tendency noted by Jacobs (1999a, b). In all of these respects this press release is a typical example of press releases issued by PowderJect. The tendency is towards a very favourable presentation of the company and its activities, combined with an air of objectivity.

The second press release is very similar. The emphasis in the text is on the progress that PowderJect has made over the year, and the headings in the 'Key highlights' section, which relate to the key themes pursued in the text, are consequently very positive: 'Strong performance from vaccines business', 'PowderJect's financial base significantly strengthened', 'Successful lidocaine clinical results', and 'Transitioning into the world's leading pure vaccines company'.

In both of these press releases we can see that the mood is very positive indeed, and that the company is looking forward to building on the new developments reported. Although a number of further developments are mentioned, such as PowderJect's decision to divest its needle-free injection business, these are not foregrounded and are not discussed in any depth.

By means of contrast, media articles based on these press releases have a different emphasis: while reporting on PowderJect's results, the acquisition of SBL Vaccin, and expectations of future growth, they place considerable emphasis on the news that PowderJect is planning to divest its needle-free injection business. This is reflected in the titles of some of the articles, such as 'Needle-free business has no point for Powder-Ject' (*The Guardian*, 4 July 2001). It is interesting and perhaps surprising that the announcement of the divestment is so prominent in the press reports given that this news has a relatively low profile in the company's statement of results. However, rather than adopting a critical stance, which might have been expected given that PowderJect has sold off the needle-free injection side of its business which was the basis on which the company was founded, the media adopt a position which is either neutral, in which case only the facts are reported, or positive, in which case the company receives praise for its recognition that the needle-free injection technology it was developing had no future and for the steps it has subsequently taken. This latter trend is reflected in extract (5):

(5)   Powderject Pharmaceuticals, the Oxford-based biotech firm, has announced plans to sell off its flagship needle-free injection business and focus on a number of vaccine products.

   Analysts welcomed this bold restructuring in the light of mounting evidence that, in most cases, drug delivery via rival liquid-based devices was likely to prove quicker and cheaper to bring to market than the powder technology. (*The Guardian*, 4 July 2001)

A positive stance is also adopted by the media in their discussions of the acquisition of SBL and of PowderJect's results. This is the case even where losses are reported: in (6) below, for example, we are told that the losses were 'in line with expectations', thereby suggesting that they do not represent a setback.

(6)   Meanwhile, losses for the year were £19.6m, in line with expectations. (*The Guardian*, 4 July 2001)

7.4.2   PowderJect's image and reputation after April 2002

From April 2002 coverage of PowderJect in some sectors of the media changed quite dramatically with the result that the manner in which PowderJect has been portrayed has been at odds with the company's (re)presentation of itself in its press releases. The example discussed here is from May 2002, i.e. just one month after the cash-for-favours scandal broke.

7.4.2.1   *Example 2: May 2002*

On 14 May 2002 PowderJect issued a press release relating to its preliminary results for the year ended 30 March 2002, a year in which the company achieved a net profit for the first time. As a result 2001–2 was a highly significant year for PowderJect: in the company's own words, it developed 'from a loss-making technology provider into a profitable products company achieving rapid growth'. The main themes in the press release include the achievement of milestones, profitability, growth, future prospects, etc., all of which carry clear positive values in the context of a company's financial results. These themes are reflected in extracts (7), (8), and (9):

(7)   PowderJect's flu franchise achieved a number of additional milestones during the year ...
(8)   PowderJect is at the beginning of an exciting new chapter as a major force in vaccination.
(9)   PowderJect now has the financial strength to extend its RandD into other commercially attractive areas of immunology.

Although based on the press release discussed above, articles from *BBC News Online*, *The Guardian* and *The Independent* do not adopt this same positive stance, however, preferring to concentrate on problems faced by the company rather than progress and achievements. These problems include most notably the 'cash-for-favours' row. Indeed, it is not until the last section of the *BBC News Online* report of 14 May 2002 (' "Cash-for-contracts" firm posts first profit') that any information at all is given about Powderject's results; until that point in the article we hear only about 'cash-for-favours'. The focus of these articles and their attitude towards PowderJect is immediately clear from their titles. For example, rather than 'PowderJect posts first profit', the title of the *BBC News Online* article is ' "Cash-for-contracts" firm posts first profit'. This would seem to suggest that cash-for-contracts has become part of PowderJect's identity and although the scare quotes used around 'cash-for-contracts' may be part of an attempt by *BBC News Online* to distance itself from this description of PowderJect, the article nonetheless goes on to describe PowderJect as 'the company recently caught up in a cash-for-favours row with the government'. Articles in *The Independent* and *The Guardian*, entitled respectively 'Powderject vows to keep bankrolling Labour' and 'I'm still a Labour man, says Drayson' also adopt a critical stance towards PowderJect, portraying PowderJect and Paul Drayson as unrepentant despite the controversy over 'cash-for-favours'. Paul Drayson in particular receives a great deal of criticism which is evidenced in the way in which he is referred to and described. For instance, although we find some objective description (e.g. 'the chairman and chief executive of Powderject'), we also find numerous references to the cash-for-favours row (e.g. 'the biotech boss and Labour donor at the centre of sleaze allegations made when his firm was awarded a £32m government contract for smallpox vaccine'). Whereas the news the company was hoping to publicize was that it has turned previous losses into profit, the general media have chosen to concentrate on cash-for-favours and to further perpetuate the image of PowderJect and its CEO as having a tarnished reputation. The business-oriented publications examined here, on the other hand, do reproduce more faithfully the news the company was wishing to send to the community of investors and the City more generally. This can be seen in extracts (10)–(12):

(10) PowderJect, the UK vaccines company, was one of the biggest risers on the FTSE 250 as it reported its first full-year profit driven by record sales of its flu vaccine, Fluvirin. (FT.com, 14 May 2002)

(11) Basic earnings per share rose 25.53p to 1.35p on turnover of GBP113m, trebling last year's GBP 40m. (FT.com, 14 May 2002)

(12) Analysts, who had been expecting a £4m loss, praised the rapid turnaround from the previous year's pre-tax loss of £20.5m. (*Financial Times*, 14 May 2002)

The focus and stance in evidence here are highly significant since these articles are the first ones based on a PowderJect press release to be published in the *FT* (*Financial Times* or FT.com) after the cash-for-favours row broke. In both *FT* articles *some* reference is made to the cash-for-contracts scandal, as exemplified in extract (13), but this only occurs towards the end of each article and is very brief and rather more fact-based than is the case in the general press.

(13)   The company is the subject of a National Audit Office inquiry into a GBP32m smallpox vaccine contract. PowderJect, run by a Labour party donor, was awarded the contract by the government without a tendering process.
    Ministers said PowderJect was the only company that could provide the specific vaccine required. (FT.com, 14 May 2002)

The message in the business press, at least as exemplified here by the *Financial Times*, is that PowderJect is making good progress and is a good investment. This message is quite different from that communicated by other media publications.

7.5   Conclusions

The aim of this chapter was to examine the way in which the corporate image and reputation of one British biotechnology company, namely PowderJect Pharmaceuticals plc, are shaped in texts. As we have seen, the company press releases indicate how PowderJect seeks to represent itself to the outside world, while the corresponding media articles give an insight into the way the media have attempted to frame news about PowderJect as well as its attitude towards the company.

As has been shown, company press releases did not change in the type of news they sought to disseminate between 2000 and 2002 or in the very positive image they presented of the company. However, such a consistent image of PowderJect has not been projected in the press. In this respect the 'cash-for-favours' row was a turning point for PowderJect Pharmaceuticals, at least as far as its image in the mainstream press is concerned. Prior to April 2002 the media presented a largely favourable picture of PowderJect and published reports which, overall, reproduced the content and stance of the company's official press releases. Means of referring to PowderJect and descriptions of the company were mostly factual and objective, but sometimes carried positive values. Since April 2002, however, coverage of PowderJect in some publications, notably mainstream newspapers such as *The Guardian* or *The Independent*, has tended to focus on the 'cash-for-favours' row, scandal and sleaze, irrespective of the developments PowderJect wishes to report and which triggered the publication of the press release in the first place.

Involvement in the scandal appears to have become a key aspect of PowderJect's corporate identity. However, a more positive message has been conveyed in articles from the specialized business press examined here, probably because of its concern with business and financial issues (share price, growth, profits, etc.) and providing advice on such matters to its readers, and the fact that PowderJect's finances have improved over the last few years with the result that prospects are good and the company represents a (potentially) good investment. Consequently, a number of different images of the company appear to be projected in texts issued by different sources: the positive image projected by the company in its press releases, a generally favourable image presented by the specialist press, and the negative image put forward by the mainstream press. The question of which source (the company itself, the general media or the financial press) has the greatest influence on the viewpoint of investors is one to which companies like PowderJect would undoubtedly like an answer.

References

Ackerman, L.D. (1988) 'Identity strategies that make a difference', *Journal of Business Strategy*, 9 (3), 28–32.

Albert, S., B.E. Ashforth and J.E. Dutton (2000) 'Organizational identity and identification: Charting new waters and building new bridges', *Academy of Management Review* 25 (1), 13–17.

Alvesson, M. (1990) 'Organization: From substance to image?', *Organization Studies*, 11 (3), 373–94.

Ashforth, B.E. and F. Mael (1989) 'Social identity theory and the organization', *Academy of Management Review*, 14, 20–39.

Bank of England (2001) *Financing of Technology-Based Small Firms* (London: Domestic Finance Division, Bank of England).

Carlivati, P.A. (1990) 'Measuring your image', *Association Management*, 42, 49–52.

Cook, T.E. (1989) *Making Laws and Making News: Media Strategies in the US House of Representatives* (Washington, DC: The Brookings Institution).

Davis, J.J. (1995) 'The effects of message framing on response to environmental communications', *Journalism and Mass Communication Quarterly*, 72 (2), 285–99.

Dowling, G.R. (1986) 'Managing your corporate images', *Industrial Marketing Management*, 15, 109–15.

Fairclough, N. (1989) *Language and Power* (London: Longman).

Fairclough, N. (1992) *Discourse and Social Change* (Cambridge: Polity Press).

Fairclough, N. (2000) *New Labour, New Language?* (London: Routledge).

Fombrun, C. and M. Shanley (1990) 'What's in a name? Reputation building and corporate strategy', *Academy of Management Journal*, 33, 233–58.

Fowler, R. (1991) *Language in the News. Discourse and Ideology in the Press* (London: Routledge).

Garbett, T.F. (1988) *How to Build a Corporation's Identity and Project Its Image* (Lexington: Lexington Books).

Gitlin, T. (1980) *The Whole World Is Watching: Mass Media in the Making and the Unmaking of the New Left* (Berkeley: University of California Press).

Gracie, S. (1998) 'Boffin brave new world', *The Sunday Times*, 5 July, 13.

Gray, E.R. and L.R. Smeltzer (1987) 'Planning a face-lift: implementing a corporate image', *Journal of Business Strategy*, 8, 4–10.

Gurău C. and Y. McLaren (2003) 'Corporate reputations in UK biotechnology: an analysis of online "company profile" texts', *Journal of Marketing Communications*, 9 (4), 241–56.

Hall, S. (1986) 'On postmodernism and articulation', *Journal of Communication Inquiry*, 10 (2), 45–60.

Hodge, R. and G. Kress (1993) *Language as Ideology*, 2nd edn (London: Routledge).

Hunston, S. and G. Thompson (2000) 'Evaluation: an introduction' in S. Hunston and G. Thompson (eds) *Evaluation in Text: Authorial Stance and the Construction of Discourse* (Oxford: OUP), 1–27.

Jacobs, G. (1999a) *Preformulating the News* (Amsterdam/Philadelphia: John Benjamins).

Jacobs, G. (1999b) 'Self-reference in press releases', *Journal of Pragmatics*, 31, 219–42.

Kazoleas, D., Y. Kim and M.A. Moffitt (2001) 'Institutional image: a case study', *Corporate Communications: an International Journal*, 6 (4), 205–16.

Knoll, H.E. and C.B. Tankersley (1991) 'Building a better image', *Sales and Marketing Management*, 143, 70–8.

Kovach, J.L. (1985) 'Corporate identity', *Industry Week*, 226, 21–2.

Lane, J.B. (1998) *The Framing of Title IX: a Textual Analysis of The New York Times and The Washington Post, 1971–1975* (Baltimore, Md: The Association for Education in Journalism and Mass Communication).

Moffitt, M.A. (1994a) 'Collapsing and integrating concepts of "public" and "image" into a new theory', *Public Relations Review*, 20 (2), 159–70.

Moffitt, M.A. (1994b) 'A cultural studies perspective toward understanding corporate image: a case study of State Farm Insurance', *Journal of Public Relations Research*, 6, 41–66.

Palenchar, M.J. (2001) *Media Coverage of Risk Events: a Framing Comparison of Two Fatal Manufacturing Accidents* (Washington, DC: The Association for Education in Journalism and Mass Communication).

Pratt, M.G. and P.O. Foreman (2000) 'Classifying managerial responses to multiple organizational identities', *Academy of Management Review*, 25 (1), 18–42.

Rogers, P. and J. Swales (1990) 'We the people? An analysis of the Dana Corporation policies document', *Journal of Business Communication*, 27, 293–313.

Simpson, P. (1993) *Language, Ideology and Point of View* (London: Routledge).

Swales, J. and P. Rogers (1995) 'Discourse and the projection of corporate culture: the Mission Statement', *Discourse and Society*, 6 (2), 223–42.

Tewksbury, D., J. Jones, M. Peske, A. Raymond and W. Vig (2000) 'The inter-action of news and advocate frames: Manipulating audience perceptions of a local public policy issue', *Journalism and Mass Communication Quarterly*, 77 (4), 804–29.

Trew, T. (1979a) 'Theory and ideology at work' in R. Fowler et al. (eds) *Language and Control* (London: Routledge and Kegan Paul), 94–116.

Trew, T. (1979b) ' "What the papers say": Linguistic variation and ideological dif-ference' in R. Fowler et al. (eds) *Language and Control* (London: Routledge and Kegan Paul), 117–56.

Van Dijk, T.A. (1988) *News as Discourse* (Hillsdale, NJ: Lawrence Erlbaum).

Williams, S.L. and M.A. Moffitt (1997) 'Corporate image as an impression forma-tion process: Prioritizing personal, organizational, and environmental audience factors', *Journal of Public Relations Research*, 9 (4), 237–58.

8
When Media Information Becomes a Business: the Case of TV Debates

Marcel Burger
University of Lausanne

8.1 Introduction: theoretical perspective, data and problem

This contribution is part of a broader research on the issue of media debates in the French-speaking media (Burger, 2000, 2002b, 2004a, b, 2005, 2006, 2008). It consists in discussing the discursive and communicative properties of a specific debate genre: the daytime talk show, which is one of the three genres of debates detailed in sections 2, 2.1, 2.2 and 2.3.

After having defined the daytime talk show genre, I will analyse an excerpt of a recent well-known French programme (*C'est mon choix*) which is representative of the genre. I adopt the theoretical background of social constructionism as termed by Shotter (1995) or social discourse analysis as termed by Van Dijk (1997). In a very broad sense, such a perspective assumes the dialogical nature of human practices as introduced by Bakhtin (1977) and Foucault (1980) and focuses on the role of discourse as a leading resource in the negotiation of meaning and the construction of social realities. In this view, the functioning of the media is very complex. As they are anchored in the public sphere, the media resort to the construction of citizenship. But at the same time, the media are economically constrained enterprises addressing customers in the private sphere.

Media debates in general and daytime talk shows in particular seem to manifest this somehow paradoxical functioning. What seems to be actually at stake with media debates is a tendency to focus on economical goals, implying that media information is becoming more and more a means to do business. As a discourse analyst, I would like to argue that taking the verbal units of discourse into close consideration helps to understand such an issue.

8.2 The complexity of media debates

A media debate can be considered as a multiple social practice (Jacobs, 1999) or a complex site of engagement (Scollon, 2001), because it involves at the same time two different interactional frames with distinct participants and distinct goals. As shown in Figure 8.1, we can identify a 'talk with' relation meant by the double arrow between a host and at least two debaters. Such a relation constructs and delimits a debate frame in which the activity of some of the participants, the debaters, is aimed at the convincing of an audience. As for the other participant, the host, he is engaged in chairing this interaction.[1]

Concurrently, a media debate obviously engages a one-way relation (meant by the single arrow) between a 'journalist' and his collective 'audience'. Such a relation constructs and delimits a media information frame in which the activity of one participant, the journalist, is aimed at informing the other participant, the absent audience, about relevant facts and opinions of public interest. According to the interactional complexity of media debates, one has to describe separately each social practice involved in it: the practice of media information first, and then the practice of debate.

8.2.1 Media information as a social practice

It is commonly assumed that media information is a practice under paradoxical constraints. On the one hand, media information has a civic function of informing about the goings-on of the public sphere. Therefore the media address an audience of citizens, and media information

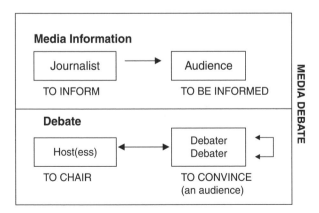

Figure 8.1 The complexity of media debates

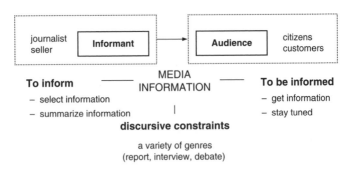

Figure 8.2   Media information as a social practice

becomes a legitimate means of constructing public opinion. On the other hand, the media are more or less important enterprises doing business in selling information. In this view, the media address an audience of buyers and media information then becomes a legitimate means to win the loyalty of customers (for a detailed presentation see Burger, 2002c, 2004a, 2005, 2006, 2008).[2]

As shown in Figure 8.2, we can define a media information process in considering the participants, their expected actions and goals, and the discursive genres that they use. I call 'informant' the role identity of a journalist engaged in the process of informing his mixed audience of citizens-customers. These identities are brought into being and best sustained by particular types of discursive actions like selecting and summarizing topics in order to attract the audience and make it stay tuned.

Media information calls for a great variety of discursive genres, from factual genres like a communiqué or a report, to genres specializing in the expression of opinions like an interview or a debate. In fact, these genres are themselves complex social practices involving specific participants, actions, goals and discursive constraints. In the broadcast we are concerned with, the media information process is linked with a debate process.

8.2.2   Debate as a social practice

A debate consists fundamentally in confronting opinions to convince an audience. Therefore, the process of debating implies a multiplicity of voices arguing against each other, and that is why a debate requires a chairman. One can represent a debate process as in Figure 8.3.

In this view, debating symbolizes the negotiation of opinions that constitutes the very core of citizenship and democracy. Therefore, a media debate process achieves best the civic function of the media. Located in the frame of media information, the journalist is a simple

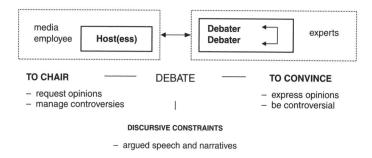

Figure 8.3   Debate as a social practice

mediator reporting opinions to the audience without interfering. But the properties of debating also serve the economic function of the media. Indeed, a debate in itself is a verbal confrontation often leading to a spectacular polemic which constitutes a good way of attracting the audience. Media information then manifests a commercial concern and displays a different and more active role, that of being the creator of an entertaining show (for a detailed presentation see Burger, 2000, 2005).[3]

8.2.3   The genres of media debates

In this respect, one can consider media debates depending on whether they reveal a rather serious and pedagogical concern linked with a civic functioning, or manifest an aspect of entertainment linked with an economic functioning.

8.2.3.1   *The civic debate*

As shown in Figure 8.4, I term 'civic debate' a process engaging a host(ess) – who is also a journalist – moving aside from the interactional scene to leave space for the debaters who are experts in a specific social domain. In this sense, the debate is focused on the debaters. These do not mostly intervene as individuals but as a spokesperson of a group (for example a political party). Therefore debaters are confronting opinions which are supposed to be shared and relevant for an audience addressed as citizens (see Cornu, 1994; Trognon and Larrue, 1994). In this sense, the discourse is manifestly anchored in the public sphere. The debaters try to impose an argumentation in order to convince the audience. In turn, the audience should compare and validate discursively expressed opinions in order to form its own. Considering the foregoing, a 'civic debate' fundamentally resorts to discourse, communication and argumentation.

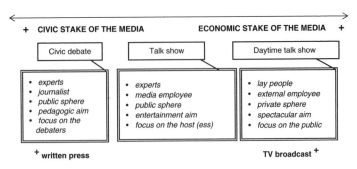

Figure 8.4   The categories of media debates

8.2.3.2   The talk-show debate

I term 'talk show' a process engaging a host – who most of the time is a popular media employee – intervening systematically with the debaters who are experts in a social domain: politics, education, science, etc. The popularity of the host(ess) puts the debaters in the shade. More precisely, the debaters are at the disposal of the host(ess) who acts as a session leader. In this sense, the debate is clearly focused on the host. Nevertheless, the issue of the debate is defined as anchored in the public sphere and therefore presented as still relevant for an audience addressed a priori as citizens. But, obviously, the aim of the 'talk-show' genre is to gain customers' loyalty by the means of entertainment (see Jost, 2002).

8.2.3.3   The daytime talk-show debate

Last, I term 'daytime talk-show debate' a process engaging a host who lets the audience participate and systematically provoke the debaters. These are not experts but lay people relating their life experiences. In this latter case, the real actor in the debate is the audience. This genre of media debates systematically offers very general and 'eye-catching' issues to discuss. Moreover the topic is regularly focused on individual opinions: for example, 'I am 30 years old and I have never made love. But I am happy', 'I am a fat woman/man . . . so what!', or 'I do not allow my daughter/son to bring her/his boyfriend/girlfriend home for the night'. Considering the foregoing, a 'daytime talk-show debate' is expected to be focused on emotions and inter-individual polemic to the detriment of argumentation which constitutes the dominant discursive anchorage of the 'civic debate' and the 'talk-show' genres. As the audience participates in endorsing the role identity of a debater, one can conclude that there is eventually no need (or not even a possibility) to convince. As for the host(ess), she/he most of the time is an external employee whose skills in leading debates have been proved. That is, the 'daytime talk-show debate' is often produced by non-media enterprises and sold to the media.

As a somewhat strange result of 'daytime talk-show debate', the lack of synthesis by the host(ess) and more globally an apparently passive role of the host(ess) increase the role of the audience participation in the construction of public opinion. More precisely, this genre of debates as it is focused on non-expert opinions offers a way to regenerate the public sphere.[4] Concurrently, the 'daytime talk-show debate' genre leads to redefining the role of the media. A 'civic debate' is preferred by the written press which cannot exploit the spectacular dimension of debates and has therefore to emphasize the pedagogical dimension of argumentation. The 'talk-show debate' is dominant on radio and television. These media can offer two fundamental dimensions of a debate: the spectacle of living text (radio) and visual emotions (television). Located in the middle of Figure 8.4, one can claim that a 'talk-show debate' constantly hesitates to manifest serious argumentation (which is the main property of a 'civic debate') or to exploit the play dimension of a show (which is the main property of a 'daytime talk-show debate').

One has to bear in mind that every media debate event manifests both the spectacular and emotional dimensions and the rational and argumentative dimensions of a debate. A debate is constituted by a suite of different sequences (see section 8.3.3) in which one of these dimensions is emphasized. Depending on the specific role identities endorsed by the participants, the debate can then be identified as dominated by argumentation or by emotion and located in one of our three categories (considering the double arrow as a continuum, that is indicating uncertain contours of each category).

8.3 Case study: broadcast *C'est mon choix* (FR3/TSR1, 2001)

8.3.1 Ethos of the broadcast

The broadcast we are concerned with clearly manifests the properties of a daytime talk-show debate. It is a popular French programme, *C'est mon choix*, which literally means 'It is my choice'. It is a very popular broadcast shown regularly two or three times a day since 1999 on French television (channel FR3). As several sessions have been sold abroad, the broadcast has also been shown on French-speaking Swiss television since 2001 (Channel TSR1). The broadcast is based on the same routine organization, so that the audience is very familiar with it. One can detail several aspects which a priori work in favour of a high polemic atmosphere to be systematically constructed in order to gain attractiveness.

First, the topic of each session always expresses a sensitive issue. In our case the title announcing the debate is: 'Collecting lovers. What do you think about it?'

The physical setting is another very important element (see Scannell, 1991). In *C'est mon choix* the debaters are on a stage facing the audience grouped in the tiered seats together with the hostess. As we will see, this position of the host is important as it allows him/her to stand aside from the scene of the debate as well as letting the audience participate.

As for the debaters, they are lay people all concerned with the very general issue, implying schematic opposition. The next section is an excerpt in which the hostess, Evelyne Thomas, is requesting the opinion of Damien, a collector of lovers conquests, and he is opposed by Fousia, a participant from the audience.

8.3.2   Excerpt[5]

STAGE 1

| 5 | HOST | Damien Yannick are you pleased that there are women who act like you do |
| | DEB. DAMIEN | I yes (..) yes yes to me she's part of I mean er (.) I feel like saying that we're part of the same family |

STAGE 2

	AUDIENCE	boo boo boo
7	DEB. DAMIEN	Yeah yeah I love
	DEB. FRÉDÉRIE	it's a game it's a game

STAGE 3

| | DEB. DAMIEN | exactly and it's the same for me yes (..) gotta make a choice (.) you either decide to be played upon or you're a player (...) |

STAGE 2

	AUDIENCE	boo b<u>oo boo</u>

STAGE 1

13	DEB. FOUSIA	Evelyne I have (.) I have a question to ask Miss it's er she said before that she's a collector but not a hunter yet the two gentlemen are hunters (.) so there's a difference between a struggle for survival and a lining up because the woman has in fact been (.) I won't say (.) I won't say frustrated but I'd say she's been er (.) sensitized in the sense that er the two men did not respect her (.) that she's always expected something good of them yet they apparently brought something only at night and only asked <u>her to work in the kitchen</u> etc etc

----

STAGE 2

	AUDIENCE	<u>ohohohohohoh</u>
	DEB. FRÉDÉRIE	<u>it's got nothing to do with that</u>
	DEB. FOUSIA	so why do you <u>line them up I suppose that</u>
	DEB. FRÉDÉRIE	to have a <u>different one every day</u>
30	AUDIENCE	<u>boo boo boo</u>
	DEB. FOUSIA	<u>and what about true love</u>
	DEB. FRÉDÉRIE	true what
	DEB FOUSIA	love <u>true love (.) you are (..) that on which we base our lives</u>
	DEB FRÉDÉRIE	true what (.) <u>how do you spell that word</u>
36	DEB. YANNICK	<u>she she she makes love to them every day she she loves them deeply every day</u>
	DEB. DAMIEN	<u>I don't see why being with the same person would mean being in love</u>
	DEB. FOUSIA	<u>no you cannot be deeply in love</u> after one night it's impossible you need time to get to know someone
	AUDIENCE	[sustained applause for Fousia]

44	DEB. FRÉDÉRIE	but I don't wanna marry all the men I sleep with
	DEB. FOUSIA	no no hang on I didn't use the word marriage but lining up goes much further than respecting oneself and respecting the other and respecting the love in which one lives (.) that's all (.) there's no need for lining up we're not on an island of ??
	AUDIENCE	[applause]
53	DEB. YANNICK	but she loves all men and the thing is we love all women (DEB. FRÉDÉRIE: precisely) she she loves all men she wants to count them she wants to seduce them (DEB. FRÉDÉRIE: that's) what you gotta understand
	DEB. FOUSIA	I love all men on the condition that they respect me (DEB YANNICK: ah I respect others and others respect you) but I don't line them up and I don't want them to line me up
64	AUDIENCE	[sustained applause for Fousia]
	DEB. FRÉDÉRIE	why would it be a lack of respect
	DEB. YANNICK	I spend an evening (.) an evening with a woman (.) that (..) while (..) I'll give myself to her from beginning to end and we'll have a great evening
	DEB. FOUSIA	why a good evening from beginning to end it's only a game of lining up (DEB.
72		FRÉDÉRIE: why) why why

STAGE 3

| | DEB. FRÉDÉRIE | why is it that if I do it it's necessarily at a given time they have no respect maybe it's I who have no respect for them |
| | DEB. YANNICK | I've preached (.) I've (.) I've preached to her about the moral of the three w's (....) eat well (.) drink well (.) f[bip] [audience: ha ha] |

NEW SEQUENCE

| 80 | HOST | Listen Fousia you're gonna get some backup because we're calling in our next guests they absolutely can't stand men who line up conquests they'll tell us if they are more tolerant when it comes to women here come Sylvie and Marilyn |
| | AUDIENCE | [applause] |

8.3.3 Structural properties of a debate sequence

The excerpt in the previous section manifests the typical organization of a debate sequence. It begins with a stage of requesting an opinion (Stage 1), then goes on to a stage of direct confrontation of the opinion (Stage 2), and is eventually concluded by a stage of stabilization of the first expressed opinion (Stage 3). The first stage engages together the hostess and one of the debaters. The hostess exposes a problematic state of affairs to discuss and asks a debater to express his opinion. This is the case at line 1. The second stage of direct confrontation engages two debaters together. More precisely, the first debater cannot develop his opinion because he is interrupted by another debater. This stage is therefore a highly polemic and interactive moment, which manifests the play dimension of a show, often to the detriment of the quality of an argument. This is clearly the case from lines 20 to 54 in our excerpt. As for the third stage of a sequence of a debate process, it can be characterized as a return back to the expression of the first debater. It again involves a debater and the hostess, once the polemic has been stopped, and that is why I term this stage 'stabilizing of an opinion'. In our case, this stage does not last long: see for example when Damien at lines 7–9 or Frédérie at line 55 try to talk after a confused polemic.

Globally, all media debates manifest such an organization in sequences of three stages. The basic distinction between a 'civic debate', a 'talk-show debate' and a 'daytime talk-show debate' lies in the peculiar role identities performed by the host(ess), that is, respectively, as a moderating or as a triggering element of each stage.

8.4 The role identities of the hostess

One can describe the role identities of the hostess in our excerpt for each stage and relate them to the discursive markers through which these identities are realized (Figure 8.5).[6]

Stage 1 of requesting an opinion:
 (a) limiting the floor (instead of allowing argumentation to develop);
   – in asking a 'closed' question;
   are you pleased that there are women who act like you do
   (line 1);
 (b) provoking a confrontation (instead of delaying);

– in supporting an alliance between the debaters:

DAMIEN: *I yes (..) yes yes to she's part of I mean er (.) I*
feel like saying that we're part of the same family (FRÉDÉRIE:
it's a game it's a game) exactly and it's the same for me yes
(..) gotta make a choice (.) you either decide to be played
upon or you're a player (...)
– in delegating her role to a person (Fousia) from the audience
the woman has in fact been (.) I won't say (.) I won't say frus-
trated but I'd say she's been er (.) sensitized in the sense that
er the two men did not respect her (.)
Stage 2 of confronting directly:
 (c) stirring up the confrontation (instead of stopping it);
   – in leaving the floor, unseen by the camera (lines 4–60);
 (d) exploiting the reactions of the audience (to benefit the show);
   – in letting the public initiate and punctuate
   boo boo boo. / ohohohohohoh (lines 4,10,20,24,35,41,64).
Stage 3 of stabilizing an opinion:
 (e) interfering in the discourse (instead of letting the debater speak);

– in obviously shortening the debater's talk (line 60);

 (f) validating the discourse (instead of taking an opinion into account);
   – in supporting implicitly a participant
   Listen Fousia you're gonna get some backup because we're
   calling in our next guests they absolutely can't stand men who
   line up conquests.

Figure 8.5   The role identities of the hostess

8.4.1   The role identities during stage 1 of the debate sequence

Thus one can observe during stage 1 that the hostess limits the floor instead of allowing the debaters to develop argumentation. Indeed, the question she asks calls for a 'yes or no' answer. Moreover the expected answer is opposed to the global opinion of the audience. This reveals a means to shorten the first stage, and virtually engage the second stage which is the most spectacular. During stage 1, one also observes that the hostess accepts that debater Fousia addresses another debater in a highly polemic way (lines 11–19). This means that the hostess delegates her role identity: she puts herself in the shade, letting someone from the audience become a debater in the spotlight.

8.4.2 The role identities during stage 2 of the debate sequence

In fact audience participation is evident during stage 2 of direct confrontation. Then, the hostess is stirring up the confrontation and exploiting the reactions to benefit the show, instead of stopping the polemic as expected in a civic or in a talk-show debate. See for example lines 4–54 how alliances are created, engaging Damien, Frédérie and Yannick together against Fousia and the audience managing the polemic alone.

Obviously, the audience constitutes the real triggering element. It initiates the polemic three times (at lines 4, 10 and 20), and becomes a participant boosting and punctuating the debate (see lines 24, 35, 41, 48). In this sense, the hostess is exploiting the polemic to benefit the show. By moving aside she is implicitly standing for, and supporting, a conflict where all opinions are equally relevant because all the participants are lay people – the debaters as well as the audience.

8.4.3 The role identities during stage 3 of the debate sequence

The focus on a show and not on argumentation seems an essential issue which explains the peculiar organization of stage 3. These stages are avoided or shortened because there is eventually no need to convince an audience. The hostess then displays a role identity consisting in intervening briefly and validating a discourse instead of letting the debaters speak and remaining neutral. See for example how she closes without any synthesis the debate sequence at line 60 and initiates a new one by announcing the arrival of two other debaters on the scene.

8.5 Concluding comments

In conclusion, what comes out of this presentation is that a debate process constitutes a kind of developer of the double functioning of the media: achieving a civic aim by means of a didactic dimension and achieving an economic aim by means of an entertaining dimension. In the broadcast we are concerned with, the civic dimension is clearly put in the shade by the constantly emerging entertaining dimension. The hostess is then a key person of the phenomenon. She supports the debaters in turn and therefore provokes the polemic. She does not allow enough space and time to develop an opinion, and does not provide any synthesis. Eventually she delegates her chairing identity to the participants from the audience.

These properties are typical of what I call the 'daytime talk-show debate' which is a genre in vogue at the moment in the broadcast media. Proposing globally the same routinized organization in the French-speaking media, the 'daytime talk-show debate' seems to reveal a change of the role of the media in participating in the construction of public opinion, and therefore the delimiting of the public sphere.[7] What is at stake with 'daytime talk-show debate' is the exploiting of media information in order to win customers' loyalty. This state of affairs is evident for a while in the practice of different media genres, but leads us – with media debates based on audience participation – to question what is or should be democracy. Of course, the role of discourse in constituting the media as specific social practices with important institutional and professional stakes is essential. Opinions cannot be expressed without discourse. A negotiation implies a discursive anchorage. Only discourse constitutes a comprehensive means to share social representations. But the role of discourse is paradoxically still minimized even if there is significant research on the media in general and media debates in particular.

8.6   Appendix

The following transcription conventions are used:

(Pauses):	(.), (..), (...) indicate appropriately timed pauses;
underlining:	indicates overlapping talk;
[square brackets]:	material in square brackets indicates transcriber's commentary regarding non-verbal events;
number in margin:	the numbers in the left margin simply indicate each line of the transcribed text;
'quotation marks':	information like 'host' or 'debater' refer to the current speaker's identity. The information on the right of the text, like 'stage 1', refers to the structural properties of a debate sequence as detailed in section 8.3.1.

This is the original French of the excerpt:

| 1 | ANIMATRICE | Damien Yannick ça vous plaît qu'il y ait des femmes qui fassent comme vous |
| | DÉB. DAMIEN | moi oui (..) oui oui moi pour moi elle fait partie enfin heu (.) on on fait partie de la même famille j'ai envie de dire |

	PUBLIC	<u>bouh bouh bouh</u>
7	DÉB. DAMIEN	<u>si si moi j'adore</u>
	DÉB. FRÉDÉRIE	<u>c'est un jeu c'est</u> un jeu

| | DÉB. DAMIEN | exactement et c'est pareil moi oui (..) faut faire un choix (.) ou on décide d'être joué ou on décide d'être joueur (…) |
| | PUBLIC | bouh b<u>ouh bouh</u> |

| 13 | DÉB. FOUSIA | <u>Evelyne j'aurais</u> (.) j'aurais une question quand même à poser à Madame c'est heu elle a dit tout à l'heure qu'elle est collectionneuse mais pas chasseur or les deux messieurs sont chasseurs (.) donc il y a une différence entre la lutte de la survie et la collection parce que la femme en fait elle a été (.) on va dire (.) pas frustrée mais je dirais qu'elle a été heu (.) sensibilisée dans le sens où heu les hommes ne l'ont pas respectée (.) où elle a toujours attendu quelque chose de bon d'eux et ne lui ont apporté apparemment <u>le soir que simplement la cuisine à faire</u> <u>étcétéra</u> |

	PUBLIC	<u>ohohohohohoh</u>
	DÉB. FRÉDÉRIE	<u>ça n'a rien à voir avec ça</u>
	DÉB. FOUSIA	alors pourquoi vous les <u>collectionnez je sup-</u> <u>pose que ??</u>
	DÉB. FRÉDÉRIE	<u>pour en avoir un différent chaque jour</u>
32	PUBLIC	<u>bouh bouh bouh</u>
	DÉB. FOUSIA	<u>et l'amour le vrai</u>
	DÉB. FRÉDÉRIE	le quoi

	DÉB FOUSIA	le vrai l'amour le vrai (.) vous êtes (..) celui sur lequel on fonde sa vie
	DÉB FRÉDÉRIE	l'a quoi (.) l'amour ça s'écrit comment l'mot
39	DÉB. YANNICK	elle elle elle fait l'amour tous les jours elle elle les aime à fond tous les jours
	DÉB. DAMIEN	j'vois pas pourquoi être avec la même personne ce serait de l'amour
	DÉB. FOUSIA	non on peut on peut pas vivre à fond l'amour sur une seule nuit c'est impossible il faut déjà du temps pour connaître quelqu'un
	PUBLIC	[applaudissements nourris pour Fousia]
48	DÉB. FRÉDÉRIE	mais j'ai pas envie de m'marier avec tous les mecs qui passent dans mon lit
	DÉB. FOUSIA	non non attendez j'ai pas dit vous marier mais le but de collectionner va beaucoup plus loin que de se respecter et de respecter l'autre et de respecter l'amour dans lequel on vit (.) c'est tout (.) y a pas besoin de la collection on est pas sur une île de ??
	PUBLIC	[applaudissements]
58	DÉB. YANNICK	mais elle aime tous les hommes et le truc c'est que nous c'est qu'on aime toutes les femmes (DÉB. FRÉDÉRIE : exactement) elle elle aime tous les hommes elle a envie de les compter elle a envie de les séduire (DÉB. FRÉDÉRIE : voilà) c'est ça qu'il faut comprendre
	DÉB. FOUSIA	moi j'aime tous les hommes à condition qu'ils me respectent (DÉB YANNICK: ah moi je respecte on vous respecte) mais je ne les collectionne pas et je ne veux pas qu'ils me collectionnent
70	PUBLIC	[applaudissements nourris pour Fousia]
	DÉB. FRÉDÉRIE	pourquoi ce serait un manque de respect
	DÉB. YANNICK	moi je passe une soirée (.) une soirée avec une femme (.) que (..) pendant (..) je vais lui donner à fond du début à la fin on va passer une bonne soirée

	DÉB. FOUSIA	pourquoi du début à la fin une bonne soirée ce n'est pas ce n'est qu'un jeu de la collec-
78		tion (DÉB. FRÉDÉRIE : pourquoi) pourquoi pourquoi

	DÉB. FRÉDÉRIE	pourquoi si je l'ai fait c'est forcément qu'à un moment donné i z'ont eu un manque de respect c'est p't'être moi qui ai eu un manque de respect pour eux
	DÉB. YANNICK	je lui ai prôné (.) je (.) j'y ai prôné la morale des trois b (....) bien bouffer (.) bien boire (.) bien b[bip] [public : ah ah]

87	ANIMATRICE	écoutez Fousia vous allez avoir du renfort puisque nous allons appeler nos prochaines invitées elles elles ne supportent absolument pas les hommes qui collectionnent les conquêtes elles nous diront si elles support-ent mieux les femmes il s'agit de Sylvie et de Marilyn
	PUBLIC	[applaudissements]

Notes

1. For the distinction between a 'talk with' and a 'talk for' relation, see Jucker (1995).
2. The paradoxical constraints on the activity of media information are discussed in Livingstone and Lunt (1994), Bourdieu (1996) and Charaudeau (1997).
3. There are numerous papers dealing with the issue of debates: Charaudeau (1991), Nel (1991), Charaudeau and Ghiglione (1997), Livingstone and Lunt (1994), Shattuc (1997) and Hutchby (1999) are important and relevant references.
4. Of course, this latter issue is polemic. On the one hand are arguments in favour of 'daytime talk-show debate' as a manifestation of a new democ-racy realized by lay participation. On the other hand are arguments in favour of the essential role of expertise and a pedagogical hosting of debates (for a discussion, see Livingstone and Lunt, 1994; Shattuc, 1997; Bourdieu, 1996).
5. See the Appendix for the transcription conventions and the original French script.
6. For a discussion of the issue of identity and the displaying of identities in dis-course, see Shotter and Gergen (1989), Zimmerman (1988) and Burger (2002a); for the construction of identities in media discourse, see Burger (2000).

7. This seems to be the case in other European media cultures: Germany, the Netherlands, the UK, Italy, Spain and Portugal at least.

References

Bakhtine, M. (Voloshinov, V.N.) (1977) *Le marxisme et la philosophie du langage* (Paris: Minuit).

Bourdieu, P. (1996) *Sur la télévision. Suivi de L'emprise du journalisme* (Paris: Ed. Raisons d'Agir).

Burger, M. (2000) 'Scènes d'actions radiophoniques et prises de rôles: informer, débattre, divertir', *Revue de Sémantique et de Pragmatique*, 7, 179–96.

Burger, M. (2002a) *Les manifestes: paroles de combat. De Marx à Breton* (Paris: Delachaux et Niestlé).

Burger, M. (2002b) 'Identities at stake in social interaction: the case of media interviews', *Studies in Communication Sciences*, 2 (2), 1–20.

Burger, M. (2002c) 'Encenaçõ discursivas na mídia: o caso do debate-espetáculo' in I. Machado, H. Mari and R. De Mello (eds) *Ensaios em análise do discurso* (Belo Horizonte: NAD/FALE/UFMG), 201–22.

Burger, M. (2004a) 'The function of the discourse of the host in a TV talk show' in C.A. Gouveia, M.C. Silvestre and L. Azuaga (eds) *Discourse, Communication and the Enterprise: Linguistic Perspectives* (Lisbon: Ulices).

Burger, M. (2004b) 'Le discours des médias comme forme de pratique sociale: l'enjeu des débats télévisés' in R. Blum (ed.) *Wes Land ich bin, des Lied ich sing: Medien und Politische Kultur* (Berne: I.M.W.).

Burger, M. (2005) 'La complexité argumentative d'une séquence de débat politique médiatique' in G. Martel and M. Burger (eds) *Argumentation et communication dans les médias* (Quebec: Nota Bene).

Burger, M. (2006) 'The discursive construction of the public and the private spheres in media debates: the case of television talk shows', *Revista Alicantina de Estudios Ingleses (RAEI)*, no. 19: *Special Issue on Linguistics and the Media*, 45–65.

Burger, M. (2008) 'Analyzing the linguistic dimension of globalization in media communication: the case of insults and violence in debates' in D. Perrin and E.L. Wyss (eds) *Media Linguistics from a European Perspective: Language Diversity and Medial Globalization in Europe*, VALS/ASLA, Special Issue, 127–50.

Charaudeau, P. (ed.) (1991) *La télévision. Les débats culturels 'Apostrophes'* (Paris: Didier Erudition).

Charaudeau, P. (1997) *Le discours d'information médiatique* (Paris: Nathan).

Charaudeau, P. and R. Ghiglione (1997) *La parole confisqué* (Paris: Dunod).

Cornu, D. (1994) *Journalisme et vérité. Pour une éthique de l'information* (Geneva: Labor et Fides).

Foucault, M. (1980) *L'ordre du discours* (Paris: Gallimard).

Hutchby, I. (1999) 'Rhetorical strategies in audience participation debates on radio and TV'. *Research on Language and Social Interaction*, 32 (3), 243–67.

Jacobs, G. (1999) *Preformulating the News* (Amsterdam: John Benjamins).

Jost, F. (2002) *La télévision du quotidien. Entre réalité et fiction* (Brussels: De Boeck).

Jucker, A.H. (1995) 'Mass media' in J. Verschueren, J.O. Ostman and J. Blommaert (eds) *Handbook of Pragmatics* (Amsterdam: John Benjamins), 1–14.

Livingstone, S. and P. Lunt (1994) *Talk on Television. Audience Participation and Public Debates* (London: Routledge).

Nel, N. (1991) *Le débat télévisé* (Paris: Colin).

Scannell, P. (1991) 'Introduction: the relevance of talk' in *Broadcast Talk* (London: Sage), 1–13.

Scollon, R. (1998) *Mediated Discourse as Social Interaction. A Study of News Discourse* (London: Longman).

Scollon, R. (2001) *Mediated Discourse. The Nexus of Practice* (London: Routledge).

Shattuc, J. (1997) *The Talking Cure* (London: Routledge).

Shotter, J. (1995) *Conversational Realities* (London: Sage).

Shotter, J. and K. Gergen (eds) (1989) *Texts of Identity* (London: Sage).

Trognon, A. and J. Larrue (1994) 'Les débats politiques télévisés' in *Pragmatique du discours politique* (Paris: Colin), 55–126.

Van Dijk, T.A. (1997) 'Discourse as interaction in society' in T.A. Van Dijk (ed.) *Discourse as Social Interaction* (London: Sage), 1–37.

Zimmerman, D.H. (1988) 'Identity, context and interaction' in C. Antaki and S. Widdicombe (eds) *Identities in Talk* (London: Sage), 87–106.

9

A Discourse-Analytic Construal of the Function of Message in Language of the Law

Piotr Cap
University of Łódź and University of Economy in Bydgoszcz

9.1 Introduction

The many different types of persuasive discourse undergo different kinds of analytic determination. Whether essentially 'top-down' (deductive) or 'bottom-up' (inductive; Beaugrande, 1991), the determination occurs according to a finite number of well-known factors such as the degree of expert knowledge in the analyst, the arrangement of data and thesis in the text, the density of macropropositional cues, or the length of the investigated text chunk. As can be seen from this exemplification, some factors determining the analytic approach to a given discourse type could be roughly classified as 'interlocutor-oriented' (i.e. stemming from, in cognitive terms, the *on/off-stage* status of the speaker and the addressee in a given discourse situation, as well as from the speaker's and the addressee's/the analyst's *viewing arrangement* of the *stage*), and some as 'message-oriented' (i.e. stemming from autonomous properties of the text). Among the many types of persuasive discourse, the analysis of, for example, the discourse of advertising undergoes mostly 'top-down' determination, while, for example, the discourse of scientific argument invites a prevailing number of 'bottom-up' prompts. The discourse of politics and political persuasion, in turn, seems positioned somewhere in between the above extremes (Cap, 2002, 2003).

The determination that affects the discourse of legal texts involves a mixture of inductive and deductive processes and in that sense compares to the determination affecting the discourse of politics (Cap, 2002, 2003). However, unlike in the discourse of politics where the logical processing of a text's function results from the heterogeneous status of the parties involved in a communicative act, the discourse of the law undergoes analytic determination largely relative to the message itself, rather than to the producer of this message (who almost invariably tends to be a lawyer; Gibbons, 1994). Since legal messages, as we shall see, are greatly different across the different types of legal texts, so is the analytic determination. Therefore, the different (by mode, style or situational context) subtypes of texts within legal discourse can give rise to different analytic approaches, either induction- or deduction-based. This follows from seeing legal discourse as a principally heterogeneous type – similar to the discourse of politics – but of a structure whose heterogeneity is a message, not an interlocutor-oriented phenomenon.

In the first part of the work I shall discuss, having first defined the concept of 'language of the law', as well as having identified its place within the domain of pragmatic persuasion, the theoretical properties of the legal discourse encouraging the particular analytic approaches adopted in order to specify the function of a given legal text. In the second part, I shall direct these observations at a number of real-life text samples.

9.2 Language of the law and language of jurisprudence

Language of the law should not be confused with language of jurisprudence, i.e. actual performance of lawyers, attorneys, judges, etc. in specific situations of legal proceedings such as trials or questionings (Conley and O'Barr, 1990, 1998; Philips, 1985, etc.). Idiolect-like in nature, language of jurisprudence carries persuasion patterns which should be approached in the way the patterns of political persuasion are; the crucial determinators of function remain the speaker, the addressee, and their relationship underlying the communicative act. In that sense, the patterns of persuasion in language of jurisprudence possess little analytic matrix, since the function of a given text chunk is not necessarily determined by the targeted message format. In contrast, language of the law, which manifests itself in less spontaneous situations (including the many predefined parts of courtroom interaction) and which, in a majority of cases, consists in formal conferring of rights of some kind, does follow such a matrix. The latter is, naturally, different in degree for different subtypes of texts, therefore allowing consideration of disparate analytic approaches to the principal discourse type.

9.3 Language of the law versus pragmatic inquiry

In order to properly prepare the discussion of analytic determinism of legal language it is crucial to look at whether and how it has been approached in the development of linguistic pragmatics and discourse analysis. A very tentative yet plausible reason that can be given at this point is that, for instance, if one can find substantial evidence of legal language falling within the latitude of interest of linguistics, then it can be presupposed that an analyst of legal language may be drawing from a large legacy of expert knowledge underlying his/her investigation. Such an analyst could hence be prompted to postulate a priori claims about the text, and generally follow a deductive track of reasoning.

It has to be noted that, obviously enough, both pragmaticists and lawyers talks about 'acts'. This analogy, however, goes deeper than the mere term may suggest. Linguists such as Kurzon (1986) point to a close correspondence between works by Austin (1962 and later ones) and works by another Oxford philosopher and lawyer H.L. Hart. Hart (1961) comments, for instance, on the parallels between illocutionary act theory and the construction of legal acts such as will-making or property transfer. He further suggests that performative utterances be called 'operative utterances', drawing on the concept of the so-called 'operative words' in legal language. Recently, Witczak-Plisiecka (2001) acknowledges more analogies. Acts in the law presuppose that the performer, in order to perform the act, needs to be able to exercise legal power. This partly corresponds to Searle's (1969, 1979) concept of necessary and sufficient conditions for successful performance of speech acts. Finally, it is recognized both in the law and in many pragmatic and discourse analysis theories (Van Dijk, 1977 and later works) that acts tend to join in sequences which generate (and at the same time subscribe to) the macro acts of highest functional value. This last observation is again crucial to the determinism of legal language analysis since the adherence to macro act derivation is a clear indication of inductivism in linguistic research. In consequence, what seems to emerge from the whole of this sketchy description is a kind of methodological paradox. When dealing with a concrete text, an analyst of 'legal language' may be well aware, as has been mentioned at the beginning of this section, of some stable characteristics of the principal discourse type. But *in effect* his/her expert knowledge may not only invite but also prevent the a priori claims, if they should be considered *necessarily* inaccurate on account of being unsupported by the derivation of the global function of the text. The logical conclusion from the above remains that it is probably only a subdivision of 'legal language' that can help resolve the analytic controversies pertaining to the genre of legal discourse as a whole.

9.4   Linguistic and paralinguistic preconditions of analytic determination

Before making this subdivision, however, it seems worthwhile to look further for some general factors under which the particular domains of legal language could fall subject to either inductive or deductive determination.

First, with the development of *forensic linguistics*, multiple professional contacts have been established between linguists and lawyers. In addition, multiple linguists have undergone substantial legal training and, vice versa, a number of lawyers have acquired language analysis skills (Gibbons, 1994; Maley and Fahey, 1991, etc.). Consequently, virtually all basic legal concepts, such as 'caution', 'sentence' or 'guilt', have been defined linguistically, according to a finite number of specific semantic features (Witczak-Plisiecka, 2001). The possession of knowledge of the exact meaning carried by the prevailing proportion of lexical items within a legal text has thus become a signpost for legally trained linguists wishing to determine the function of the text upon the mere skimming of it. Whether this finds plausible reflection in actual data analysis will be discussed later in the contribution, but the undeniable fact remains that the relatively short forensic legacy has incidentally created potential for a 'top-down' approach to persuasion patterns used in some of the legal texts.

Second, as a consequence of the American trend of the early 1980s which advocated simplification of legal documents or even the complete rewriting of some (Charrow and Charrow, 1979), the analysis of legal language has been jeopardized by perception of legal texts as *necessarily* vague, in order to bring concrete persuasion benefits to their authors. The simultaneous coinage of such pejorative terms as, for example, 'gobbledegook' (Lewis and Pucelik, 1982), has only increased a temptation to approach a legal text with a certain dose of analytic cynicism and a ready-made conclusion about it at hand. As we shall see, several analysts such as Lutz (1990) have already fallen victim to this temptation.

Yet another 'top-down' prompt has emerged from historical transformation of legal language. In countries where the process of codification was, for social or other reasons, somewhat delayed (as was the case, for instance, in Britain), interpreters of legal language were given a chance to pre-postulate about functions of some legal discourses only when dealing with chunks which had already been (literally) written down and brought to light (Gibbons, 1994). Consequently, it was also the titling or naming of legal documents that started to play a significant role in approaching the text from an analytic standpoint. For a present-day linguist this means that, at least apparently, legal texts from more recent times stand a better chance of being interpreted deductively than the older, less worked-out ones do. The same phenomenon bears responsibility for perception of older 'texts' (such as, for example, the as yet non-institutionalized instances of wills or the early statutes – cf. Gibbons, 1994; Bhatia, 1994, etc.) as more 'friendly' data for 'bottom-up' research.

The last remark points to the possibility of finding some further prompts for inductive analysis of legal texts. As Goodrich (1987) suggests, certain instances of language of the law, being on the one hand apparently fixed and all-inclusive in meaning, on the other have to be flexible enough to enable future interpretation and adjustment. This concerns mainly all legal systems which have developed, less or more directly, from the British common law tradition: in particular, the contemporary legal systems in the USA, Canada, Australia and New Zealand. The common law heritage is in fact responsible for a mental paradox that is often addressed by legal experts (MacCormick, 1990): *how* can the law be certain and stable and yet achieve flexibility? Certainty is demanded by justice and the rule of law which require *predictability* of outcome: like cases must be decided alike (this naturally translates into the above-mentioned suggestion that, from an analytic standpoint, a legal provision should possess a definite function which is traceable upon a glance-like look).

When the facts are the same, the outcome should be the same. But no set of facts is ever *quite* the same and, again, the question arises: does the new set of facts arising from different times and different circumstances really fall within the ambit of the same legal rule as the earlier set? What are the mechanisms by which the legal rule can be adjusted, made flexible, in order to accommodate the new set of circumstances? How is the rule extended or restricted in order to do justice to this particular case? Parallel are the questions that could be posed by a legal language analyst: is it not possible that in a given legal text the function of its contents can be stretched to embrace more than the 'label' of the text originally suggests? If so, is it not worthwhile to reconsider the initial, deduction-based conclusions by a thorough, linear investigation of particular words and phrases? Hesitations of that kind seem to apply to analysis of both the written language and some (initially) spoken (yet institutionalized) instances of legal discourse such as, for instance, judicial resolutions in courtroom situations.

Also, an analyst of legal language whose expert knowledge is as yet incomplete for a given field of investigation may become somewhat baffled by the text chunks containing a high number of nominalizations representing processes, as well as passive clauses with agents deleted. As they are used in some legal discourses (for instance, written legislation), nominalizations and passive structures plus their immediate contexts constitute, for extremely qualified experts, the ultra-clear indicators of meaning and function of the text, though these features may remain relatively vague for analysts of slightly lower expertise (Maley, 1994). The latter are thus forced to work out the function of the text by looking at the *series of like constructions* involving the 'vague' phenomena (naturally, if the text format allows) and thereby reach conclusions about the particular structures, whether nominal or passive, inductively and not sooner than toward the end of the text.

To illustrate this, let us consider the following example. In most English-written legislations the term 'homicide' is technically a superordinate category for a number of subordinate terms such as 'murder' or 'manslaughter'. Yet for a less expert analyst, it only covers up the important technical differences between these terms. Whether 'homicide' should be considered synonymous to 'murder' or 'manslaughter' remains, in 100 per cent probability, to be worked out from the immediate context that follows its initial use in the text chunk, but it does take the knowledge of a full paradigm of its lexical collocations to derive the correct conclusion. Since with the repetition of the principal term 'homicide' the number of contexts increases, so does the chance that an analyst will interpret the term correctly, from finally knowing a consecutive collocation in the paradigm.

9.5   Determinism of sample subtypes of legal discourse

Having discussed the analytic determinants of legal discourse as a whole, let us look at the construction of a number of real-life samples, exemplifying some more specialized discourse domains. In order to talk about analytic determination of specific instances of legal discourse, one needs to make a plausible subdivision of the principal type. It is frequently maintained (Shuy, 1986; Danet, 1990; Maley, 1994) that the classification of legal discourse is best laid out by the consecutive stages in what might be called a 'conflict resolution' scheme.

Let us assume that there is a 'social conflict' between parties which comes under the rubric of a rule of law, either a statutory or a common law one. If the parties decide to litigate, each party will consult a lawyer and the case will be *prepared* (Stage 2), with all the attendant *documentation* (Stage 1). If the next step is taken, the parties appear in court and a *trial* before a judge (and sometimes a jury) follows (Stage 3). At the end of the trial, the judge will give judgment which is an integral part of the trial process itself. However, if the judgment has any significance in terms of extending or restricting a rule of law, or establishing a rule of statutory interpretation (Maley, 1994), then it is *reported* and becomes part of the huge volume of precedents that constitute case law (Stage 4). There is, apparently, some *circularity* in the process: once a case is reported and becomes a precedent for later cases, it is then a source of law and potentially an originating point for a new trial process with a new set of parties (Stage 1, Stage 2). Thus, the classification of subtypes of legal discourse based on a sequence of conflict resolution might look as shown in Figure 9.1.

STAGE 1

SOURCES OF LAW; ORIGINATING POINTS OF LEGAL PROCESS			
Legislature	Regulations, by-laws, etc.	Precedents	Wills, contracts, etc.

↓
STAGE 2

PRE-TRIAL PROCESSES			
Police interviews	Lawyer pleadings	Lawyer/client consultations	Subpoena and jury summons

↓
STAGE 3

TRIAL PROCESSES			
Witness examination and cross-examination	Judge/counsel interaction	Jury summation	Judge's decision

↓
STAGE 4

RECORDING AND LAW-MAKING
Case reports

Figure 9.1　Classification of subtypes of legal discourse based on a sequence of conflict resolution

Obviously, this sequence is not inevitable. Wills and contracts, for instance, once drafted and made effective, may never give rise to legal process; or, after consultation with lawyers, the parties may settle the dispute privately; some, perhaps a majority of cases, are recorded but not reported and collected in law reports. But these different structural and discourse situations exist, as a potential, where needed, for the regulation and facilitation of social life. They also provide a feasible classification of major subtypes of legal discourse, one that allows for discernible function differences between constructions of each of them.

As the notion of circularity of legal discourse situations indicates, the most significant structural differences can be derived from the confrontation of the subtypes which fall within the very 'distant' domains of Stage 1 and Stage 3. Consequently, the member discourses of Stage 1 and Stage 3 seem to offer the most promising observations as regards the heterogeneity of legal discourse and its reflection in different kinds of analytic determination. Therefore, in what follows we shall discuss the internal structure and analytic construal of some sample instances of legislature (a member discourse of Stage 1) and witness examination and cross-examination (a member discourse of Stage 3).

9.5.1   Legislation: statutes

The construction of statutes, i.e. acts of parliament, allows to a large extent an a priori specification of the function of a given text.[1] This is possible because, first of all, all modern statutes follow a regular form (Maley, 1994) which constitutes their generic structure. The actual configuration of elements, both obligatory and optional, may be dictated by jurisdiction and certain types of statute have a specific generic structure. However, some generalizations across the different types and jurisdictions can be made. There is first pre-material, giving long title, year and number, short title, preamble and, importantly, an *enacting formula*. The body of the statute follows, divided into numbered sections, subsections and paragraphs. Larger units may be used; for example, a definitions part or division, followed by a substantive part and a procedural part. Schedules are appended as end material. Definitions may occur here as a schedule, if they do not constitute a separate part in the body of the act. Some elements are optional, e.g. short title and preamble, division into parts, but the sequence of elements is invariable.

It is frequently argued that (e.g. Maley, 1994), apart from the meaning and function constituting the specifics of individual legislative documents, the universal performative function underlying most English-written statutes is that of expressing a perpetual command from the sovereign power to its subjects. The rule expressed in a statute is assumed to be forever-speaking; it is supposed to acquire continuity and permanence as an authoritative text. This function is initially realized in the 'enacting formula', a textual chunk such as (1), which precedes all British statutes:

> (1) Be it enacted by the Queen's Most Excellent Majesty, by and with the advice and consent of the Lords Spiritual and Temporal, and the Commons, in this present Parliament assembled, and by the authority of the same, as follows:

The enacting formula makes law the entire text which follows it. The positioning of the enacting formula is crucial for the performative function of the text; the formula comes early enough to be a cue for perpetuity and permanence of the law it announces. Therefore, its lexical structure involves a number of regularities which help the addressee establish and accept this function. The most important element of the structure is naturally the archaic jussive subjunctive which expresses the relationship between the speaker and the addressee. As has been noted, this relationship is based on a huge power differential which fosters the authoritative character of the later words. Also, the enacting formula usually makes use of the pattern of repetition which is supposed to stress the globality and perpetuity of the message. In (1) this is done with the help of *by*-repetitions which not only reiterate the many authority parties from which the legal message originates, but again, underline the profundity of the addressee's subordination to the rule enforced.

From an analytic standpoint, of crucial importance is the fact that all these lexical devices are part of a structure which appears right at the outset of the message expressed in a statute. This makes it easy for the analyst of the statute to work out such functions as perpetuity, globality or permanence relatively early in the analysis of the text. It can thus be pre-postulated that the body message of the statute is going to have as its central task the identifying and empowering of rights and duties in a manner which follows the initiated overtone of permanence and authority, as well as allows the presence of lexical structures capable of enacting these functions. What occurs in the process of analysis is then a deduction of a certain fixed form and function of the text (the statute), out of a 'frozen' structure underlying the main functional indicator of it (the enacting formula of the statute).

Fixed lexical data is a chief instrument whereby the analyst of a statute can postulate about its function at an early point of analysis. Let us consider the following example:

(2) 1. A person, whatever his nationality, who, in the United Kingdom or elsewhere,

(a) detains any other person (the hostage), and

(b) in order to compel a State, international governmental organisation or person to do or abstain from doing any act, threatens to kill, injure or continue to detain the hostage, commits an offence.[2]

In this statute, the words *whatever, elsewhere,* and the defining relative clause serve to establish a range of application of the legal rule that follows, a spectrum that is broad enough to cover as many foreseeable cases of violation of the rule as possible. The use of such lexis is typical of most kinds of prohibitive legislation or the legislation which is supposed to specify all the conditions under which a person may be labelled as 'guilty'. Interestingly, the use of *whatever* or *elsewhere* in discretionary (i.e. permissive) legislation is much less common. This shows that the analyst can readily work out a prohibitive function of a statute by looking at some specific instances of lexical data occurring early in the text. At the same time, discretionary legislation requires the analyst to go beyond such a deductive approach.

The certainty of law which is sought by the application of fixed lexical terms and other textual features entails a number of ensuing considerations which may ultimately give rise to a paradoxical situation wherein the analyst admits to the inaccuracy of 'top-down' analysis and, in consequence, makes an expert assumption about the need for componential study of the whole of the text. In other words, he/she 'deductively' draws upon his/her expertise, only to postulate an 'inductive' approach further in analysis, which then turns into a series of mutual confrontations of lexical environments surrounding each consecutive occurrence of the item in question (cf. Section 9.3). Subordinate to this problem are some micro-concerns: about the analytic value of technical terms such as, for example, nominalizations and passive structures (cf. Section 9.3), or about the many words and phrases which are, by virtue of being perceived by some analysts as 'too technical', often reduced to the function of vagueness-carriers (Lutz, 1990). Consider the following example:[3]

(3) 1. A person who attempts or incites another to commit, or becomes an accessory after the fact to an offence (in this subsection called 'the principal offence') commits-

(a) if the principal offence is an indictable offence, the indictable offence; or

(b) if the principal offence is a simple offence, the simple offence, but is liable on conviction-

(c) to a fine not exceeding half of the fine; and additionally or alternatively,

(d) to imprisonment for a term not exceeding half of the term, to which a person who commits the principal offence is liable.

2. A person who conspires with another to commit an offence (in this subsection called 'the principal offence') commits-

(a) if the principal offence is an indictable offence under section 6(1) or 7(1), the indictable offence, but is liable on conviction to the penalty referred to in section 34(1); . . . .

This section has some technical, nominal-phrase terms or nominalizations ('accessory after the fact', 'indictable offence', 'on conviction'), and is a general rule ('a person who . . .'). The present tense of the rule ('attempts', 'commits', 'is liable') provides continuity over time, a function which we have seen to be normally deducible at an early stage of analysis. There is also a typical pattern of participants, processes and circumstances – in legal terms, the legal subject, the legal operative verb and the conditions (Renton, 1975). In addition, textual features, in the sense of the management and packaging of information (the retention of one-sentence layout of consecutive subsections, the use of repetition rather than pronouns, etc.), are intended to make the section explicit and precise and therefore certain as to the function. The global function is to be inferred, as we have seen before, as enactment of permanence or continuity of prohibition and penalty for ignoring it. On a micro-scale, however, it is tempting to postulate that subsection 1 also seeks to enact the concept of penalty for inciting a rule violation as imposed in some way *proportionate* to the principal penalty imposed for the actual commitment of the principal offence.

But despite the lexicogrammatical and textual contributions to precision, Section 33 is not, as it turns out, entirely clear or certain, especially with regard to the last function above. Its uncertainty derives from an intertextual clash between it and the section referred to in the final subsection, which provides a *different* way of penalizing a person for the same offence. Ambiguity of this kind can be attributable either to the wish to allow some judicial flexibility (most statutes have to be understood and interpreted against a background legislation) or, as is the case here (Maley, 1994), plainly to faulty drafting. For the analyst this situation means a continual risk of overinterpreting texts of such high lexical density as in Section 33. Furthermore, it sometimes means approaching the text with a tendency for treating fixed lexical data not in terms of its primary function (which remains to be the precision of reference), but in terms of an analytic 'catch' about which no functional presupposition should be made, at least not until further contextual and confrontative testing has been performed.

Finally, the density of fixed lexical data in legal texts (not necessarily statutes) may, in extreme though imaginable cases, contribute to the perception of legal language as not just flexible to allow judicial interpretation but merely vague on purpose, to serve the benefit of a specific party engaged in a legal dispute. However infrequently, preconceptions of that kind do exist in some studies, especially those immediately following the campaign for simplification of legal language as a whole (cf. Section 9.4). A good example of such cynical predisposition affecting the actual analysis is Lutz's (1990, p. 4) discussion of a legal concept termed *involuntary conversion*:

> [...] Lawyers speak of an 'involuntary conversion' of property when discussing the loss or destruction of property through theft, accident or condemnation [...]. When used by lawyers in a legal situation, such jargon is a legitimate use of language, since lawyers can be expected to understand the term. However, when a member of a specialized group uses its jargon to communicate with a person outside the group, and uses it knowing that the nonmember does not understand such language, then there is doublespeak. For example, on May 9, 1978, a National Airlines 727 airplane crashed while attempting to land at the Pensacola, Florida airport. Three of the fifty-two passengers aboard the airplane were killed. As a result of the crash, National made an after-tax insurance benefit of $1.7 million, or an extra 18c a share dividend for its stockholders. Now National Airlines had two problems: It did not want to talk about one of its airplanes crashing, and it had to account for the $1.7 million when it issued its annual report to its stockholders. National solved the problem by inserting a footnote in its annual report which explained that the $1.7 million income was due to 'the involuntary conversion of a 727'. National thus acknowledged the crash of its airplane and the subsequent profit it made from the crash, without once mentioning the accident or the deaths. However, because airline officials knew that most stockholders in the company, and indeed most of the general public, were not familiar with legal jargon, the use of such jargon constituted doublespeak.

Clearly, the early positioning of the (hypo)thesis claim ('..., then there is doublespeak') indicates Lutz's firm perception of some legal texts as instruments of manipulation. This analytic attitude affects the data part of the argument. Within the data part, most lexical choices serve the purpose of presenting National Airlines as parasiting on the consequences of the accident. For example, there is a metonymic relation established between 'the crash' and 'the after-tax insurance benefit'. Thereby, National Airlines side is shown to have derived the $1.7 million income 'from the crash', and not, as it *really* happened, from insurance compensation. Instances of that kind of data presentation reinforce the predisposition voiced in the initial claim.

However, analyses such as Lutz's have little to do with the many approaches recognizing the *constructive* aspect of legal flexibility and the inevitable intricacies that follow it (Goodrich, 1987; Bhatia, 1994). It is well known and accepted that many legal texts, and statutes in particular, make use of the so-called 'legal fiction'. Legal fiction is a kind of enabling or facilitating device which enables a lawyer to say, 'X is Y', or, more precisely, 'For the purposes of this enactment or statute, X is *deemed* to be Y' (Maley, 1994). Because deeming clauses of this kind bring together two disparate elements into a temporary text-specific equative relationship, they have affinities with metaphor (which, incidentally, entails a necessarily *inductive* computation of meaning). Just as a literary metaphor enables readers (or analysts) to think of an entity as being in some sense the same as another and thus enlarges the system of meaning relations for the literary work, so the legal fiction allows lawyers (or legal analysts) to treat disparate entities as similar and thus enlarges the legal meaning relationships for the purpose of the particular statute or section. Therefore, the constructive effect of deeming consists in the fact that a new rule for a new circumstance does *not* have to be made. The existing rule applies, simply by 'deeming' one circumstance, participant or process to be the same as another. Naturally, acknowledgement of the positive aspects of the legal fiction and deeming means adopting an inductive approach to analysis, since, as is the case with metaphoric expressions, it is mostly linear processing of lexical data that is crucial to working out the meaning and function of a given text.

9.5.2 Courtroom discourse: witness examination and cross-examination

Compared to study of legislation, analysis of courtroom discourse entails substantially more of inductive computation of meaning and function behind each discourse subtype, whether it be a 'text proper' or merely a recorded oral performance of any of the session participants. This is so because of a number of analytic beliefs concerning the conceptual framing of courtroom discourse, as well as because of the autonomous, generic structure of the discourse itself. It seems plausible to say that many approaches to courtroom discourse have been deeply affected by the common conceptualization of the discourse situation and structure as that of a 'story'. The initial impetus toward such trial-as-story metaphor came from Bennett and Feldman's pioneering study (1981) in which they claimed that in a criminal trial a jury interprets the evidence presented to it from the opposing sides and constructs a story. That is to say the jury accepts from the opposing versions or 'stories' of the event placed before them a single story which fits with their everyday knowledge of what people are likely to do and should do. It is true that in many cases, counsel, particularly defending counsel, may be more concerned to throw doubt on the prosecution story than to construct an alternative version, but in raising a 'reasonable doubt' in the minds of jury members, an alternative version is normally implied. The trial-as-story metaphor, despite a certain vagueness about the linguistic and discoursal criteria for storiness, has proved to be a very fertile one and has been the framework around which a great deal of analysis and comment has been made of courtroom language from expert linguists and lawyers (Kurzon, 1986; Den Boer, 1990; Maley and Fahey, 1991; Maley, 1994, etc.). These studies have come to reveal a necessarily linear and componential investigation of textual properties, as if to demonstrate the need to look at the accumulation of all possible cues that might lead toward the 'point' of the story. In this way, they have simultaneously acknowledged the existence of autonomous generic features of courtroom language which thus prompt its 'bottom-up' analysis, for instance the changing degree of cue density and the accumulation speed across the different subtypes of the principal discourse, or the variations of function caused by the apparent margin of unpredictability in participants' interaction.

An illuminating instance of 'bottom-up' analysis of courtroom discourse is Maley's (1994, pp. 36–8) study of witness examination (by prosecution counsel, example (4)) and cross-examination (by defence counsel, example (5)) in an Australian trial. The witness is a key witness for the prosecution, a criminal who has turned police informer:

(4)

Counsel   After having given those documents to Mr. H, did you see Mr. H again?

Witness   Yes, I did.

Counsel   When was that?

Witness   About the second or third week of June.

Counsel   Did you have a conversation with him regarding M?

Witness   Yes, I did.

Counsel   What did you say?

Witness   I said to him, 'There seems to be some holdup with the M money. The chap didn't turn up. I'll have to wait for the weekend and go out and see M'.

Counsel   Then Mr. H said something to you?

Witness   That is correct.

Counsel   After that meeting with Mr. H, when was the next time that you saw him?

Witness   In July of 1983.

(5)

Counsel   And I suppose it would be fair to say that as they came to recognize the extent of your knowledge about overseas drugs, so they became more and more interested?

Witness   No, that would be incorrect. They already knew where I stood, much prior to July of 1982.

Counsel   You say that their own intelligence was sufficient to let them know how important you were even before you spoke to them?

Witness   They had been following me...

Counsel   Is that right or not?

His Honour   Just a moment, Mr. B. I am allowing the witness to answer that question.

Counsel   With respect, Your Honour...

His Honour   I am allowing him to answer it.

Counsel   I am asking that my objection be noted.

His Honour   Every objection that you have ever made in this case has been noted, Mr. B.

Counsel   I must be allowed to make it, with respect, or it does not go down.

His Honour   Would you say what you were saying, Mr. C?

Witness   They had been following me, monitoring telephones that I was associated with and raiding premises that I was associated with since 1979.

The global function of the exchanges in (4) is, Maley suggests, to build up a 'story' in which both sides are congruent and cooperative enough to make the whole of the sequence plausible. The counsel is thus reluctant to 'lead' or ask questions which presuppose their answer, so his questions tend to alternate between indefinite polars ('Did you have a conversation ... ?') and open information-seeking questions ('When was that?'). The witness, right on cue, responds with the required information, in the desired sequence. His composure and consistency, Maley observes, are enacted in the easy and appropriate way in which he quotes conversations, that is in direct, as against indirect, reported speech, thus conforming to evidential requirements. Closing the analysis, Maley notes that the question 'Then Mr. H said something to you?' is answered only by a confirmation, since the witness does not elaborate unless his counsel gives him a prompt. This, Maley concludes, enhances the character of the examination as that of a 'carefully rehearsed performance' (Maley, 1994, p. 38).

Methodologically, Maley's study of (4) relies heavily on continual accumulation of lexical cues for the macro function of the text. The cues are varied (two different types of questions, direct speech chunks, two different patterns of confirmation, etc.) and distributed freely around the text. The macro function of the text is thus derived dynamically, from analysis of consecutive 'regularity spots' revealing the accomplishment of plausibility of the interaction through smoothness of cooperation between the interactants. Even though, at the beginning of analysis, Maley does make a presupposition about the tentative function of 'storiness' and cooperation, he is nonetheless reluctant to reiterate it ('carefully rehearsed performance') until a thorough study of the particular lexical data has been completed. This is no surprise since the analysed text does not possess any early or immediate indicators of function, at least not of the kind we have seen from, for example, the enacting formulae in written legislation (cf. Section 9.5.1). As a result, it is a '(theory)–data–thesis' sequence that underlies the analysis. Given the remaining variety of lexical choices which were *not* made by the interactants to contribute to the macro function but *could* have been, it is problematic to imagine this sequence otherwise.

In his analysis of (5), Maley stresses the adversarial character of the counsel's performance; the counsel apparently targets at elucidating the fact that the Australian Federal Police ('they') could have managed without the involvement of the witness. Although Maley fails to acknowledge it explicitly, the macro function of the counsel's performance is thus to discredit the witness, by showing superficiality of his expertise in the workings of the drug gang. Since the witness, motivated by prospects of mitigation, has exactly opposite goals, the global meaning and function of the event consist in the clashing 'stories' presented by both interactants. The lexical manifestations of the occurring conflict are again to be found across the entire text and, as has been the case with the examination in (4), none of the cues seems significantly more important than any other. They are also comparably heterogeneous, in terms of length, grammatical mode or prosodic load (the counsel's alternating between encouraging and curbing the answers, his posing the questions as true interrogatives or a declarative with a rising tone, the different length of particular confirmation or denial phrases by the witness, etc.).

Thus, the mechanisms governing the inference of macro function of the cross-examination in (5) reflect largely the same 'bottom-up' processes as they underlie the analysis of the examination in example (4). Naturally, there are some hypotheses that can be made about both texts, prior to actual analysis. They include, for instance, the preconception of the witness examination as necessarily supportive and of the cross-examination as necessarily adversarial; also, and perhaps more importantly, they involve the very basic belief that the undertaking of analysis of courtroom discourse as such *entails* an inductive quest for function of the investigated text.

9.6   Conclusion

Approached in terms of an analytic determinant, language of the law can be defined as follows:

1. As a principal discourse type, it invites both the 'top-down' and the 'bottom-up' modes of analysis;
2. It is according to the lexical and semiotic construction of a subtype of the principal discourse that either of the analytic approaches is better adopted; the discourse of legislation, for instance, entails mostly the deductive approach, while the discourse of the courtroom is more feasibly analysable in an inductive manner;
3. Thus, the major cues for macropropositions in legal language involve the *message as such*, rather than the discourse participants or interlocutors;
4. The assumption of an inductive study in a subtype of legal language (for instance, in witness (cross)-examination patterns) is nonetheless predefined deductively, from the general analytic construal of language of the law as a whole;
5. In random cases, the density of fixed lexical data may cause legal language to be accounted for in a necessarily deductive manner, which may in turn render the analysis superficial (cf. Lutz's case in Section 9.5.1).

Notes

1. The forthcoming observations apply to the legal systems in the 'post-common-law' countries. This includes, predominantly, Britain, the USA, Canada, Australia and New Zealand.
2. Taking of Hostages Act 1982, United Kingdom.
3. Requoted after Maley (1994, p. 24). The text is an excerpt from Section 33 of Drugs Act, Western Australia 1981.

References

Austin, J.L. (1962) *How to Do Things with Words* (Oxford: Clarendon Press).
Beaugrande, R. de (1991) *Linguistic Theory: the Discourse of Fundamental Works* (London: Longman).
Bennett, W.L. and M.S. Feldman (1981) *Reconstructing Reality in the Courtroom* (New Brunswick, NJ: Rutgers University Press).
Bhatia, V. (1994) 'Cognitive structuring in legislative provisions' in J. Gibbons (ed.) *Language and the Law* (London: Longman), 136–55.
Cap, P. (2002) *Explorations in Political Discourse* (Frankfurt am Main: Peter Lang).
Cap, P. (2003) *Analytic Determinism of the Study of Persuasive Discourse: Inductive and Deductive Processes* (Łódź: University of Łódź Press).
Charrow, R. and V. Charrow (1979) 'Making legal language understandable'. *Columbia Law Review*, 79, 80–96.
Conley, J. and W. O'Barr (1990) 'Rules versus relationships in small claims disputes' in A.D. Grimshaw (ed.) *Conflict Talk* (Cambridge: Cambridge University Press), 22–44.
Conley, J. and W. O'Barr (1998) *Just Words: Law, Language, and Power* (Chicago: University of Chicago Press).
Danet, B. (1990) 'Language and law: an overview of fifteen years of research' in H. Giles and W. Robinson (eds) *Handbook of Language and Social Psychology* (Chichester: Wiley), 537–59.
Den Boer, M. (1990) 'A linguistic analysis of narrative coherence in the courtroom' in P. Herhot (ed.) *Law, Interpretation and Reality* (Dordrecht: Kluwer Academic Publisher), 346–78.
Gibbons, J. (ed.) (1994) *Language and the Law* (London: Longman).
Goodrich, P. (1987) *Legal Discourse* (London: Macmillan).
Hart, H.L. (1961) *The Concept of Law* (Oxford: Oxford University Press).
Kurzon, D. (1986) *It Is Hereby Performed: Explorations in Legal Speech Acts* (Philadelphia, Pa: John Benjamins).
Lewis, B. and F. Pucelik (1982) *Magic Demystified* (Lake Oswego, Ore.: Metamorphous Press).
Lutz, W. (1990) *Doublespeak* (New York: HarperPerennial).
MacCormick, N. (1990) 'Reconstruction after deconstruction: a response to critical legal studies', *Oxford Journal of Legal Studies*, 10, 539–58.
Maley, Y. (1994) 'The language of the law' in J. Gibbons (ed.) *Language and the Law* (London: Longman), 11–50.
Maley, Y. and R. Fahey (1991) 'Presenting the evidence: Constructions of reality in court', *International Journal for the Semiotics of Law*, 4, 10–21.

Philips, S.U. (1985) 'Strategies of clarification in judges' use of language: From the written to the spoken', *Discourse Processes*, 8, 421–36.

Renton, D. (1975) *The Preparation of Legislation: Report of a Committee Appointed by the Lord President of the Council* (London: HMSO).

Searle, J.R. (1969) *Speech Acts* (Cambridge: Cambridge University Press).

Searle, J.R. (1979) *Expression and Meaning: Studies in the Theory of Speech Acts* (Cambridge: Cambridge University Press).

Shuy, R. (1986) 'Language and the law', *Annual Review of Applied Linguistics*, 7, 50–63.

Van Dijk, T.A. (1977) *Text and Context* (London: Longman).

Witczak-Plisiecka, I. (2001) 'Semantic and pragmatic aspects of speech acts in English legal texts'. Unpublished PhD thesis, University of Łódź.

10
Conflict-Softening in Thai–Japanese Business Discourse

U-maporn Kardkarnklai
Department of Western Languages, Faculty of Humanities,
Srinakharinwirot University, Thailand

10.1 Introduction

Conflict avoidance has been characterized as a preferred means of communication for Japanese as well as Thais. In business interaction, pressure arising from the job can cause potential conflict between co-workers. Both Thais and Japanese tend to adopt a strategy of conflict-softening as a means of dealing with conflict in intercultural business communication.

The avoidance of open discussion of conflict has been well documented in the literature of anthropology and sociology. For example, Bilmes (1992) in a study of the mediator's role in a negotiation between northern Thai villagers found that Thai villagers place a value on social harmony and non-confrontation, which makes them rely on trust and goodwill. He observed that when conflict occurs, the villagers feel uncomfortable. He further noted that when two persons had a conflict, they 'do not like to look one another in the face' or 'cannot look each other in the face', and avoid one another (Bilmes, 1992, p. 578). Moeran (1989) studied the heated arguments in ritual drinking parties in Japan. He reported that drinking arguments allow people to express their confrontational thoughts which are not openly discussed in daily conversation. In general, previous studies suggest that Thais and Japanese avoid confrontation and deal with conflict indirectly.

There have been relatively few examinations of the interaction between Asian speakers, in particular how two similar cultural backgrounds manage conflict in intercultural communication. It is this area that is the central focus of this study.

10.2   Purpose of the study

The purpose of this work is to explore how Thais and Japanese manage conflicts in intercultural business meetings; what conflict-softening strategies are employed by Thais and Japanese in these meetings; and what significant cultural values underlie the use of these conflict-softening strategies. The results of this study should add to an understanding of cultural values that influence communicative strategies.

In what follows, I first give an overview of recent studies in language and conflict on which this contribution is based. I then present a brief description of data collection and methodology. Next, a number of conflict-softening strategies, which were adopted as a means to achieve transactional and interactional goals in the meetings, are examined and illustrated with examples from the data. Finally, some significant cultural values underlying the use of these strategies are discussed.

10.3   Communicative strategies of managing conflict

In this section, I review the literature which particularly focuses on interpersonal conflict and linguistic issues. Lebra (1984), for example, contends that conflict exists in Japan, but that the Japanese seek non-confrontational methods of resolving that conflict. This is because they place a high value on harmony and social interdependence.

Based on Japanese data, Jones (1990) studied conflicts in three different contexts: debate talk, office talk and family talk. She found that conflicts were managed differently in these contexts. In office talk, when the conflict occurred, co-workers expressed it explicitly but less directly than in debate talk. They managed conflict through switches in speech style, parallelism and laughter. In addition, they relieved tension through 'play'[1] (Bateson, 1979).

Yamada (1997), in a study of a Japanese business meeting, found that the Japanese lowered their voices to express their negative opinions. This lowering of the voice is a 'talk-distancing' strategy which helps a smooth exchange of conflicting ideas and to achieve the interactional goals.

Turning to Korean data, Song (1993) provided a qualitative analysis of the linguistic strategies in conflict. These strategies are formulaic expressive adverbials, repetition, code-switching, silence and personal experience stories among others. In Taiwanese data, Kuo (1991) studied a way of negotiating conflict in formal and informal conversations. She found that in the parliamentary interpellations, sarcasm and accusatory questions were included in the list of forms and types of disagreement. Among friends, participants employed various forms of argumentative strategies: formulaic expressions, initiations of disagreement latching onto each other's talk with the Chinese equivalent of the contrastive marker 'but', uncooperative interruptions, and wh-questions with partial repetitions and substitutions marked forthcoming disagreement.

Some studies relate conflict to facework. For example, Muntigl and Turnbull (1998) examined the conversational structure of disagreement and how the negotiation to save face influences the argument. They claimed that facework is a main determinant of the type of turn sequence that speakers will use. Four main types of disagreement are identified: irrelevancy claims, challenges, contradictions and counterclaims. They found that the more a second turn threatens the position of the speaker who made a claim as a first turn, the more likely it is that the third turn will contain further support of that first speaker's claim.

Tang and Kirkbride (1986) examined differences in conflict management styles between Hong Kong Chinese and Western managers. They reported that when an interpersonal problem occurs in an organization, Chinese bosses often solve the problem with the subordinates individually and privately without loss of face. This practice helps to preserve harmony. On the other hand, Western bosses often deal with interpersonal conflict openly in order that the cause of a problem can be fully solved. This results in 'better understanding, mutual trust, constructive competition and creativity' (Tang and Kirkbride, 1986, p. 294). This view is in line with Ting-Toomey (1992). She reported that Chinese from Taiwan, Hong Kong and the People's Republic of China use more compromising strategies in dealing with conflict. Similarly, Bilbow (1997) asserted that Chinese attempt to avoid interpersonal conflict because they place great value on social harmony.

According to Ting-Toomey (1992, p. 5), conflict is related to saving face, which determines the use of strategies in managing conflict. She suggested that American people are oriented to strategies to save their own face, whereas Asian people focus on mutual face-saving strategies. Table 10.1 shows the comparison of strategies in managing conflict between American and Asian people.

This brief review shows that conflicts are marked linguistically and they tend to be dealt with differently in different contexts. In the next section, I will summarize the data collection and introduce the various approaches used for analysis and interpretation of the data for the present study.

Table 10.1 Comparison of managing conflict strategies between American and Asian people

American people	Asian people
• concern for one's own image – own face-saving strategies • control-focused conflict strategies • confrontational strategies • displaying win–lose orientations	• concern for both parties' image – mutual face-saving strategies • face-saving strategies • conflict avoidance strategies • displaying win–win orientations

10.4 Data collection and methods of analysis

The main data for this study comprised 7.43 hours of tape-recorded meetings between the Thai and Japanese employees of two large Japanese companies in Thailand. I chose the context in which English is used in Thai–Japanese interaction in the workplace as the basis of this study because English is the most common language in Japanese organizations in Thailand (JETRO, 2001). For this chapter, I am using the data from company A, which involves monthly meetings. The purposes of these meetings were project planning, routine checking, making arrangements, problem solving and taking decisions. In the meetings, Thai participants outnumbered Japanese participants: 6 Thais (1 director, 4 managers and 1 assistant manager), compared to 4 Japanese (1 managing director and 3 managers). Table 10.2 shows the profile of the participants.

Various approaches were used to analyse and interpret the data. I employed an ethnographic approach, using the SPEAKING framework of Hymes (1972), to organize the analysis of the relevant sociocultural backgrounds of the participants. Discourse analysis was utilized to explain how the business people used conflict-softening strategies

Table 10.2 Profile of the participants in company A meetings

Management level	Thais (6)	Japanese (4)
Senior	1 director	1 managing director
Middle	4 managers and 1 assistant manager	3 managers

in business discourse and to understand the discourse patterns in an ongoing interaction. Politeness theory was also used to analyse the discourse in particular contexts.

10.5   Definition of conflict-softening

To analyse conflict in Japanese data, Jones (1990) developed a framework which consists of two kinds of strategies in managing conflict: explicit and inexplicit strategies. The former refers to ways in which participants discuss a conflict in words. The latter involves strategies used to manage a conflict without referring to it directly. They may be verbal, non-verbal or non-vocal. Table 10.3 shows examples of explicit and inexplicit strategies.

Following Jones's framework, I will differentiate between explicit and inexplicit strategies. In this study, I will relate conflict-softening to linguistic strategies employed to reduce tension arising from disagreement or potential disagreement between interlocutors with opposing ideas. As Thais and Japanese are less likely to be involved in open confrontation, I also include features at discourse level, such as repetition, hesitation, hedges and vowel lengthening to identify conflict. This detailed framework can provide greater insight into the sensitive nature of conflict management.

10.6   Strategies for conflict-softening

It would not be sensible to claim that Thais and Japanese have never disagreed, or never had conflicts with others. Rather, we can observe how speakers select linguistic or non-linguistic forms to express their conflicting views. For example, one may prefer to keep silent instead of saying bluntly 'no'. In this chapter, I will present three strategies that Thais and Japanese adopt in softening conflict.

Table 10.3   Framework for identifying conflict by Jones (1990, p. 20)

Explicit strategies	Inexplicit strategies
• statements of opposition, i.e. mitigated or blunt • compromise • explicit concession	• ignoring a conflict • asking a question • shifting speech style • frequent laughter

10.6.1   *Sa-nuk* and non-task talk

The first strategy which Thais and Japanese use to reduce potential disagreement is lightening the tone when engaged in discussion of a serious issue. I have discussed this point in more detail elsewhere (Kard-karnklai, 2003) that Thais tend to employ *sa-nuk* talk and Japanese adopt non-task talk.

10.6.1.1   *Sa-nuk talk*

The word *sa-nuk* literally means 'fun' or 'pleasure'. *Sa-nuk* talk in this study involves non-serious, non-task discussion, jokes and talk about personal matters. This kind of talk is introduced as 'play' in Jones's framework. *Sa-nuk* talk is shown in extract 1: A12/30-31. The Thai director (TM1) employs *sa-nuk* talk as a means of softening potential disagreement, creating an easy-going atmosphere, strengthening a close relationship, and minimizing status differences.

The context here is that the participants are discussing rearranging furniture in the office, i.e. relocating the copy machine and staff desks. While the Japanese managing director (J2) is elaborating his idea about arranging the space in the office for staff, TM1 suddenly steps in to express a contradictory idea, which is an unexpected proposal to move the copy machine out of the room. It appears from the shared laughter that all participants treat this remark as *sa-nuk*.

Extract 1: A12/30-31 Thai director (TM1) speaking to Japanese managing director (J2)

Context: **The participants are discussing where to place a copy-machine in the office.**		
1	TF3:	*de* copy copy machine *wa kono mama desuka*
		(and) *(do we leave it like this?)*
2	J1 :	copy machine umm

| 3 | TM1: | *koe pid dan-nok* | partition | *dan-nok* |
| | | *(close outside)* | | *(outside)* |

| 4 | J1: | *naruhodo* | *hai* | *takusan* XX |
| | | *(I see)* | | *(yes many XX)* |

| 5 | TM1: | open door | *yuu-lei* |
| | | | *(like that)* |

| 6 | J2: | XX | XX | *a-no* | expand | office |
| | | | | *(ah)* | | |

| 7 | TM1: | @@@ |

| 8 | J2: | also we if we even | we | another | estimator |
| 9 | TM1: | | | | yeah yeah |

10	J2:	*kocchi wa* design section *no a-no sales to* [
		(this is the design section's ah sales)
11 >>>>>TM1:		[*ja au ook rue*]
		(take it out, will you?)
		<laughing voice>

| 12 | | All @@@@ |

One possible explanation for using *sa-nuk* talk here is to soften possible conflict and promote an easy-going atmosphere, which results in less formality. Grindsted (1997, p. 159) points out the advantage of this strategy in which *sa-nuk* expressed as a form of joke-telling is that it can 'relieve tension in double-bind situations',[2] where it is necessary to balance the conflict. Clearly, no one in the meeting perceives this event as a face-threatening act because all participants laugh together. This shared laughter on the part of participants confirms that a special relationship exists in the ongoing conversation (Schenkein, 1972). In line with this view, Miller (1994, p. 224) argues that laughter covers 'ideas or opinions in goodwill', therefore 'maintaining collegiality and harmony'.

A second possible explanation for using *sa-nuk* talk in an amusing way is to maintain a close relationship. Although both the Thai director (TM1) and the Japanese managing director (J2) in this study are classified as senior management, it is J2 who is in a higher position than TM1. *Sa-nuk* talk by TM1 indicates that their relationship has been well established for a considerable length of time. There is no evidence that J2 regards this *sa-nuk* talk as offensive. This kind of *sa-nuk* talk signals and strengthens solidarity (Grindsted, 1997) and also contributes to social relationships (Holmes, 2001). Thus, the use of *sa-nuk* talk here by TM1 clearly promotes a close relationship between the participants.

Another interesting point is that *sa-nuk* talk with a hedge functions to reduce unequal status, and avoid confrontation. In this example, TM1 introduces his *sa-nuk* talk by the hedge word *rue* in Thai (line 11) which is roughly equivalent to a tag question in English. The tag *rue*, in this example, is slightly less questioning than a direct question. This form of a tag question seems to reduce the force of the utterance, and helps smooth conversational interaction (Coates, 1993) and avoids conflict (Holmes, 1995). Thus, this tag form is clearly used to show facilitative politeness, which expresses concern for the needs of others. Without the tag *rue*, the statement 'take it out' simply indicates a directive form which, in contrast, shows a certain forcefulness. In a way, the tag question allows TM1 to express his challenging idea in a more acceptable way. In addition, the use of interruptions co-occurring with a tag question is used as a device to minimize inequalities and sustain conversation.

In sum, *sa-nuk* talk or play functions to reduce conflict, promote an easy-going atmosphere, create a close relationship, and reduce imbalances in status.

10.6.1.2 Non-task talk

Japanese business people tend to place importance on what Graham and Sano (1989) called 'nontask sounding'. This term involves activities which aim to create rapport, such as finding out what the other feels.

The next example shows non-task talk used to avoid interpersonal conflict by a Japanese. This example is illustrated in extract 2: A12/40. The context is that the female manager in the personnel and public relations section (TF2) asks *shacho* (the Japanese managing director or J2) for a new camera for use in the company. Before TF2 has finished her request, she is interrupted by J2's spontaneous joke, saying 'I have' (line 8). This brief amusing remark could convey the meaning that 'I have the kind of camera that will do the job, so there is no need to get a new one'. This indicates conflicting views because J2 disapproves of TF2's request to purchase a new camera. The non-task talk in the form of brief amusing joke successfully invites shared laughter. Later, J2 continues his non-task talk, which is jointly produced by the Thai director (TM1). The evidence shows that J2 makes use of non-task talk to indirectly refuse TF2's request.

Extract 2: A 12/40 Japanese managing director (J2) speaking to Thai female manager (TF2) in the personnel and public relations section

Context:	**TF2 requests a new camera for use in the company.**
1 TF2:	I have one more thing for the ah camera of the company
2 TF2:	I don't know now we have spare in the good condition or not
3 TF2:	because sometimes
4 J2:	camera *ga nain dayo na* *(no camera)* *<low voice>*
5 TF2:	I I need to er use ah like signing
6 TF2:	contract ceremony or new year party always er

7	TF2:	borrow from employee	because [
8 >>>>>	J2:	@@	[I have]
			<laughing voice>

| 9 | | ALL @@@@ | |

| 10 | TM1: | XX |

| 11 | J2: | good good camera |

| 12 | TM1: | special good camera |

| 13 | J2: | special camera |

| 14 | TM1: | cannot use very very special @@@@@ |

Softening disagreement and maintaining good relationships are possible explanations for the use of non-task talk. This talk suggests that J2, a superior, shares concern for a subordinate's (TF2) positive face needs. If J2 used a direct refusal, it could be seen as a potential threat or might turn out to be an offensive remark. Instead, he shifts his disgreement by replying to TF2 with a humorous statement. In turn, TF2's face is saved by not having her request refused point-blank. It is clear that shared laughter confirms the success of this non-task talk. The use of joke-telling here indicates that there are some explanations for why he disagrees with the purchase. Both J2 and TF2, in fact, may know whether the camera he refers to works or not.

Non-task talk seems to be a good device to 'sugar the pill' (Holmes 2000b, p. 172), that is, it serves to mask the tension that might arise from unequal status. As Holmes (2000a) notes, humour can be an effective means of 'doing power' implicitly. This is on the grounds that the context is made less formal and status differences become less important. In this context, J2 also makes use of jokes in combination with implicit power to maintain good relationships. Non-task talk in the form of joke-telling, therefore, functions to minimize the unacceptability of face-attacking acts (FAAs)[3] (Austin, 1990), to de-emphasize status differences and to promote interpersonal rapport.

In sum, non-task talk in the form of joke-telling and laughter is used to soften disagreement, promote close relationships, and de-emphasize status differences. Consistent with this result, Jones (1990, p. 305) found that colleagues in office talk use elements of 'play' and laughter to try to make their conflict acceptable. When conflict cannot be resolved, it is dropped. Then, a new topic is brought up in order to relieve the tension and restore harmony to their relationships.

10.6.2 The repeated soft 'no'

The second strategy of conflict-softening is the repeated soft 'no', which is commonly used by Thais and Japanese throughout the data. As pointed out earlier, direct disagreement is not encouraged, in particular towards a senior. However, sometimes participants find it necessary to present corrections to the information offered in the transactional portion of meetings.

An example of the repeated soft 'no' in extract 3: A10/4 shows an explicit disagreement by the Japanese managing director (J2). This kind of explicit disagreement is classified as 'blunt opposition' in Jones's framework. In the present data, the blunt opposition 'no' is softened by repetition and the low tone of voice.

The context here is that when J2 finishes his utterance (line 11), TM1 tries to summarize what J2 has said. In TM1's understanding, two quotations have been prepared for submission for the NS project. One is a quotation for renovation; the other, for decoration. TM1 would like J2 to confirm whether what he had understood about the quotation is right or not. Before TM1 has finished his explanation, J2 butts in to show his disagreement with TM1 saying 'no no no' (line 14).

Extract 3: A10/4 Japanese managing director (J2) speaking to Thai director (TM1)

Context: J2 is talking about the submission of the quotation for the NS project.		
1	J2 :	one (X) now flood
2	TM1:	*oorh* *<umm>*
3	J2:	the owner want to stop it (.) twenty-sixth up the this week and

4	J2:	also the last week (.) eh :: S building XX er export and import

5	J2:	bank (.) below er that office XX to the *T* *<company's name>*

6	J2:	now er X that office change to X building eh ::: that er er er

7	J2:	export and import bank Mr *K* ah into XX then he
		                                  <title+Japanese
		                                  family name>

8	J2:	want to move to the now existing office they try the tenth of next

9	J2:	month but er ::: within this week he want urgently submit the

10	J2:	quotation then that quotation send to me XX and

11	J2:	XXX XX then start it

12	TM1:	*shacho* you so you have meant we have two quotations one is *<Japanese MD>*

13	TM1:	renovate [and make] ing good to the existing *na* and [now] decoration
14>>>>>	J2:	[no no no] [no no no] *<fast and soft voice>* *<fast and soft voice>*

15	J2:	now that company now (shift) already

16	TM1:	yes

17	J2:	demolish *kanaa ::* only demolishing work *(demolish isn't it :::?)*

18	TM1:	making good

19	J2:	yes

20	J1:	where xxx until

Getting the information right is the reason for J2's expression of direct disagreement. J2 displays his rejection of TM1's idea without aggressive confrontation. With the first and second interjections, he repeats 'no' six times with a fast and soft voice which displays his explicit disagreement. This indicates that disagreement is not necessarily an exercise of power. It is, indeed, on the content that J2 disagrees with TM1. To weaken his disagreement, J2 uses repetitions with a soft tone of voice. In this way, his disagreement seems to be less confrontational. According to Brown and Levinson (1987) and Leech (1983), softening disagreement is one way of being polite. This is a clear example of expressing contradictory ideas without exercising power. In sum, the repeated soft 'no' is motivated by the desire to get the right information which contributes to the progress of the meeting.

This result is confirmed by Miller (1994), who examined directness and indirectness in business communication between Japanese and American co-workers. She found that a Japanese uses the repeated 'no' to express his direct disagreement. She explained that the Japanese does not hesitate to express disagreement explicitly because he and co-workers have been colleagues in the same group and have a close working relationship. Yamada (1992), in a study of a Japanese meeting, asserted that the use of various lengthened sounds such as vowels, aspirations, and nasals can decrease order of frequency (Yamada, 1992, p. 124). She reported that when Japanese co-workers detect a potential conflict of views in a meeting, they lengthen the talk by using hesitation markers together with filled pauses and silent pauses.

10.6.3 Compromising

The third strategy used to soften conflict is compromising. An example of compromising takes place when the participants discuss an issue related to a potential conflict. In extract 4: A6/5, the context is the complaint by the Thai female manager in the personnel public relations section (TF2) about the increase in paper used for a copy machine on the SA project. Her complaint might be due to the company's policy of reducing costs in each section. A Japanese project manager (J4), who is in charge of the SA project, argues that the amount of paper used on the SA project is not high when compared to the average use by the head office. To prevent any further conflict, TM1 shifts the dispute to *sa-nuk* talk by saying 'seventy percent ok (1.0) negotiation more X' (line 18) which successfully provokes shared laughter (line 19). Then he goes on to say 'so ok ok discount discount fifty fifty percent' (line 22) which generates more shared laughter (line 23) to provide support for TM1's amusing remark.

Extract 4: A6/5 Thai director (TM1) speaking to Thai female manager in the personnel and public relations section (TF2) and Japanese project manager (J4)

Context: TF2 complains about the increase of paper use for a copy machine.

---

1   TF2:   ah next we go to the use of stationery in July two thousand (.) also have

---

2   TF2:   a lot of detail please take a look   *ha*   only at ah   *shacho*   and
                                  <polite   *<Japanese MD>*
                                  Thai particle>

---

3   TF2:   *J4 san*   copy has a   *SA*   detail that to order which
         <Japanese family   *<project's name>*
         name+title>

---

4   TF2:   er kinds of stationery maybe next this month ah the purchasing amount

---

5   TF2:   will be reduced because ah we separate from *SA* and   *T*
                                            <company's name>

---

6   T21:   separately (2.0)

---

7   J4:   from on August

---

8   TF2:   Yes

---

9   J4:   first of all July XX XXX

---

10   TF2:   @@ @@

---

11   J4:   *a-no* suggestion did I [X X X X   ]
         (ah)

12   TF2:   [no no no I mean] like paper now

13	TF2:	we last month we already divide ah something make still
14	TF2:	make some copy at eight floor still high amount of paper
15	J4:	no no no you can imagine average of the head office
16	J4:	our average charge to the *SA*
17	TF2:	@@@@
18	TM1:	seventy percent ok (1.0) negotiation more X
19		All @@@@
20	TM1:	ok discount fifth percent
21	J4:	XXXXX
22	TM1:	so ok ok discount discount fifty fifty percent
23		All @@@@
24	TM1:	ok discount fifth percent

Compromising is introduced here to minimize disagreement between TF2 and J4 about the high paper use. TM1, acting as a mediator, turns a possibly serious situation, which may jeopardize the harmony of the group, to a *sa-nuk* tone by telling a joke (lines 18–24). This joke successfully provokes shared laughter (lines 19, 23). The evidence of TF2's laughter and the shared laughter indicates that, despite their disagreement, the participants can maintain a good relationship. Thus, compromising with *sa-nuk* talk serves to reduce possible tension and maintain in-group membership.

10.7 Conclusion

This work explores conflict-softening strategies by Thais and Japanese in business discourse. Both Thais and Japanese employed similar strategies of conflict-softening to achieve the shared goals. For both groups, the preferred strategies of conflict-softening are *sa-nuk* and non-task talk, the repeated soft 'no', and compromising.

In a business context in which conflict arises, Thai and Japanese speakers express their implicit and explicit disagreement through various strategies. These strategies of softening conflict function as a smoothener of interaction in double-bind situations and maintain group harmony. In other words, the use of conflict-softening strategies can achieve both transactional and interactional goals. The analysis of the data showed that *sa-nuk* talk and non-task talk are used to mask disagreement and make the conflict less confrontational (for more details, see Kardkarnklai, 2004). When direct disagreement is necessary, the repeated soft 'no' is used to tone down conflicting views. In addition, the role of the mediator in compromising is crucial in settling a dispute between participants. This is in line with Jones (1990, 1995) who studied conflict and negotiation in Japanese conversations and found that mediation is an important technique for reducing conflict. As Jones cautions, it is important to look beyond the myth of culture to how people in different cultures behave, and acknowledge that there are other constraints which influence language use. The analysis of managing conflict in this chapter gives some evidence to support the myth of harmony and non-confrontational style of communication between Asian speakers.

Appendix: transcription conventions

[ ]	square brackets indicate the point at which an interruption begins and ends
>>>>>	arrows indicate that the line on the right of the arrow is the interruption to pay attention to
(1.0)	a number in round brackets indicate pauses in tenths of seconds
(I see)	italic words in italic round brackets indicate literal translation
<laughing voice>	italic words in italic angle brackets indicate clarificatory information
a-no	a word/words in italics indicate Thai/Japanese language
XXX	crosses show indecipherable speech
@@@@	one or more 'at' symbols indicate laughter
::::	one or more colons indicate vowel lengthening

Acknowledgements

I would like to thank my supervisors, Ms Pauline Robinson and Professor Paul Kerswill, for their constructive comments on an earlier draft of this contribution.

Notes

1. Certain actions and interactions made less threatening.
2. Occurs because both poles in a continuum are desirable and necessary, and because interactants are obliged to balance the conflicting poles simultaneously (cited in Yamada, 1992, p. 45).
3. 'Those communicative acts which are injurious to the hearer's positive or negative face, and are introduced in a situation which could have been avoided, but where their inclusion is perceived by the hearer to be intentional' (Austin, 1990 p. 279).

References

Austin, P. (1990) 'Politeness revisited: the dark side' in A. Bell and J. Holmes (eds) *New Zealand Ways of Speaking English* (Clevedon, Philadelphia: Multilingual Matters), 277–93.

Bateson, G. (1979) *Mind and Nature: a Necessary Unity* (New York: Dutton).

Bilbow, G. T. (1997) 'Spoken discourse in the multicultural workplace in Hong Kong: Applying a model of discourse as "impression management"' in F. Bargiela-Chiappini and S. Harris (eds) *The Language of Business: an International Perspective* (Edinburgh: Edinburgh University Press), 21–48.

Bilmes, J. (1992) 'Dividing the rice: a microanalysis of the mediator's role in a northern Thai negotiation', *Language in Society,* 21, 569–602.

Brown, P. and S. Levinson (1987) *Politeness: Some Universals in Language Usage* (Cambridge: Cambridge University Press).

Coates, J. (1993) *Women, Men, and Language: a Socio-Linguistics Account of Gender Difference in Language* (London and New York: Longman).

Graham, J. and Y. Sano (1989) *Smart Bargaining: Doing Business with the Japanese* (New York: Harper and Row Publisher).

Grindsted, A. (1997) 'Joking as strategy in Spanish and Danish negotiations' in F. Bargiela-Chiappini and S. Harris (eds) *The Languages of Business: an International Perspective* (Edinburgh: Edinburgh University Press), 159–82.

Holmes, J. (1995) *Women, Men and Politeness* (London: Longman).

Holmes, J. (2000a) 'Politeness, power and provocation: How humour functions in the workplace', *Discourse Studies,* 2 (2), 159–85.

Holmes, J. (2000b) 'Doing collegiality and keeping control at work: Small talk in government departments' in J. Coupland (ed.) *Small Talk* (London: Longman), 32–61.

Holmes, J. (2001) *Introduction to Sociolinguistics* (London: Pearson Education Limited).

Hymes, D. (1972) 'Models of the interaction of language and social life' in J. Gumperz and D. Hymes (eds) *Directions in Sociolinguistics: the Ethnography of Communication* (New York: Holt, Rinehart and Winston), 35–71.

JETRO (Japanese External Trade Organization) (2001) Seminar documents on 'The Guidelines for Personnel Development in Japanese Organisations', at Hyatt Erawan Hotel, Bangkok, Thailand, 8 December 2000.

Jones, K. (1990) 'Conflict in Japanese conversation'. Unpublished PhD dissertation, University of Michigan, Ann Arbor, Michigan.

Jones, K. (1995) 'Masked negotiation in a Japanese work setting' in A. Firth (ed.) *The Discourse of Negotiation: Studies of Language in the Workplace* (Oxford: Pergamon), 141–58.

Kardkarnklai, U. (2003) 'The facilitative role of interruptions in Thai–Japanese business meetings: *Sa-nuk* versus non-task orientation', *CamLing Proceedings*, 1.

Kardkarnklai, U. (2004) 'The facilitative role of interruptions in Thai–Japanese business meetings: Some inter-cultural perspectives'. Unpublished PhD thesis, the University of Reading.

Kuo, S. (1991) 'Conflict and Its Management in Chinese Verbal Interactions: Casual Conversations and Parliamentary Interpellations'. Unpublished PhD thesis, Georgetown University, Washington, DC.

Lebra, T. (1984) 'Non-confrontational strategies for management of interpersonal conflicts' in E. Kraus, T. Rohlen, and P. Steinhoff (eds) *Conflict in Japan* (Honolulu: University of Hawaii Press), 41–60.

Leech, G. (1983) *Principles of Pragmatics* (London: Longman).

Miller, L. (1994) 'Giving good listening: Interaction and identity in Japan's bicultural workplace', *The World and I*, 9 (12), 221–9.

Moeran, B. (1989) *Language and Popular Cultural in Japan* (Manchester and New York: Manchester University Press).

Muntigl, P. and W. Turnbull (1998) 'Conversational structure and facework in arguing', *Journal of Pragmatics*, 29, 225–56.

Schenkein, J. N. (1972) 'Towards the analysis of natural conversation and the sense of heheh', *Semiotica*, 6, 344–77.

Song, K. (1993) 'An interactional sociolinguistic analysis of argument strategies in Korean conversational discourse: Negotiating disagreement and conflict'. Unpublished PhD thesis, Georgetown University, Washington, DC.

Tang, S. F. Y. and P. S. Kirkbride (1986) 'Developing conflict management skills in Hong Kong: an analysis of some cross-cultural implications', *Management Education and Development*, 17 (3), 287–301.

Ting-Toomey, S. (1992) 'Cross-cultural face-negotiation: an analytical overview'. Presented at Pacific Region Forum on Business and Management Communication, David See-Chai Lam Centre for International Communication, Simon Fraser University at Harbour Centre, 15 April 1992, 1–8. http://www.cic.sfu.ca/forum/ting-too.html, date accessed 31 January 2008.

Yamada, H. (1992) *American and Japanese Business Discourse: a Comparison of Interactional Styles* (Norwood, NJ: Ablex).

Yamada, H. (1997) 'Organisation in American and Japanese meetings: Task versus relationship' in F. Bargiela-Chiappini and S. Harris (eds) *The Languages of Business: an International Perspective* (Edinburgh: Edinburgh University Press), 117–135.

11

The Co-Construction of the Transition Relevance Place in a Brazilian Consumers' Product Safety Commission Meeting: Some Structural Properties of Institutional Interaction in a Conflict Situation

Paulo Cortes Gago and Sonia Bittencourt Silveira
Universidade Federal de Juiz de Fora, Minas Gerais, Brazil

11.1 Introduction

Following recent trends in modern societies, conflict episodes tend be solved on an alternative basis. Going to court seems to be the last option nowadays. Several institutions have been created in many countries to serve this goal. As positive aspects, it is normally cheaper and people can be helped faster with their troubles (Carnevale and Pruit, 1992; Folger and Jones, 1994). This work reports research on talk-in-interaction conducted in one of such alternative dispute resolution institutions in Brazil: PROCON, an abbreviation for Consumers' Product Safety Commission. It is a public mediation institution sponsored by the state and municipalities, whose function is to inform consumers on their rights in consumer relations and help them solve problems with providers of goods and services. A Brazilian Federal Law from 1990 gives the necessary legal support.

When consumers ask PROCON to intervene and mediate in a specific problem, it means that the parties involved could not reach a solution on their own. PROCON specialists call them to a meeting – the Confrontation Session – in which the problem will be discussed.

Conflict is then an inherent 'ingredient' in the talk at PROCON. For this reason, it belongs to the institutional discourse genre called *conflict talk* (Grimshaw, 1990).

It is widely assumed in discourse studies that institutional talk differs from ordinary conversation in many aspects (Drew and Heritage, 1992; Heritage, 1997; Schegloff, 1992). One way to look at these differences is through the *turn-taking system* developed in conversation analysis (Sacks et al., 1974). Since most of the business in a society is done through talk-in-interaction, and the turn-taking system (and its special-izations) is assumed to be what regulates people's participation in social life, it can furnish a basis to get to *structural properties* of institutional talk.

In the turn-taking model, the 'grossly apparent facts' (Sacks et al., 1974, p. 700) about ordinary conversation are, among others: each party talks at a time, more than one speaker at a time is common but brief, transitions occur normally with no gap and no overlap and speakers' change occurs overwhelmingly at the end of turn constructional units, which constitute a *transition relevance place*. Speaker transition is seen, then, as a smooth process.

Based on this description, in this contribution we will pay closer attention to the *speaker change process* at PROCON, with the following questions as guidelines: (1) Where does speaker change occur? (2) How does it occur? (3) What motivates it? (4) What does it tell us about the conversational floor and this kind of interaction? We hope that through these questions we can get at important *structural properties* of social par-ticipation at PROCON, and, thus, enlarge the contribution to research on conflict talk. Given that discourse analysis is an applied field, we hope also that our findings can serve, at least, as reflection tools for mediators in this setting.

The issues raised above will be illuminated through a case study of two discourse fragments in one confrontation session at PROCON. Data analysis combines tools from conversation analysis, especially the sequential analysis of talk and the turn-taking process (following basi-cally Sacks et al., 1974) and from interactional sociolinguistics, with the notion of frame in discourse (Goffman, 1974; Tannen and Wallat, 1993; Ribeiro, 1993; Ribeiro and Hoyle, 2002).

11.2　Theoretical remarks

In a central way, talk-in-interaction is considered the home environ-ment for language use and the workings of society at large. When people go to a party, most of their social work of being together as a group is done through talking; if someone needs information at a service counter, s/he will get it through talk; and if someone has problems in consumer relations and lodges a complaint at PROCON, as is the case here, people will most of their time be busy in talking to each other in order to get their problems solved. Thus most of the social work is done through direct face-to-face verbal interaction (Sacks et al., 1974; Atkinson and Heritage, 1984). As for the interface between discourse, interaction and the institutions, communication is a constitutive part of the very institution, or, as Sarangi and Roberts formulate it, 'workplaces are held together by communicative practices' (1999, p. 1).

Another important theoretical background aspect for the study of language use and interaction is that, in the face-to-face focused situation, people are constantly monitoring each other's behaviour so that they can act appropriately as a competent social being. This situation of possible mutual monitoring is what Goffman defined as the social situation, for the author a 'neglected situation' until recently (1972). Therefore, the unit of microsocial analysis is the face-to-face encounter, a privileged locus for the study of social order and meaning (Goffman, 1967, 1983; Sacks, 1984).

Following recent theoretical orientation in the humanities, construction of meaning in talk is seen not as a product of a single speaker, responsible for the whole meaning process, but rather as a product of a joint construction of participants in the encounter. Therefore, we adopt here the multidisciplinary concept of co-construction to refer to 'a joint creation of form, interpretation, position, action, activity, identity, emotion or any other culturally significant reality' (Jacoby and Ochs, 1995, p. 171).

The hosting space for language use in spoken discourse is the turn at talking (Schegloff, 1996; Ford and Thompson, 1996). Although this notion is vital for spoken discourse, it is also a very difficult one to define. Edelsky (1981) points out this difficulty, but does not offer a satisfactory definition, nor does the classical turn-taking paper (Sacks et al., 1974) offer a clear-cut definition. Roughly speaking, a turn at talking is the access a person has to utter speech in interaction with others. A correlated concept is the notion of floor: 'The *right* of access by an individual to a turn at speaking that is attended to by other individuals, who occupy at that moment the role of listener' (Schultz et al., 1982, p. 95, emphasis added). It seems that what distinguishes turn from floor, close in meaning, is the aspect of legitimacy: floor refers to the interactional right to occupy the turn at that moment. In some situations it is legitimate that more than one person occupy the floor, as for example in chorals, in church services. So we can speak of speech situations with a single speaker's floor or a multiple speakers' floor. The literature warns us that this right must be 'measured' against cultural patterns of acceptance of communicative behaviour (Schultz et al., 1982; Philips 1993[1983]).

The turn-taking 'machinery' is a system composed of two basic components: a turn constructional component and a turn allocation component. For the construction of turns, four types of units can be employed: (1) one word or lexical units; (2) phrasal units; (3) clausal units; and (4) sentential units. These units of talk are called turn constructional units (from now on TCUs). The unit types allow people in interaction to predict roughly what it will take for the unit type under way to be completed, i.e. these units provide talk with the feature of projectability. It is not surprising that many speaker's changes begin in the turn of other speakers in places where recognition of his/her TCU has already been made (it is a recognitional overlap, one of the places Jefferson points out where others can start to speak [1984]). The allocation of turns can be done by interactants by way of two groups of techniques: (1) the current speaker selects the next speaker; (2) the next speaker self-selects (Sacks et al., 1974). These units of talk are responsible for the process of speaker's change in conversation.

At the end of each of these units the turn reaches a possible completion point, defined by syntactical, intonational (prosodic) and pragmatic completion. Rather than being a conversation analyst's criterion, completion is 'emic': we can see people in conversation orienting to it. Possible completion is what people monitor in the other's talk in order to start to speak and it is where, therefore, transition between speakers becomes relevant, at a transition relevance place.

What exactly the end of a turn at talking is in relation to the ending of the speaking units (the TCUs) has been a subject of reflection by Jefferson (1984). She points out that 'there is some flexibility as to what "at" a possible turn-ending is, which is why we talk of transition *place* instead of a transition *point*' (1984, p. 13, emphasis in the original). Sometimes speaker's change occurs 'on time' at the end of a TCU; sometimes a little bit before; and sometimes still a little bit after that. She states that transcripts can evidence some 'instability' as to where exactly those places are. Since transcriptions rely on the auditory systems of human beings, which are not the same and can vary in the same person from moment to moment, transcripts will show variability in the location of these places from person to person and by the same person from hearing to hearing. And it is normal that it is so; it is just human.

The talk in the Confrontation Session at PROCON, as an institutional genre of discourse, is based on ordinary conversation, which is considered the sociological bedrock in talk-in-interaction, i.e. the matrix genre of talk, from which all other forms depart (Sacks et al., 1974), but at the same time it differs from it in some aspects. Silveira (2001) points out its main difference in the turn-taking-system, defined by the author as semi-structured. Although the job of talking is done very conversationally, participants have some notion of ordering in speaking and in the distribution of turns: the mediator is normally the one who initiates the interaction and opens the meeting; (s)he also allocates turns to respondent and complainant and conducts talk to negotiation of an agreement; as for the parties, while one of them is telling his or her 'side of the story', the other one should remain silent and not interrupt him/her, while (s)he is talking. So, participants do have some specific rights and obligations in talk-in-interaction in this context, which render their behaviour, verbal and non-verbal, as appropriate or not. We will see participants' orientation in the analysis to these rules.[1]

One word of caution here. Although we can locate discourse 'fields' or 'areas' of human social activity represented as institutional talk, one should be aware that labels like medicine discourse, forensic discourse, etc. are only generic names that encompass, in reality, a variety of forms of talk in them. For example, under the rubric 'forensic discourse' one can classify a specific area, courtroom communication (Atkinson and Drew, 1979; Maher and Rokosz, 1991; O'Barr, 1981, 1983), in which many speech activities take place, e.g. jury instructions, lawyers questioning of witnesses, witnesses' narratives.

Throughout analysis, an important concept to understand meaning in discourse is the concept of *frame*. According to Goffman, frames are 'principles of organization which govern events – at least social ones – and our subjective involvement in them' (1974, p. 10). The notion lies in the interface between cognition and interaction and 'focuses on the construction, conveying and interpretation of meaning' (Ribeiro and Hoyle, 2002, p. 36). In the cognitive perspective, frames are anchored in research in artificial intelligence and cognitive psychology and are understood as knowledge structures saved in long-term memory with which we interpret events in the world. They are cognitive constructs, blocks of cognition, and are related to the similar notions of *script*, *schema* and *prototype* (Tannen and Wallat, 1993). For example, the *taxi schema* will contain a taxi driver, a taximeter, money for the fare, etc., in most cities in the Western world.

Bateson (1972), however, uses the term 'frame' in a different sense. He is interested in the implicit ways in which messages are contextualized in communication and how frames furnish a basis for people's interpretation of events – if it is meant to be a joke or serious talk. The author uses two analogies to explain how the framing activities work. One is the analogy of the *picture frames*: they tell people how to direct their look and highlight figure and ground relationships. Applied to communicative situations, frames furnish ways to distinguish what is relevant from what is secondary in understanding meaning. The second analogy is the *mathematical set* – a frame establishes logical membership relationships as to what shall be considered as belonging to the same set of messages: an irritated tone of voice, fast pace in speech and short sentences can frame one person's mood as angry. Tannen and Wallat (1993) worked up Bateson's and Goffman's definition and argued that the concept of *frame* encapsulated in reality two aspects: a cognitive and an interactional one. They distinguished accordingly between *knowledge schemas* for the cognitive part of the frames and *interpretative frame* for their interactional part.[2] This distinction will be followed here.

11.3   Research methodology and data

Research methodology is qualitative, in many respects. As a set of practices, it combines in the analysis tools from two different approaches to discourse – conversation analysis and interactional sociolinguistics. The main source from which we will gain knowledge on interaction and institutional practices is discourse. Data collection was carried out with ethnographic methods, using audio-tape material to record naturally occurring scenes of social conduct, field notes and interviews with participants to gain more accurate insight into the 'foreign field', all executed during field experience that took a six-month period, during the years 2000 to 2001. Analysis will concentrate vertically on a single encounter, with detailed analysis of samples of talk.

The data was collected in the state of Minas Gerais, south-east Brazil, within the research project 'Talk-in-interaction in institutional contexts', coordinated by the second author in our home university. Transcription conventions follow those of the conversation analysis method, developed by Gail Jefferson (in Sacks et al., 1974). We offered readers a three-line transcript, with the original version in Portuguese (first line); a word by word translation (second line) and a free translation in English (third line) (Duranti, 1997), on which analysis will be based. Transfer of prosodic cues was made only in the third line and is, of course, by its 'translatable nature' imperfect. Readers shall rely therefore on the first line in the Portuguese for an accurate view of the prosodic phenomena.[3]

The confrontation sessions at PROCON are always mediated by a third party – a mediator. Where data was collected, mediation is done generally by a trainee law student from a local law school. An experienced lawyer intervenes only in cases in which conflict is diagnosed a priori as very complex or when any kind of stand-off emerges in the sessions. The parties – complainant and respondent – may represent themselves or delegate the representation to lawyers. Silveira (2001) identified three phases in the talk at PROCON: (1) the case presentation phase, where each party presents his/her own view of the problem; (2) the discussion phase, when people discuss the problems; and (3) the conclusion phase, in which the mediator tries to bring parties to reach an agreement. Although these phases seem to be clear, they interweave with each other. If an agreement is not possible, the complainant is advised to take the issue further and prosecute the respondent in court. That is to say, PROCON is a parajuridical institution and only mediates the conflict; it does not have juridical force *strictu sensu* to initiate a prosecution.

The case selected for analysis is coded as 'OK VEÍCULOS'.[4] Participants were *José*[5] – the complainant, *Pedro* – a friend of the complainant, *Lucas* – the respondent, and *Marta* – a mediator law student. José bought a second-hand car at Lucas' garage that has been out of order since then, almost three months ago from the time of the recording (December 2000). The issue in the meeting concerns the guarantee term for the product. Analysis will show three extracts from the first phase of the hearing. The two extracts represent two moments in the first phase in which each of the parties (complainant and respondent) has 'the right to speak'. By describing the speaker's change process in these moments, we wish to show, in the scope of this work, what happens to the conversational floor in this interactional setting. In each fragment, analysis will be focused on the interactional work of one of the parties, but of course the other participant's reaction to these moves will also be taken into account. We begin with the first extract.

11.4 'No! it's wrong' (José, the complainant)

This fragment is at the beginning of the interaction (p. 2 of the transcript) and reflects the moment when Lucas (the respondent) holds the floor and tells his 'side of the story' about the complaint against him. On line 11, he highlights the successive car changes José made: he returned two cars to the garage, claiming they had problems, and got a third one. The title of the section – 'No! it's wrong' – voices José's incursion into Lucas' talk and the main action executed in it – disagreement – which will receive the main analytical focus (the arrowed turns).

[02:11–02:28][6]

11	Lucas:	[(.) >lá] na na< nu <u>sá</u>bado (num sei) na segunda-feira, >ele=
		[( ) then] on on on saturday (don't know) on monday he
		[( ) >then] on on< on <u>sa</u>turday (I don't know) on monday, > he=
12	Marta:	[↑uhum.]
13	Lucas:	=ligou dizendo que <u>não</u> queria< o carro.
		called up saying that didn't want the car
		=called up and said he didn't <u>want</u>< the car.
14	José:	nã[o.
		no.
→		n[o.
15	Lucas:	[então tudo ↑bem.=
		[so all right.=
		[so that's all ↑right.=
16	José:	=tá er<u>ra</u>do.
		is wrong.
→		=it's <u>wrong</u>.
17	Lucas:	deixa eu contar a his [to[ria. depois cê fala?,] ((irritado))
		let I tell the s[to[ry. then you talk] ((irritated))
		let me tell the s[to[ry. then you talk,?] ((irritated))
18	José:	[nã[o,
		[no[
→		[no[,
19	Marta:	[deixa o- d e i x a [ele depois-]
		[let the- let [him then-]
		[let the- let [him then-]
20	José:	[tá. então tá] bom.
		[ok. so all] right
→		[ok. all] right.
21		(.)
22	Lucas:	depois [ce fala. >senão nó- (nós ( ) vamos] (começar) discu]tir<=
		then [you talk otherwise we (we ( ) will] (start) argue
		then [you talk. >otherwise we (we ( ) will] (start) to arg]ue<=
23	Marta:	[p a s s a a p a l a v r a p r a v o c ê.]=<não, pera aí<.]
		[passes on the word to you] no wait
		[he passes on to you.]=<no wait a minute<]
24	Lucas:	=>uma [c o i s a] que não vai ter nad-<=
		one [thing] that not will has noth-
		=>on [something] that has nothing to d-<=
25	José:	[então tá:.]
		[so ok]
→		[so ok:.]
26	José:	=já começou er<u>ra</u>do.
		already started wrong
		=it started already <u>wrong</u>.

```
27            (0.5)
28  Lucas:   Aí, (0.8) >>ele falou que não<< queria ficar com o    carro.
             then       he said  that not   want   keep  with the car
             THEN, (0.8) >>he said that he didn't<< want to keep the car.
```

José's first disagreement – 'n[o' (line 14) – has to be analysed in relation
to Lucas' turn, on lines 11, 13 – '>he called up and said he didn't want<
the car'. It states that José announced over the phone that he was returning the first car and emphasizes particularly the fact that José 'didn't
want' the car, i.e. it is a matter of desire, and not necessarily a problem
with a product. In TCU terms, the unit is a sentential TCU. José certainly
makes use of the transition space opened by Lucas' TCU completion,
which was reached in syntax and prosody, but *not pragmatically*. The
notion of *unit* relevance here is not TCU completion, but *story* completion. In technical terms, a story projects an *extended multi-unit turn* that
can comprise several TCUs and will be complete, in the pragmatic sense,
only at its end; action completion is here story completion. As the turn-
taking system at PROCON is not so rigid as at court, there are no formal
sanctions for speaking out of place. Theoretically, any speaker can self-
select and start to speak. So, José self-selects at the end of Lucas' TCU,
which is actually the beginning of his story, and utters a disagreement
at a place *not* appropriate for a speaker's transition.

Why did José do it? Lucas is not just telling a story. His 'version of
the facts' is, at the same time, a creation of a legal interpretive frame
in the conversation that can have consequences for the case at hand.
If some facts are established in this first version, it can affect people's
judgement about the guarantee term for the product. In this case, it is
being affirmed that the consumer 'didn't want' the product. The way to
block it or interfere in it is to place disagreement as soon as possible, so
that a 'wrong version' of the facts does not crystallize. This explains the
quality of Jose's participation: in the form of a lexical TCU – 'n[o' – i.e. a
'minimal participation', restricted to a blunt disagreement form, uttered
with louder volume, partially overlapped by the continuation of Lucas'
talk, on line 15. It is the most economic form of disagreement possible
in the context, expressing urgency, in a place not appropriate to speak.
As a 'general no', it only points out problems with the telling so far and
intends to stop the action.

José's second disagreement – '=it's wrong' – (line 16) can be explained
by Lucas' reaction to his first disagreement, on line 15. Lucas does not
stop the telling sequence to deal with the objection José has just made.
Quite the contrary, he ignores his contribution and continues the turn's
project with the next instalment of it – an assessment of this part of the

story – '[so that's all ↑right.=', which expresses his reaction to the car being returned: he accepted the consumer's return of a product supposed to have a problem. The second disagreement is an upgraded version of the first one. It is also an assessment and also has general properties: it only qualifies the version as *wrong*. As with the previous one, although it is at the speech unit's syntactic and prosodic completion (actually latched into his talk), it is still in the midst of Lucas' telling and is therefore not a place of pragmatic story completion, nor of the speaker's transition relevance.

The third disagreement, on line 18 – '[no[,' – can be understood as an *echo* from the second one. It does not address Lucas' current talk on line 17 – 'let me tell the s[to[ry. then you talk,?] ((irritated))' – but still deals with the previous turn. Lucas' reaction – an admonition that his right to speak was violated, in an irritated mood – shows an orientation to the story unit as the pragmatic relevant unit. Again, José's disagreement is a compact version – '[no[,' – as the first one.

The next two arrows in José's talk ('[ok. all] right.' (line 20) and '[so ok:.]' (line 25)) show him apparently agreeing in realigning himself as a non-contesting participant, due to the other participants' strong reaction to his turn incursion, on lines 17, 19, 22, 23 and 24. They invoke a principle of rationality in talk: each has his turn to speak and shall wait until the other is finished: Lucas – 'let me tell the s[to[ry. then you talk,?]' (line 17); and Marta – '[let [the- let] [him then-] [he passes on to you.]' (lines 19, 23) – mediator and respondent are here aligned with each other. In this moment, three people occupy the floor simultaneously.

But José latches into Lucas' talk with a fourth disagreement, on line 26, again in the form of an assessment – '=it started already <u>wrong</u>', an upgraded disagreement version, a little bit more formulated than the others, expressing a more precise opinion about the story: It's '*wrong*'. Lucas actually cuts himself off to let José speak, i.e. José clearly violates his speaking rights. After 5/10 seconds of pause (line 27), Lucas continues the telling, not dealing again with the disagreement, only registering it with higher volume – 'THEN, (0.8) >>he said that he didn't<< want to keep the car' (line 28), expressing an irritated mood. We move on to the second excerpt.

11.5   'Not at all' (Lucas, the respondent)

This segment maintains a temporal closeness with the previous one, being distant from it by only 30 lines, about one page of transcript. It shows the moment when José holds the floor to tell his side of the story. The title of this section – 'Not at all' – expresses Lucas' move, also with disagreements, which will receive analytical emphasis (the arrowed turns). Line 28 in the transcript is the beginning of the story.

[03:28-04:10]

```
28   José:     [ele- [ele falou que  eu peguei a   u:no:,
               [he-  [he said   that  I got       the uno
               [he-  [he said   that  I got       the u:no:,
29   Marta:    >> t[á.= cês  trou]xeram u::m- [a  l i s t i n h a,]  n é ?      ]<<
               o[k   you brou]ght    a      [a    list         ]  didn't you]
               >>o[k.= you brou]ght   a::    [a    list,        ]  didn't you?]
30   José:     [>> fiquei- <<]
               [   kept      ]
               [>> I kept- <<]
31   José:                           [>>o final de semana] com a    u]no. fique-
                                     [   the     weekend] with the u]no. kep-
                                     [>>the car      over] the weekend] . I kep-
32             não peguei. <<= eu peguei a    uno na quinta-feira, (0.8)
               not get        I got      the uno on Thursday
               I didn't get. <<= I got     the car on thursday, (0.8)
               <na quinta-feira,> (.)  s:[::-
               on thursday       fry:[::
               <on thursday,>    (.) fry:[::-
33   Marta:                               [unhum.=
01   José:     =no sábado  eu voltei    à.
               on saturday I came back  there
               =on saturday I came back  there.
02             (.)
03   José:     dois dias.
               two days
               two days.
04   Lucas:    então cê   ficou com ela.
               so     you kept it
→              so     you kept it.
05   José:     >>doi- eu- eu andei- eu peguei ela na [quinta-feira de [noite.]<<
               two-  I   I drov-  I got    it on [thursday     eve[ning.]
               >>two- I-  I got-           I got it on [thursday     eve[ning.]<<
06   Marta:                                        [ e s p e r a  a í, [você falou.]
               agora deixa ele-=
                                                   [wait          [you spoke]
                                                   [wait,         [you spoke.]
               now let him-
07   Lucas:                                                       [(não senhor.)]
                                                                  [(no   sir)]
→                                                                 [(not at all.)]
08   José:     = (peguei) na quinta-feira de noite. fui    trabalhar sexta
                 (got)    on thursday   evening. went  to work Friday
               = (got)    on thursday   evening.  I went to work Friday
```

09		nem usei o carro. (1.2) (peguei) na quinta-feira a noite. sexta
		even used the car. (got) on thursday evening Friday
		I didn't even use the car. (1.2) (I got it) on thursday evening. Friday
		nem usei o carro.
		even used the car.
		I didn't even use the car.
10	Pedro:	un<u>hum</u>.

The transcript begins in a strong overlap environment, reflecting a previous conflict that emerged in the interaction (not shown here), as Pedro (José's friend) tried to get a turn to participate in the talk and give his opinion, which was not allowed by the mediator. José begins to speak, on line 28, building his turn on what Lucas had said before, in his account of the facts – '(…) [he- [he said that I got the u:no:,'. By doing so, José selects what he will be the main topic in his talk – the time he kept the car – before returning it to the store, information that will be disputed in the talk. As we can see in the transcript on line 29, the mediator at the same time makes a first move – a prelude – into the possibility of negotiation. She accelerates the pace of her talk in order to ask José, before he launches into his story, if he had brought to the meeting the list with all the costs he has already had to fix the car – '>> o[k.= you brou]ght a:: [a list,] didn't you?]' (line 29). This list will be the basis for future negotiation later on.

José's talk is aimed at establishing his version of the facts, which seems to differ from Lucas'. First, he mentions when exactly he got the car from the garage. 'It is plenty of self-repairs. The repairable is the action *keeping the car*, which is replaced to *getting the car*' – '[>>I kept- <<]', '[>>the car over] the weekend]. I kep- I didn't get. <<= I got the car on <u>thursday</u>, (0.8)' (lines 30, 31, 32). The final action is when he got the car – 'on <u>thursday</u>'. As a next instalment, he adds on the day he returned the car to the store – '=on saturday I came back there' (line 01). After a small gap (line 02), he tells how long it took him to report the trouble to the store – '<u>two</u> days' (line 03).

As happened in the previous fragment, the interactional project of the participant who has the right to hold the floor at that moment is intercepted by the counterparty – Lucas, also with an act of disagreement. But now, what is the object of disagreement is something that derives implicitly from what José has said, and not something available on the surface of the discourse; it works on the level of inference. That is why Lucas' disagreement, on line 04, is introduced by a conclusive form – 'so you kept it'. It is a 'mathematical calculation': if José got the car on Thursday and returned it on Saturday, 'so' he kept it anyway, even if for a short period of time. In TCU terms, Lucas makes use of syntactic and prosodic unit completion, but not of pragmatic completion, for the unit in progress is a story, that projects an extended multi-unit turn for José. Disagreement comes, again, right after the fact to be disputed, in a place not relevant for a speaker's transition. The motivation is also the legal interpretive frame being established in the talk. It refers to the guarantee term of the product: when the consumer wants to return a product, he has to do it within a certain period of time. Delay in returning may invalidate the guarantee term. As a reaction to this turn incursion, José repeats, now with emphasis, when he got the car, on line 05 – '>>two- I- I got- I got it on [thursday eve[ning.]<<'.

In the next turn, partially overlapping with José, the mediator sanctions Lucas's behaviour, reminding him that he has already had his right to speak and is now violating José's right – '[wait, [you spoke.] now let him-='. Nevertheless, overlapping with José's turn, Lucas reinforces his position taken before, uttering another disagreement, on line 07 – '(not at all.)]'. It is now an open disagreement and has a specific target – the day José got the car. By way of recognition of what is available in José's talk, Lucas disagrees immediately with it, so to speak, in the middle of his talk and overlapping with the mediator too, ignoring her contribution. It is an open conflict episode. As for the form, it is also a 'minimal' but strong participation, reflecting the fact that it is done 'in the speaking rights' of another person.

11.6 Concluding discussion

The study of the speaker's change process examined in the talk here evidenced some features about the conversational floor in this kind of interaction. As we saw in the participants' sanctioning behaviour, the rule *one speaker at a time* is clearly operative in this setting. Moreover, when one of the parties is doing the job of telling his side of the story, (s)he shall have his/her right unimpeded by others. Data analysis showed that speaker's transition occurred in places not transition relevant, in relation to the conversational activity executed at that moment – a story being told by the other party. Sometimes speaker change occurred at places of unit syntactic and prosodic completion, but not of pragmatic completion (first fragment, José in lines 14, 16; second fragment, Lucas, line 04). Other times it occurred in the middle of the other participants' talk (first segment, José, lines 18, 20, 24, 26, Marta, lines 19, 23; second fragment, Lucas, line 07, Marta, line 06). In each fragment, we saw instances of three at a time trying to occupy the floor to deal with interactional matters relevant to the talk at hand.

The main interaction project underlying this turn-taking behaviour was disagreement. Sacks et al. (1974) describe a natural built-in pressure in the turn-taking system for speaker's change in ordinary conversation, because at the end of each TCU any participant can self-select and start to talk, if no one has been selected. In conflict situations, as in the one at PROCON, this pressure becomes even more potentialized: it seems that whenever legal frames are being established in the talk with which the other party does not agree, it has to be signalled or 'corrected' right away. It explains participants' urgency to take a turn, at places not of transition relevance. Turn-taking practices in the talk render the notion of floor here as a highly competitive one.

The topic *disagreement* has to be connected with the wider literature on preference structure and disagreement. In ordinary conversation, it has been amply demonstrated that disagreement is a *dispreferred* social action. As a consequence, when it is done, it is executed with features such as delays, modalization, late placement of the oppositional element in the turn, etc. (Pomerantz, 1984). This shape of turns is not, however, operative at PROCON. Quite the contrary; when parties did not agree, disagreement came blunt, unmitigated, in the first position of the utterance, sometimes in the middle of the other's turn, and in the most economic form. Our data corroborates Gruber's empirical findings about 'the dissent organization of talk' in conflict episodes: 'Speaker changes (or attempted speaker changes) do not occur at transition relevant places but at *disagreement relevant points* (i.e., the opponent produces disagreements immediately when propositions, etc., in the current speaker's turn occur which she does not agree with)' (1998, p. 476, emphasis added). In this sense, disagreement is a *structural property* of some interactions and can be seen as *endemic*, i.e. highly expected. Our larger corpus confirms that this is how part of the social work of having problems in consumer relations discussed at PROCON is done. The features described here would be one aspect of the context-sensitiveness of the turn-taking system formulated by Sacks et al. (1974) and what renders this talk as belonging to the genre of *conflict talk* (Grimshaw, 1990), furnishing also the connection between the social/institutional order and interactional order, as the recent tendency in sociolinguistics attempts to do (for example, Erickson 1999, 2001).

The issue of participants' motivation for producing disagreement talk – the establishment of legal interpretive frames – must receive more serious attention. In our view, this process is at the very heart of all legal disputes, in court and also at PROCON. In legal processes, and in dispute processes in general, the whole issue is people's differences in *framing* regarding the case at hand; each party has a different view of what happened – if the defendant has committed a crime or not, if someone has accused the other or not, if the respondent has disrespected the consumer's right or not, etc. In the example analysed here, José and Lucas seemed to differ on their versions of the facts. What generated prompt disagreement by José was Lucas' version that José 'didn't want< the car'; for Lucas, what generated his disagreement was José's statement that he got the car 'on [thursday eve[ning.]'. All these facts can have legal consequences for a juridical discussion on the guarantee term, if parties take the issue further.

The dispute we saw in order not to let a certain version of the facts get crystallized has to be connected with another issue: the *ordering of speakers*. It seems that the person who has the right to speak first will also have the opportunity to establish the first frame for the case. In formal legal contexts, this issue can have important consequences for the parties involved: the first frame built can be the most difficult one to be deconstructed. The first author has already observed this fact in judges' criminal sentences, where the prosecution established the first interpretive frame and knowledge schema applicable to the case (see Gago, 1997). At PROCON, the second author brought attention to the fact that, in many confrontation sessions, the mediator gives the respondent first chance to talk, as happened in OK VEÌCULOS. This issue deserves more profound reflection and more research, in depth and expanded to other legal situations.

Research on framing thus seems to offer a solid way to understand the argumentative process and, in general, the organization of discourse and the institution, especially legal ones. It is a promising research tool to be developed.

As a last point in our discussion, we want to address the issue of a *principle of rationality* in communication speakers' transition. As we saw, in the talk at PROCON, the turn-taking system in operation, although being a semi-specialized one, did not prevent participants from voicing their dissent during the speaking rights of the other participants, violating those rights. In our larger corpus, this fact seems to be more the rule than the exception. The question we want to leave open for reflection is this: given, on the one hand, that direct conflict is unavoidable and disagreement comes as early as possible in conversation, as research shows, and, on the other hand, that PROCON should bring people to an agreement, should it not combine in its mode of operation *social action* with *communicative practice*, trying to apply a more rational principle of communication, like Grice's cooperative principle (1975 [1967]) or Habermas' communicative action principle (1988), in order to promote consensus talk? How could such a model of communication be negotiated with the parties? What would it look like? Should the mediator try to negotiate with parties for a more efficient turn-taking system that would promote less dissent? Given the democratic principles of PROCON, perhaps this institutional setting would be a perfect arena for experimenting with *models of communication*. Such a model would necessarily need to rethink the turn-taking system.

We hope the reflections made here can somehow be transformed into an applied contribution of discourse analysis to the 'success' of communication at PROCON. At least, there are problems to be discussed, and it can be the first step to improvement.

Appendix: transcription symbols

[	A left-hand bracket indicates overlap onset.
]	A right-hand bracket indicates end of overlap.
(.)	A dot in parentheses indicates a micro pause, less than 2/10 of a second, hearable, but not readily measurable.
(0.8)	Numbers in parentheses indicate time, in tenths of second.
=	Equal signs indicate latching into the talk from same speaker or different speakers.
.	Period indicates falling intonation contour, not necessarily the end of the sentence.
?	Question mark is used for rising intonation, not necessarily a question.
,	Comma indicates continuing intonation, not necessarily a clause boundary.
? ,	A combination of a question mark and a comma indicates a rise stronger than a comma but weaker than a question mark.
Word:	Underlined colon indicates inflected rising intonation.
Word:	Letter underlined preceding a colon means inflected falling intonation.
↑	Arrow pointing upwards marks sharper rise in pitch.
↓	Arrow pointing downwards marks sharper falls in pitch.
:	Colons signal stretching of a sound.
-	A hyphen after a word indicates a cut-off or self-interruption.
Underlining	Underlining stresses emphasis.
UPPER CASE	Speech in upper case indicates stronger emphasis.
°words	Degree sign to the right indicates quieter beginning of speech.
°words°	Words between degree signs indicate quieter speech.
> words<	The combination 'more than' 'less than' indicates compressed talk in between.
<words>	The combination 'less than' 'more than' indicates compressed talk in between.

<words	Talk after 'more than' sign means it starts with a rush.
h	Letter 'h' marks hearable aspiration (breathing, laughter, etc.).
w(h)o(h)r(h)d(h)s	Letter 'h' in parentheses means aspiration during the uttering of the word.
.h	A dot before the letter 'h' means inhalation.
((cough))	Transcriber's comments on the transcript/interaction.
(doubt)	Transcription doubt.
( )	Transcription impossible.

Acknowledgements

This chapter has benefited from research grants FAPEMIG-SHA-APQ-2129-5.06/ for PCE and FAPEMIG-SHA-APQ-2586-5.06/07 for SBS.

Notes

1. In formal juridical settings, the organization of the turn-taking-system becomes even more complex and rigid, as for example in court, where parties' opportunities to talk (judges, lawyers, defendant and witnesses) are well defined, fixed and ritualized, as Atkinson and Drew (1979) amply demonstrate.
2. For a more comprehensive review of the state of the art on frames, see Ribeiro and Hoyle (2002).
3. The authors wish to thank all students involved in the transcription work, specially Fernanda Motta, Luciana Arruda, Maurita Sartori and Vivian Weiss.
4. Data was selected among a corpus of 16 audio-recorded confrontation sessions, available at that moment.
5. See Garcez (2002) for a discussion on the problem of speaker's identification in transcripts. Accordingly, we took the option of using first names, instead of institutional names.
6. The notational system was used in Gago (2002). Numbers between brackets refer, respectively, to the beginning and ending of pages and line numbers in the original transcript: [01:10-02:02] must be read as the transcript begins on page 01 line 10 and ends on page 02 line 02. Each new page receives a new (continuous) number (page 01, 02, 03, etc.) and each first line of each new page begins again with number 01.

References

Atkinson, J, and P. Drew (1979) *Order in Court: the Organization of Verbal Interaction in Judicial Settings* (New Jersey: Humanities Press).

Atkinson, J.M. and J. Heritage (1984) 'Introduction' in J.M. Atkinson and J. Heritage (eds) *Structures of Social Action: Studies in Conversation Analysis* (Cambridge, UK: Cambridge University Press), 1–16.

Bateson, G. (1972) 'A theory of play and fantasy' in *Steps to an Ecology of Mind* (New York: Ballantine).

Carnevale, P. and D. Pruitt (1992) 'Negotiation and mediation', *Annual Review of Psychology*, 43, 531–82.

Drew, P. and J. Heritage (1992) 'Analyzing talk at work: an introduction' in P. Drew and J. Heritage (eds) *Talk at Work* (New York: Cambridge University Press), 3–65.

Duranti, A. (1997) 'Transcription: From writing to digitized images' in *Linguistic Anthropology* (Cambridge, UK: Cambridge University Press), 122–61.

Edelsky, C. (1981) 'Who's got the floor?', *Language in Society*, 10, 383–421.

Erickson, F. (1999) 'Appropriation of voice and presentation of self as a fellow physician: Aspects of a discourse of apprenticeship in medicine' in S. Sarangi and C. Roberts (eds) *Talk, Work and Institutional Order: Discourse in Medical, Mediation and Management Settings* (New York: Mouton de Gruyter), 109–44.

Erickson, F. (2001) 'Co-membership and wiggle room: Some implications of the study of talk for the development of social theory' in N. Coupland, S. Sarangi and C. Candlin (eds) *Sociolinguistics and Social Theory* (London: Longman), 152–81.

Folger, J.P. and T.S. Jones (1994) 'Introduction' in J.P. Folger and T.S. Jones *New Directions in Mediation: Communication Research and Perspectives* (Thousand Oaks, Calif.: Sage).

Ford, C. and S. Thompson (1996) 'Interactional units in conversation: Syntactic, intonational, and pragmatic resources for the management of turns' in E. Ochs, E. Schegloff and S. Thompson (eds) *Interaction and Grammar* (New York: Cambridge University Press), 134–84.

Gago, P.C. (1997) 'Análise do discurso da sentença judicial penal'. Master's thesis in Applied Linguistics, Faculdade de Letras da Universidade Federal do Rio de Janeiro, 207 pp.

Gago, P.C. (2002) 'A relevância da convergência num contexto de negociação: um estudo de caso de uma reunião empresarial na cultura portuguesa'. PhD dissertation in Linguistics and Portuguese Language, Faculdade de Letras, Pontifícia Universidade Católica do Rio de Janeiro, 350 pp.

Garcez, P. (2002) 'Transcrição como teoria: a identificação dos falantes como atividade analítica plena' in L.P. Moita Lopes and L.C. Bastos (eds) *Identidades: recortes multi e interdisciplinares* (Campinas: Mercado de Letras), 7–22.

Goffman, E. (1967) *Interaction Ritual* (New Yok: Pantheon Books).

Goffman, E. (1972) 'The neglected situation' in P.P. Giglioli (ed.) *Language and Social Context* (New York: Penguin), 61–6.

Goffman, E. (1974) *Frame Analysis* (New York: Harper Torchbooks).

Goffman, E. (1981) 'Footing' in *Forms of Talk* (Philadelphia: University of Pennsylvania Press), 124–59.

Grice, H.P. (1975 [1967]) 'Lógica e conversação' in M. Pascal (ed.) *Fundamentos metodológicos da lingüística* (Rio de Janeiro: Editora do Autor), 81–103.

Grimshaw, A. (1990) 'Introduction' in A. Grimshaw (ed.) *Conflict Talk: Sociolinguistic Investigations of Arguments in Conversations* (New York: Cambridge University Press), 1–20.

Gruber, H. (1998) 'Disagreeing: Sequential placement and internal structure of disagreements in conflict episodes', *Text*, 18 (4), 467–503.

Heritage, J. (1997) 'Conversation analysis and institutional talk: Analyzing data' in D. Silverman (ed.) *Qualitative Research: Theory, Method and Practice* (Thousand Oaks, Calif.: Sage), 222–44.

Jacoby, S. and E. Ochs (1995) 'Co-construction: an introduction', *Research on Language and Social Interaction* (Special issue: 'Co-construction', edited by S. Jacoby and E. Ochs), 28 (3), 171–83.

Habermas, J. (1988) *Theorie des Kommunikativen Handels* (Frankfurt: Suhrkamp), vol. 1.

Jefferson, G. (1984) 'Notes on some orderliness of overlap onset' in V. D'Urso and P. Leonardi (eds) *Discourse Analysis and Natural Rhetoric* (Padua: Cleup), 11–38.

Maher, J. and D. Rokosz (1991) 'Language use and the professions' in W. Grabe and R. Kaplan (eds) *Introduction to Applied Linguistics* (Reading, Mass.: Addison-Wesley), 231–53.

O'Barr, W. (1981) 'The language of the law' in C. Ferguson and S.B. Heath (eds) *Language in the USA* (New York: Cambridge University Press), 386–406.

O'Barr, W. (1983) 'The study of language in institutional contexts', *Journal of Language and Social Psychology*, 2 (2/3), 241–51.

Philips, S.A. (1993) [1983] *The Invisible Culture: Communication in Classroom and Community on the Warm Springs Indian Reservation* (New York: Prospect High).

Pomerantz, A. (1984) 'Agreeing and disagreeing with assessments: Some features of preferred/dispreferred turn shapes' in J.M. Atkinson and J. Heritage (eds) *Structures of Social Action: Studies in Conversation Analysis* (Cambridge, UK: Cambridge University Press), 57–101.

Ribeiro, B.T. (1993) 'Framing in psychotic discourse' in D. Tannen (ed.) *Framing in Discourse* (New York: Oxford University Press), 77–113.

Ribeiro, B.T. and S.M. Hoyle (2002) *Frame Analysis*. Palavra, Rio de Janeiro, no. 8, 36–49.

Sacks, H. (1984) 'Notes on methodology' in J.M. Atkinson and J. Heritage (eds) *Structures of Social Action: Studies in Conversation Analysis* (Cambridge, UK: Cambridge University Press), 21–7.

Sacks, H. E. Schegloff and G. Jefferson (1974) 'A simplest systematics for the organization of turn taking for conversation', *Language*, 50 (4), 696–735.

Sarangi, S. and C. Roberts (1999) 'The dynamics of interactional and institutional orders in work-related settings' in S. Sarangi and C. Roberts (eds) *Talk, Work and Institutional Order: Discourse in Medical, Mediation and Management Settings* (New York: Mouton de Gruyter), 1–57.

Schegloff, E. (1992) 'On talk and its institutional occasions' in P. Drew and J. Heritage (eds) *Talk at Work* (New York: Cambridge University Press), 101–35.

Schegloff, E. (1996) 'Turn organization: One intersection of grammar and interaction' in E. Ochs, E. Schegloff and S. Thompson (eds) *Interaction and Grammar* (New York: Cambridge University Press), 52–133.

Schultz, J., S. Florio and F. Erickson (1982) 'Where is the floor? Aspects of the cultural organization of social relationships in communication at home and in school' in P. Gilmore and A. Glatthorn (eds) *Ethnography and Education: Children in and out of School* (Washington, DC: Center for Applied Linguistics), 88–123.

Silveira, S.B. (2001) 'Mediation strategies in institutional confrontation setting'. Paper presented at the 1st International Conference on Discourse, Communication and the Enterprise, Lisbon.

Tannen, D. and C. Wallat (1993) 'Interactive frames and knowledge schemas in interaction: Examples from a medical examination/interview' in D. Tannen (ed.) *Framing in Discourse* (New York: Oxford University Press), 57–76.

12
The Composition of a Participative View for the Management of Organizational Communications

Maria do Carmo Leite de Oliveira and José Roberto Gomes da Silva
Pontifícia Universidade Católica do Rio de Janeiro

12.1 Introduction

The development of a communications management viewpoint able to strengthen the participation of individuals is perhaps one of the most complex challenges faced by organizations today. First, because the context of major transformations creates a growing need to obtain employees' conscious involvement, so that they can contribute intensely to the development of such important requirements for the competitiveness of organizations, such as learning, capacity to change and to innovate (Argyris, 1994; Garvin, 2000; Nonaka, 2000). Secondly, the development of a participative focus becomes a challenge for organizations since, as Zarifian (2001) observes, organizational communications have been dealt with in an instrumental way, merely as a resource for the exercise of power and control, as a mechanism for the controlled management of employees. This instrumental view, based essentially on an emphasis on subordination and hierarchical one-way relationships, tends to reduce the notion of communications to a mere matter of transmitting orders and guidelines to be executed without any questioning in general.

Authors such as Ford and Ford (1995) and Giordano (1998) argue that, first of all, the development of a notion of authentic participation implies the need to constitute a new concept of the role of communications in the organization, to abandon the traditional instrumental view and to conceive communications as an arena for the collective construction of meaning. The first step towards this transformation is taking into account the subjectivity of individuals, the multiplicity of relationships involved and the diversity of forms, means and contents of the interactions that exist in the daily life of organizations, without, however, ignoring the context and power structure in which the subjects are inserted (Boden, 1994; Giordano, 1998; Silva, 2001; Taylor, 1993).

The main implication of this type of approach is an attempt to conceive communication as an integrated process that recognizes the importance of the actors and their relationships, as well as the means they use. Similarly, it is necessary to understand the structures that provide the context for their everyday action and, at the same time, that are continually transformed by them (Giddens, 1984; Giordano, 1998; Rojot, 1998).

This study aims to contribute to this discussion by trying to identify different aspects that affect the construction of a focus for the management of organizational communications, favouring the development of a model of participative management. Based on a case study of a large Brazilian company working in the field of energy infrastructure services, we will outline a reference framework that can inspire managers' action in creating a view that reinforces the notion of participation.

12.2 The consequences of an instrumental focus for organizational communications

Giordano (1998) observes that the main characteristic of the instrumental perspective, still dominant in the literature on management science, is a tendency to focus on instruments and technical devices of message transmission as the determinants of *good communications*. This perspective is continually reinforced by the constant development of new technologies that are supposed to create new, innovative and increasingly sophisticated opportunities for an enlargement of means. It is also a type of focus still based as if communications were only the transmission of a message according to an appropriate code.

According to Giordano (1998), the main consequence of this overvaluation of the language structure and of a *technological determinism* has been the relegation of individuals, i.e. those who are the real authors and actors of communications, to the status of mere accessories in the process, creating a kind of organizational schizophrenia, whose consequences are unforeseen and hard to administer.

The exaggerated confidence placed by organizations in the transforming power of technology is a good example of this schizophrenic viewpoint of communications. One of the biggest investments organizations have been making, for the development of a more participative viewpoint in management mechanisms, is exactly the adoption of an increasing number of varied solutions, based on the use of information and communications technology (Dewett and Jones, 2001). However, many questions have been raised with regard to the capacity of this kind of technology itself to promote or cause effective change of human behaviour and organizational culture (Cabrera and Cabrera, 2002; Davenport, 1998; Scott et al., 1998; Silva, 2000).

Based on research carried out by a big consulting group, Cabrera and Cabrera (2002) observe, for example, that the path usually trodden by organizations in order to implement the concept of knowledge management, which is strongly based on the notion of participation, is based on developing solutions linked to information and communications technology. However, in most cases, the biggest impediments to the implementation of this concept are caused by non-technological aspects, such as the difficulties employees have in understanding the importance of sharing knowledge, lack of time for this sharing and lack of incentive for the production of new ideas.

Similarly, studies done by Silva (2000) on the adoption of electronic mail in a big Brazilian company, indicate the limited capacity of this technology in terms of promoting the desired change the organization wants, abandoning a bureaucratic culture which called forth the personnel's defensive attitudes in favour of constructing a participative culture.

Similar results about power limitations to change organizational behaviour were obtained by Scott et al. (1998) in a study on the use of communications technology for assisting group decision-making (or GDDS – group decision support systems). One of the main objectives of employing this kind of technology is mediation between the participants in projects that involve multiple processes of collective decision-making, so as to grant three important characteristics to these processes: the preservation of the participants' anonymity; the equalization of opportunities for participation; and the elimination of undesired influences of some individuals on others, resulting from power inequalities. The results of the study show that the users of the system develop several types of parallel mechanisms in order to circumvent these characteristics: creating devices that allow the recognition of interlocutors; searching for language styles that strengthen the power of their ideas to convince others; including content marks that highlight imbalances of power, favouring the opinion of certain individuals. As a consequence, individuals spend much of their time developing countermeasures to protect against these devices, reducing the efficacy of the objectives for which systems are projected.

12.3 The importance of an integrating focus for organizational communications

According to Giordano (1998), a second type of limited reasoning used by some authors to conceive organizational communications refers to a perspective that concentrates almost exclusively on the diversity of perceptions and on the capacity of both senders and receivers to interpret organizational messages. It is, therefore, a kind of approach that endeavours to revert the logic of the actors' subordination to the structure of language and environment, to put them in the position of almost absolute masters of the fate of communications. From this point of view, the construction of social reality is seen as a process related to the way individuals interpret events in accordance with a personal logic, in a way that is almost independent of the impositions of a context.

In addition to questioning the instrumental view, authors such as Giddens (1984) and Olivier (1995) also criticize this kind of belief in the imperialism of the individual subject. By concentrating all their attention on individual interpretation, such approaches do not take into account that, when involved in interaction situations, individuals are also engaged in a process of group construction of meaning, based on a shared knowledge of social reality, in the same way as, from interaction, they change their knowledge of the context. Thus, according to Giddens, social reality is a process in a permanent state of structuring, in which macro and micro levels have the same degree of importance and influence over each other.

This notion of social reality as a continuous and collective process of construction of meaning has inspired some authors to develop an approach to communications that takes into account a more integrated view, which recognizes, conjointly, the weight and evolutionary character of context, the quality of relationships, the content of interactive exchanges and the interpretation of meaning by participants (Clark, 1996; Silva, 2001).

12.4 Communications as an arena for the construction of meaning

Taylor (1993) proposes a metaphor for the notion of organizational communications that integrates both macro and micro views of organizational reality. For Taylor, the organization is a virtual reality supported by communications. The organization arises and is mediated by communications. Furthermore, it is an artefact of communications. But the mere existence of individuals or their composition in a network by the transmission of messages is not, in itself, a guarantee of organizational existence. An organization exists from the moment at which there is the recognition of mutual engagements. Being organized means being in a relationship. Relationships are the *raw material* of the organization.

Taylor (1993) proposes, thus, a metaphor that takes into account the universe of relationships, as a communications context comprised of a *text* and a *conversation*, which is equivalent to saying that 'the organization is semantically and pragmatically structured' (1993, p. 70). The author assumes that the organization needs to become an object of discourse before becoming an object of management and planning. It must be perceived before being recognized. In other words, it must pass through a process of *textualization*. The organization, as intersubjectivity manifested in interaction, remains inevitably virtual. It is in textualization that intersubjectivity acquires meaning. This notion of the importance of constructing an *organizational text* is shared by Dunford and Jones (2000) for whom the managers of the organization must be able to construct a coherent corporate discourse, especially in times of great change. The coherence of this discourse lies in its capacity to propose meanings to individuals, to bring together ideology and practice, to construct a consensus about reality, to develop an *identity* for the organization (Gioia et al., 2000; Pratt and Foreman, 2000).

At the conversational level, the organization can be understood as a system of interactions by means of which relationships are materialized. However, at this level, the organization, still according to Taylor, is not real. It is, above all, hyper-real: an overlapping of all its members' realities, not necessarily coherent with one another, and even, sometimes, strongly contradicting each other. The transformation of the organization into an object of sharing among individuals is possible since, by means of conversations multiple visions of the world are shared and *social identities* are constructed (Brickson, 2000; Hogg and Terry, 2000).

As in Giddens' point of view (1984), for Taylor, organizational reality is constructed in a continuous way, to the extent that the *text* enables the constitution of a common reference for the conversations and, through them, is continually rewritten by the participants in their interactions. According to this perspective, the notion of *good organizational communications* is linked not only to the existence of a well-planned discourse guided by the top management of the organization, although this discourse is also important for the construction of the *text*. Equally important will be the conditions by which this discourse can be adopted by the participants as their own, as well as the level of openness they will have in order to contribute to the continuous writing of the *organizational text,* so as to load it with meaning.

In the same way, the conditions in which the conversation will be developed in the middle of daily interactions will be important, be it in terms of the available means of interaction, the possibility of meetings among participants, their capacity to share a meaning for the *text,* or the construction of social identities that reinforce this sharing.

12.5 Scope of the study

This study focuses on a Brazilian company that supplies infrastructure services in the energy field. The work was conducted in the middle of 2002, approximately six years after its privatization, at which time the company was purchased by a consortium, formed by various private and state-owned companies of both Brazilian and foreign capital. It is managed today by the major shareholders of this consortium, a European company that works in the same field in its country of origin.

After the first years of privatization, the predominant feeling among the participants of the study is that the company is going through a phase of *stabilization* or maturation of its new profile as a private organization that aims to be competitive. Thus, a major part of the efforts of the organization's top management is aimed at trying to consolidate a management model that promotes individual and team commitment, in order to strengthen the chances of the success of the strategy. One of the biggest challenges faced by the organization's top management was to improve the internal communications processes, taking into account the heavy turnover in personnel in recent years and the fact that it operates, at present, through alliances with a variety of companies that provide outsourced services. This study was conducted with the support of the organization, whose name, however, will not be revealed for ethical reasons.

12.6 Methodology

The data collection methodology comprised a combination of: a set of semi-structured interviews with company employees; the analysis of institutional documents; and the participation of the researchers, as observers, in three meetings to discuss action plans for important projects prepared by the company. The three meetings were observed. The first was related to the Quality project, the second to document management and the third one related to the implementation of a system for managing customer relations. The objective of observing the meetings was to see the way interactions develop for problem-solving as part of the organization's routine.

Twenty people working in different areas and at several hierarchical levels of the company were interviewed, of which 19 were employees and one was hired on a contract basis. The theme of the interviews was the aspects that, in the individual's opinion, influenced communications positively or negatively within the organization. The interviews were transcribed and their content analysed with the help of Atlas/TI software.

The documents analysed were institutional communications instruments, such as internal newsletters and e-mails for policy dissemination to the employees. This analysis aimed to complement the participants' opinions with a more refined view of the manner and type of content of the message.

The final analysis comprised a detailed qualitative presentation of the data obtained from the three methods of data collection, which were classified according to the types of content relevant to the understanding of the study's objectives, in accordance with the categories presented in the results section.

12.7   Results

The varied perceptions of the interviewees and the analysis of the content of formal documents and other communications, such as those occurring during meetings, permitted the identification of a set of representative categories of the elements that affect the development of a participative view.

12.7.1   Issues related to the general guidelines of the organization

The employees' discourses reveal a high degree of homogeneity regarding the challenges faced by the organization. The necessity to develop a greater focus on competition, an increase in concern for customers' expectations and a strengthening of the company's image in society are some of the aspects that seem to draw the attention of people located in different sectors and across hierarchical levels. The existence of a common discourse can be observed, reinforcing the feeling that it is necessary to join together, to involve everybody in the organization in order to face these challenges.

At the same time, however, the employees reveal a high degree of uncertainty about the general guidelines of the organization, as well as a feeling that this effort needs to be better coordinated so that each individual and the team can decide on the best way to align their actions with these guidelines. In the interviewees' opinion, this is one of the factors that make their participation more difficult.

Among the most frequently mentioned factors regarding the difficulties faced by individuals to align their efforts with the guidelines of the organization are: limited knowledge of the viewpoint of foreign headquarters; existence of a variety of perceptions of the company's mission and strategy; weak institutional reinforcement regarding the official definition of mission to current and new employees; insufficient dissemination of official objectives linked to the strategy, which, in the interviewees' opinion, should be reinforced both for employees and for contracted workers who directly affect the result of the business (e.g. receptionists and subcontracted maintenance workers); excessively fragmented goals in sectors, which are clear only for the management level and are not updated; lack of knowledge of the goals of other sectors; goals defined in a vertical non-participative way; lack of feedback about results; lack of knowledge about the company's human resources policy, especially with regard to the management of performance, training and development, salary policy, and acknowledgement and management of career opportunities.

12.7.2   Issues related to organizational and team identities

The intense changes in the company's operational environment in recent years, as well as significant turnover in personnel, have led to some difficulties in forging a strong organizational identity that can be perceived by all in a shared form. In the discourse of some interviewees, the view of an eminently technical company of the past, which emphasized quality, safety and the maintenance of installations, sometimes seems to conflict with the image of a company that needs to be concerned with the *demands of the market*, in which commercial objectives seem to be the main focus. Similarly, one can perceive a certain difficulty of articulation between the view of an organization with a local focus, with a long history as a parastatal company committed to public policies, and a multinational company, whose identity needs to become closer to the one of a competitive foreign group.

The search for the construction of a strong organizational identity seems to be, however, a concern not only for the company's top management, but also for all individuals, who see this search as an essential condition for promoting internal integrity, as well as strengthening its image in the market. At the same time, the changes occurring in recent years have accentuated the existence of *identity conflicts* among groups, some of which already existed before the privatization. Among the main identity conflicts are: those who think they are responsible for the continuity and success of the company, with a more collective vision, and those who, in their opinion, put their personal objectives first, with a more individualistic perspective; those who consider themselves qualified and/or experienced and those who are seen as having low qualification; those who feel they were marginalized by the company and those who they see as being privileged or more valued by the company; and those who seek to guide their career according to the logic of the market and those whose professional expectations seem to be directed solely towards the company.

The participants' discourse shows that these categories are strongly influenced by stereotypes that were constructed or reinforced during the process of changes in recent years. The main causes for the appearance of these stereotypes are considered to be: differences in treatment or lack of clearer policies regarding the professional profile desired and valued by the organization; the intense movement of people, due to the dismissal of a large number of established employees and the hiring of new professionals, generally younger, more updated and with a higher level of education; the mutual adaptation between foreigners belonging to headquarters and the Brazilians.

With special regard to the adaptation between foreign and Brazilian professionals, some factors continue to work against a closer identity: differences in personal style, since the foreigners have a more direct and frank style, which to the Brazilian ear can sometimes sound rude, while for the foreigners the Brazilian's indirect style sometimes is perceived as dissimulation; differences in power, since foreigners, in general, occupy higher positions in the organization; the scarcity of occasions for social and informal interaction between members of both groups; the fact that headquarters does not seem to take into account the specific circumstances of Brazil.

12.7.3   Issues related to integration between areas

One of the main difficulties identified by the interviewees, with regard to the possibility of developing a focus on communications management that gives priority to a sense of participation, is related to the low operational integration among different areas of the company. This lack of integration has become apparent since it has impacted the progress of some important projects being implemented by the organization, such as quality management and the integration of information systems.

The main sources of difficulties for the construction of a more integrated view among the different areas of the company highlighted by the employees were: ignorance about the mission and the strategy; lack of a common focus on the customer and on external demands in general; lack of a formal system for management of multifunctional processes; excessive workload in each sector; high level of personnel turnover in the organization as a whole and in each sector; lack of common goals among sectors, as well as a clear delimitation of their scope of action; lack of knowledge of each individual about the work of other sectors; lack of opportunities for acquaintanceship among people from different work teams who, often, interact only by telephone or e-mail, without getting to know each other personally; lack of integration among the information systems that serve different sectors; lack of sensitivity to the problems of other teams, existence of individualistic attitudes, lack of a systemic view about problems, power struggles and attempts to protect positions; physical distance among the sectors which, although concentrated in one place, are spread out in different buildings; lack of a routine of meetings among sectors; excessively hierarchical position of some sectors that hampers direct access among professionals at the operational level; and existence of fixed procedures that impede the flexibilization of integrated actions.

12.7.4   Issues related to personal integration

The general opinion of the participants in this study is that, after the critical period of changes due to privatization has passed, a friendly atmosphere, without conflicts or exaggerated disputes, will prevail among the company staff. However, relationships are distant, people do not know each other, contacts are restricted to the minimal necessities of work and in general mediated by technology (telephone or e-mail). In the current context, in which the volume of work is growing and work teams have few members, the problem of distant relationships is a frequent complaint not only regarding colleagues in other sectors, but also regarding colleagues in the same room or from other parts of the same sector. In the words of some interviewees, one can see today the lack of a *culture of communications* that increasingly causes personal relationships to be restricted to formal work routines.

There is also a feeling that this distance has been, to a certain extent, engendered by the company when, during the changes due to privatization and even in the period immediately prior, the supposed *privileges* existing in the old parastatal company were fought by means that caused a fragmentation of the collective spirit. In this sense, the distance in relationships is a kind of 'side effect' due to, among other aspects: the end of all fraternization activities that existed in the past, such as end-of-year parties and sports events which were held at the company's football field; the dismissal of a large number of veteran employees and high personnel turnover; the almost defunct employees' association and other kinds of associations that employees maintained in the past and that used to play an important role in their integration; the fact that even the union, which used to be active, has been losing significance in the current context.

Among the reasons for the existence of this difficulty of integration cited during the interviews were: lack of spaces for fraternization within the company; low quality of the restaurant which leads people to leave the company during lunch time; unresolved identity stereotypes among groups (example, new and old, Brazilians and foreigners); 'laziness' caused by e-mail and telephone technology, which makes people prefer to maintain contacts from a distance rather than to leave their offices and solve work problems personally; increasingly individualistic focus, reinforced by a more internally competitive view promoted by the company; location of the company's installations in a dangerous neighbourhood that is isolated from major entertainment centres, forcing everybody to go straight home after work and making any fraternization difficult after work hours; lack of an effective programme of integration for new employees; and lack of a routine of meetings promoted by the company.

Despite all these difficulties of integration, the company has visibly become sensitive to the problem and, during recent years, has implemented initiatives aimed at recovering some of the old spirit of closeness. Thus, there exists a recent effort to promote again end-of-year parties, in addition to the establishment of group activities, such as group gymnastics sessions and an employee choir. Furthermore, the human resources newsletter has created a monthly section that presents the profile of an employee, providing information about his background and activities within the organization. Recently, further aiming to improve negotiations during collective bargaining, the company itself promoted a campaign for employees to take part in union meetings, so as to contribute more actively to a negotiated solution. In the employees' opinion, these measures have helped increase the level of individual engagement in different areas and, little by little, contributed to the development of a more participative management.

12.7.5   Issues related to the means of institutional communications

The main means of institutional communications used by the company are: an institutional newsletter, intended to reinforce the internal and external image of the company, as well as to disseminate information about programmes implemented by the organization; online newsletters used in order to disseminate information to employees about the company's policies and actions; a monthly human resources newsletter, normally inserted into the institutional newsletter and aimed mainly at disseminating news about personnel management; official HR communiqués, distributed in printed form and by e-mail, in order to inform of instructions or important news on subjects of interest to employees, such as changes in benefits; and sector bulletin boards.

With regard to these different types of resources, the research examined the perceptions of the employees as to their level of contribution and their limitations as instruments of reinforcement of communications between the company and its employees. This was complemented by the analysis of the content of institutional documents. The results of this evaluation are presented in Table 12.1.

Table 12.1   Evaluation of the main means of institutional communications

Means	Positive aspects	Negative aspects
Institutional newsletter	Considered to have a good visual quality; has been increasing space for news about activities of the sectors; has relevant information about the company and especially about some of its more important projects	Represents only the institution's voice and does not reflect the employees' perspective; shows an idealized image of the institution, with little discussion of problems; does not promote dissemination and integration of people and sectors (photographs and subjects favour certain sectors, projects or people who hold power) – does not include a focus on socialization with subjects that motivate integration; does not explicitly reinforce the values of the company; does not provide space for people to speak and obtain feedback about their communications

202

Table 12.1   (Continued)

Means	Positive aspects	Negative aspects
Online newsletters	Considered to be the main means for employees to be updated with the viewpoint and image of the company	The texts are frequently long and numerous, making reading difficult, due to the pressure of work routine
Monthly human resources newsletter	Deals with subjects that interest employees; has opened an important space to hear them by inviting them to send suggestions to the human resources sector; has created a section for presenting profiles of some employees; has created, through the editorial written by the Human Resources Director, a language of greater proximity to employees	Does not make explicit enough the formal human resource policy of the company; subjects in general are not democratic – does not provide exposure to the employees at lower levels, chooses photos and interviews with persons of great projection or power in the company; interviewees' speech are directed, not leaving space for them to be able to present freely their more critical opinions; there is no feedback on suggestions sent by employees
HR communiqués	Considered as the most important means for the employee to keep abreast of the company's HR policy, as well as to obtain news of interest in the field of personnel management	Adopts, in general, an unnecessarily formal and distant style, with a standardized language, independent of the subject in question; terms used sometimes reinforce conflicts of interest with the union
Sector bulletin boards	Some sectors use the local bulletin board as a resource to promote personnel integration and team spirit, with news of interest to the team and organized in a participative manner	Not all sectors give the same importance to this resource; lack of standardization or stimulus for using it; no organizational board that people from all sectors can access – the existing board at the company entrance is not updated and is located at a place that is invisible to employees who arrive by car

In summary, the most important criticisms of the interviewees with regard to the means of institutional communications refer to their limited application, in terms of their possible usefulness in helping to disseminate the viewpoint and general policies of the organization, as well as the fact that they are not adequately used to promote a stronger identification of employees with the company or to stimulate greater integration.

12.7.6 Issues regarding means of interpersonal communications

The main means of interpersonal communications considered relevant by the interviewees are: e-mail, telephone, meetings, personal contact, and in some operational sectors, radio. The evaluations of the main strong points and limitations of each one of these means are summarized in Table 12.2.

Table 12.2 Evaluation of the main means of interpersonal communications

Means	Positive aspects	Negative aspects
E-mail	Considered to be a support tool that makes communications faster, shortens distances and allows follow-up processes; a means of integrating the teamwork, when the manager shares information and motivates his employees; a main source of information and access to people	Abusive use, an excessive number of messages, discouraging reading and creating storage problems in computer memory and expenses with printing; inadequate use in situations in which telephone and personal contact would be more adequate; distorted use, as a means of not assuming responsibility, create problems, or show up others; *cold communications*, because the style adopted strengthens distant and formal relationships; fails in contact, if mailbox is full or password has expired, if one does not work with one's e-mail open or does not have an e-mail address (as is the case of subcontracted people and some who work externally)
Telephone	Considered to be a practical means to avoid and solve misunderstandings, bring people together and enable faster solutions to problems	The heavy work routine makes it difficult for a person to spend time on the phone; not as efficient as personal contact, in terms of its potential to bring people together

Table 12.2   (Continued)

Means	Positive aspects	Negative aspects
Meetings	Considered to be an important means to get to know people, understand different points of view, integrate teams, managers and sectors, solve problems that demand joint decisions, disseminate and update information	There is no culture of meetings in the company, whether between managers and the base, a manager and his team, or among departments; even in areas in which there are meetings, the periodicity is not considered to be adequate; the predominant formal style in conducting meetings increases distance and hierarchy
Personal contact	Considered to be the most important means of knowing people and their activities, as well as to improve relationships	Opportunities for personal contact are increasingly rare, either due to lack of opportunities or due to the constant pressure of work
Radio	Used mainly by people in external field activities; seen as a means that helps to shorten distances, intervenes rapidly, and permits access to people who, because of their external work, are difficult to find	Use limited to some specific activities and not viable, therefore, as a means of general integration

In summary, the main criticisms made by employees refer to the fact that, in recent years, the company has promoted electronic communications as the main tool for interpersonal communications, weakening other more efficient ways for the development of a sense of integration, such as personal contact, meetings or even the telephone. Thus, interpersonal communications have become increasingly formal and distant. In addition, the use of e-mail is not accessible to all and demands better systematization and learning, in order to avoid the excess of messages and lack or delay in answering. The formalism of language is also another aspect that limits integration.

12.7.7   Issues related to sectors responsible for improving communications

Two sectors of the company are recognized by the interviewees as the main channels for making their opinions heard by the organization managers: the human resources and social communications sectors. It is also in these sectors that the company concentrates its biggest efforts to promote a dialogue with employees.

The main compliments regarding the performance of these areas, especially the human resources department, are: easy access to the professionals of the sector, who are attentive and respectful with employees; significant efforts to become closer to employees in recent years; extremely positive and charismatic image of the director, a foreigner who is very well adapted to the local culture; perceived to be the main (and sometimes only) channel of communications of the employees; work of arousing awareness that it has been trying to develop with directors and managers with regard to the need for promoting a more intense dialogue within teams and among departments; transparent way in which it has been trying to inform employees about the conduct of collective bargaining; promotion of different events of integration, such as end-of-year parties, breakfasts with the President and creation of the choir.

The main criticisms are: lack of clarity when disseminating HR policies; excessive centralization with regard to personnel management initiatives, leaving little space for team managers' action, since all demands from employees must necessarily be addressed to the human resources department; reduced attention given to sectors located outside the physical environment of headquarters; timid attitude regarding the dissemination of initiatives aiming to increase integration; lack of clarity on the specific responsibilities of each person in the HR and social communications departments with regard to communications management in the organization, creating conflicts and difficulties for employees to identify who they should turn to in each type of situation.

12.7.8   Issues regarding hierarchical structures

The mid-level managers occupy a limited space with regard to their work as elements of integration between the base and the top management of the organization. They feel that they are put in a position of information *disseminators,* from the top down to the base, and they believe they do not have sufficient autonomy, time and information to perform the role of negotiators between the base and the top management of the organization.

On the other hand, in the opinion of those in the base, some managers are not well qualified to deal with people management, since they have a centralized and authoritarian style, and are not sensitive to the needs of the people at the base. In general, a large gap can be observed between the base and the top management of the organization, and the mid-level managers mediate this relationship excessively, since the company is still very hierarchical. As a result of this hierarchical viewpoint, the access to employees from other areas is difficult and must be routed through middle managers.

12.7.9   Predominant characteristics in the culture and atmosphere of the organization

Finally, in the interviewees' opinion, the characteristics related to the culture and atmosphere of the organization most helpful to the development of a more participative view are: the organization charisma, its capacity to captivate employees and to make them feel proud to be part of its staff; and the emphasis on results, developed in recent years, which stimulates individuals and teams to better align their efforts.

With regard to the characteristics that most negatively affect the development of a sense of participation, the participants report: excessive hierarchy and formality as well as insufficient flexibility of norms and routines; existence of a paternalistic relationship with regard to employees, creating few opportunities to act consciously and autonomously with regard to the objectives of their jobs; insufficient dialogue, not being listened to enough, few opportunities for participation in decision-making.

12.8   A framework for communications management

This study aimed to identify aspects of the organization's communications management that can affect the possibility of constructing an enhanced sense of participation. The variety of positive and negative aspects considered relevant by participants of the company analysed allows the proposal of a framework to help managers of the organizations to move forward in this direction, as presented in Figure 12.1.

12.8.1   Aspects regarding knowledge of the organizational context

The organization's mechanisms of communications management must be especially sensitive to the need to create a referential basis for the individuals that enables the construction of a common language, of a shared meaning for actions. The results of the study suggest some essential factors for the construction of this common referential basis: clarity about the challenges faced by the organization; transparency in the dissemination of strategic guidelines; continuous reinforcement of the officially declared mission by the organization to all individuals, making them think and debate its meaning; wide dissemination and

Figure 12.1   Reference chart for management of organizational communications

constant updating of objectives and strategic global goals, as well as the objectives and goals defined by each part; involvement of individuals in the dissemination and review of these objectives and goals; continuous supply of feedback for individuals and teams about the results achieved by the organization and its different parts, as well as the level of contribution of each person to these results; and dissemination of human resource management policies and programmes.

In addition, the results of the study demonstrated the fundamental importance of a collective effort, orchestrated by the top management and desired by all, for the construction of a strong organizational identity that is fully shared. This process, however, cannot be imposed on individuals and needs to be renewed every day, by an intense dialogue and a constant attempt to bring closer together the *multiple organizational identities* that arise. In an environment of intense change, it seems utopian to imagine that it is possible to avoid the appearance of multiple identities perceived by the different members of the organization. However, to ignore their existence or believe that the existence of a cohesive viewpoint among only the leaders is sufficient, to be simply *transmitted* to other individuals, can lead the organization to an identity crisis that can reinforce fragmentation.

12.8.2   Aspects regarding management structure

Other aspects that significantly influence the efficiency of organizational communications management, in terms of a capacity to promote a sense of participation, are the structure and type of the management system that prevail in the organization. Vertically, the results of this study suggest that aspects such as excessive hierarchy, formality, centralization of authority and distance of power seem to undermine the conditions for the different members of the organization to develop a greater sense of involvement, as well as a greater command of their work. Thus, the intensification of dialogue without excess formality among different levels seems to be the most adequate remedy against this vertical fragmented vision.

In addition, the results demonstrated that excessive *vertical fragmentation* also strengthens *horizontal fragmentation*, since it reduces the possibility that individuals from different parts of the organization can routinely, in a natural way without unnecessary mediation, discuss problems arising from their work.

Still regarding horizontal fragmentation, the results obtained highlight the importance for the organization to strengthen the development of a processes view for its management systems. The processes view, in addition to attracting the attention of individuals towards customer needs, enables the composition of a permanent arena to discuss problems and solutions and to facilitate mutual knowledge, creating conditions for each person to develop with others a systemic and shared view about the organization.

Another aspect that contributes to strengthening vertical and horizontal fragmentation are the difficulties of sharing information. Thus, a very important type of initiative to improve communications is also a greater integration of the bases and the systems that regulate information flow.

12.8.3   Aspects regarding communications tools

The results of this study suggest that the notion of communications that still predominates in the organization follows the traditional linear model, of a *sender–receiver type*, in which the literal content of the message issued and the quality of the means of transmission is privileged, in detriment to the form of communication and the capacity of the actors to construct a shared meaning.

One idea that can be clearly extracted from the perceptions of the participants of this research is that technological resources cannot substitute for personal interaction or be the main element in the promotion of the socialization of individuals. The results suggest also that the power of technology tends to be limited when it is used in an abusive or inadequately systematized way, creating noise that can even weaken the quality of communications. Thus, it is very important that organizations evaluate the way they use such kinds of resources. At the same time, it is essential that the employment of these resources be balanced with support for other more efficient means to help individuals socialize, especially those that strengthen personal contact.

With regard to the institutional channels of communications, the existence of an adequate means of disseminating the official vision appears to be recognized as important by individuals, as an element that enables the construction of a referential basis for action. The most important message resulting from this study is, however, that, instead of *selling* the image of an ideal organization to employees, these channels must be capable of strengthening the collective construction of a common identity. And for this, it is necessary for them to be capable of promoting, above all, the *identification* of individuals with the organization. When reading institutional newsletters – when it is possible to read them, if they are not excessive in number or too long – individuals not only seek to know the *face of power* or the expectations of top management. First of all, they look for elements that can bring answers to their own expectations and, for this, they need to see *their own and their colleagues' faces* recognized by the organization.

12.8.4   Aspects regarding social interaction

In their drive to reduce costs or emphasize results, many organizations have weakened a variety of initiatives that can promote greater integration among employees. In recent years, many companies have cancelled fraternization programmes, reduced spaces for interaction, discouraged professional associations, fought against unions, encouraged a spirit of competition, classified the sense of cooperation as a synonym for *privileges*, discouraged socialization in and outside the workplace. The result of this process of excessive *rationalization* of work relations can be observed in this study when individuals perceive a *loss of enthusiasm* for relationships and an excessive formality, two of the main obstacles for the development of communications that lead to engagement and to the construction of a shared feeling for the organization.

Therefore, the construction or recovery of this *interactive context* seems to be one of the main goals to be considered for the organization's communications management. Some of the elements that can contribute significantly to this goal are the development of meeting practices within and among teams, the creation of fraternization programmes, the encouragement of contacts among individuals, the availability of spaces and resources that encourage personal acquaintances.

12.9   Conclusion

The perceptions of the participants of this study suggest that, above all, the management of organizational communications needs to seek a shared construction – involving the leaders and those who are led, top management and base – of values that strengthen mutual respect, closer identification, sense of collaboration, pride in sharing a common project. The greater objective to be pursued must be to gradually transform a paternalistic culture, of *guidance* of individuals, which has dominated the classic view of organization management, into a new culture capable of recognizing the best contributions from individuals as subjects of their action.

References

Argyris, C. (1994) 'Good communications that blocks learning', *Harvard Business Review*, 72 (4), 77–85.

Boden, D. (1994) *The Business of Talking: Organizations in Action* (Cambridge, UK: Polity Press).

Brickson, S. (2000) 'The impact of identity orientation on individual and organizational outcomes in demographically diverse settings', *Academy of Management Review*, 25 (1), 82–101.

Cabrera A. and E.F. Cabrera (2002) 'Knowledge-sharing dilemmas', *Organization Studies*, 23 (5), 687–710.

Clark, H. (1996) *Using Language* (Cambridge: Cambridge University Press).

Davenport, T. H. (1998) 'Putting the enterprise into the enterprise system', *Harvard Business Review*, 76 (4), 121–31.

Dewett, T. and G.R. Jones (2001) 'The role of information technology in the organization: a review, model, and assessment', *Journal of Management*, 27, 313–46.

Dunford, R and D. Jones (2000) 'Narrative in strategic change' *Human Relations*, 53 (9), 1207–26.

Ford, J. D. and L. W. Ford (1995) 'The role of conversations in producing intentional change in organizations', *Academy of Management Review*, 20 (3), 541–70.

Garvin, D.A. (2000) 'Construindo a organização que aprende' in *Harvard Business Review (coletânea) Gestão do Conhecimento* (Rio de Janeiro: Ed. Campus), 50–81.

Giddens, A. (1984) *The Constitution of Society* (Berkeley: University of California Press).

Gioia, D.A., M. Schultz and K.G. Corley (2000) 'Organizational identity, image, and adaptative instability', *Academy of Management Review*, 25 (1), 63–81.

Giordano, Y. (1998) 'Communications et organisations: une reconsidération par la théorie de la structuration', *Revue de Gestion des Ressources Humaines*, 26/27, 20–35.

Hogg, M.A and D.J. Terry (2000) 'Social identity and self-categorization processes in organizational contexts', *Academy of Management Review*, 25 (1), 121–40.

Nonaka, I. A (2000) 'Empresa criadora de conhecimento' in *Harvard Business Review (coletânea) Gestão do Conhecimento* (Rio de Janeiro: Ed. Campus), 27–49.

Olivier, B. (1995) *L'acteur et le Sujet* (Paris: Desclée de Brouwer).

Pratt, M.G. and P.O. Foreman (2000) 'Classifying managerial responses to multiple organizational identities', *Academy of Management Review*, 25 (1), 18–42.

Rojot, J. (1998) 'Communications et organisations: une reconsidération par la théorie de la structuration', *Revue de Gestion de Ressources Humaines*, 26/27, 20–35.

Scott, C.R., L. Quinn, C.E. Timmerman and D.M. Garret (1998) 'Ironic uses of group communications and interviews with group decision support system users', *Communications Quarterly*, 46 (3), 353–74.

Silva, J.R.G. (2000) 'O poder da tecnologia da informação e da comunicação e a tentativa de mudança das relações de trabalho em uma organização brasileira', *Anais do III Congresso da ALAST*, Buenos Aires.

Silva, J.R.G. (2001) 'Comunicação e mudança em organizações brasileiras: desvendando um quadro de referência sob a ótica do sujeito e da reconstrução de identidades'. Unpublished PhD thesis, Departamento de Administração da PUC-Rio, Rio de Janeiro.

Taylor, J.R. (1093) 'La Dynamique de Changement Organisationnel: une théorie conversation/texte de la communications et ses implications', *Communications et Organisation*, 3, 50–93.

Zarifian, P. (2001) 'Comunicação e subjetividade nas organizações' in E. Davel and S.C. Vergara (eds) *Gestão com Pessoas e Subjetividade* (São Paulo: Atlas).

13

'What Alter Says and Ego Hears': a Discourse-Based Analysis of Control, Trust and Information in a Professional Organization

Fabienne Alvarez
University of Antilles and Guyane and University of Paris-Dauphine

13.1 Introduction

Addressing the question of change and questioning the emergence of new realities in today's world requires a global perspective (from the individual to the societal level) that challenges traditional paradigms. The traditional way of addressing these issues focuses on problem-solving solutions with formally designed and structured investigation modes, which fail to recognize the subject-grounded nature of social dynamics. As a result, traditional inquiry methods in organizational settings are epistemologically unsound and contribute to a depersonalized view of organizations.

To illustrate this point, this contribution will examine a postmodern organizational strategy for investigating critical organizational issues. The case study illustrates how to obtain a more comprehensive understanding of the organization and its issues by simply challenging and changing the investigation strategy and the organizational modern paradigms. We analyse how an organization implements change and favours the support and socialization of individuals towards new devices. In order to show how the introduction of managerial devices in the merger process changes work organization and power equilibrium, we focused on control relationships[1] of various groups of actors in a professional organization, the Georges Pompidou European Hospital, the result of one of the largest mergers in the French health care industry. The aim was to analyse the nature and dynamics of control relationships, to identify the reasons for the ability of clinicians to resist the change process and their repeated conflicting position towards local and/or headquarters controllers.

An innovative 'seven step' discourse analysis process[2] was designed to investigate organizational behaviours and representations. Although discourse 'produces a particular version of social reality' (Chia, 2000), the analytical process made it possible to identify factors critical to the success of the merger, and to change processes in general. It was shown that the participants supporting the project developed strong exchange relationships and networks in which information flowed. The importance of trust in the communication process was crucial in terms of how it could condition sense-making. More specifically, trust allowed the dynamics of information exchange to take place, as it influenced in a favourable way the actor's interpretation of the information received. We assume that trust or distrust relationships, by determining the bases of information exchange, contextualize the scheme through which information is considered, sometimes as 'objective data', sometimes as 'subjective message'.

The chapter is organized in three parts. The first section presents a challenging theoretical and epistemological framework for the study of organizational control and communication processes. Discourse analysis gives more room for the individual level of analysis, while at the same time allowing the construction of collective representations. The case study is presented in the second section, as is the investigation process that was built in order to provide a deep analysis and to understand how individuals and groups felt about the change process. The last section discusses the results and presents the perspectives for future research.

13.2 Organizational control as a set of social exchange relationships

13.2.1 Revisiting organizations' traditional theoretical frameworks

Although control in organizations has often been viewed through the lens of tools, particularly in the agency theory and transactions cost theory, we consider control relationships as social exchange relationships. Breton and Wintrobe (1982) have developed a theory of control and trust in bureaucracies. This theory[3] which represents an extension of the agency theory, gives the first economic explanation of the existence and functioning of informal structures and provides a concrete answer to the work of Granovetter (1985) for whom economic action and social structures are embedded.

Following White (1991), we considered agency relationships as social relationships, since 'agency [...] is intensively social in its mechanism, since it gets one person to do something for another vis-à-vis a third person, but only with heavy reliance on the lay of the social landscape. Opportunism and flexibility, in both the short and the long term, are the key to agency's perennial robustness.' Moreover, the form of control exacted upon a worker or employed by a worker will, to an extent, influence or be associated with the nature of that worker's informal relations in the workplace (Ghidina, 1993). For White (1991), the embeddedness of control, networks and agency relationships requires control to be

> [...] crafted continuously out of what are residuals as seen by the bulk of persons involved: their central cognitive and emotional investments are put into keeping going their social acts together, into keeping going a show not apparently concerned with the strategy and change that are crucial to the controller. The awesome social pressure from which control is bled off at the margin comes and must come from the self selected, self interested, self directed 'natural' actions and emotions of the actors, constrained, to be sure, by corporate cultures and in more tangible ways.

Thus, we consider organizational control as a process aimed at controlling or influencing the behaviour of individuals, as part of a formal organization, in order to increase the probability that they reach the organizational goals (Flamholtz, 1996). By defining control as the capacity that some actors or groups of actors have to influence the actions of others, Giddens (1984, p. 345) and Hofstede (1978) underline the social aspect of this process. Management control tools cannot be appreciated only through their technical dimension, since they are 'embedded' in social networks (Granovetter, 1985, 1992). Therefore they are at the same time tools for management and means to articulate social relationships (Berry, 1983).

Numerous existing theoretical researches on trust proposed various definitions, typologies, dimensions or foundations (Lewis and Weigert, 1985; Zucker, 1986; Luhmann, 1988; Williamson, 1993; Servet, 1994), in order to clarify a concept whose analysis remains subtle. Its importance can be illustrated by the work of Zucker (1986) who defines trust as 'a set of expectations shared by all those involved in an exchange'. For Lewis and Weigert (1985) 'trust may be thought of as a functional prerequisite for the possibility of society'. Confronted with this dense literature, we elaborated a typology of organizational trust that fitted field observation and discourse patterns. As trust remains complex to observe and often relies on non-discursive elements, we focused on its foundations. Those dimensions of trust are observable in organizational life and express the wide variety of trust relationships, the various ways of creating and sustaining it and the impact organizational and individual features can have on trust. The five foundations identified are the following:

1. Trust based on competencies or experience of individuals;
2. Trust based on intentions or morality of individuals;
3. Trust based on reputation;
4. Trust based on formal rules, procedures, systems or structures;
5. Trust based on institution (organizational level).

There is a crucial need to adapt theoretical frameworks and investigation modes to the new challenges organizations are facing, in particular the role of trust in organizational control. The necessity to understand individuals and groups calls for deep analysis of the functioning of contemporary organizations. Yet, when answers are sought to address such issues, there is a propensity to address new problems with old response patterns, which are typically based upon data-bound analyses. Inherent in the concept of change is the necessity to challenge beliefs and interpretative schemas to accommodate emerging realities. But the actual implementation of the research is very slow.

13.2.2   Revisiting the organization through a discourse perspective

Concurrent with the rapidity of change is also a redefinition of the worker that makes up today's organizations. Organizations posit that they seek to find and develop knowledge workers who possess strong behavioural competencies, believe that learning is a lifelong process, are flexible in their outlook, are readily able to adapt concepts within abstract frameworks and are not afraid to venture into new paradigms. However, today's knowledge workers comprise more than just an expansion of behavioural competencies; they are also in a quest for meaning and purpose to their lives (Easley and Alvarez-Pompilius, 2003). The emerging needs of this workforce suggest that organizational leaders must also be ready to listen to their employees. Proponents of postmodernist organizational change theory refer to this level of deep listening as polyphonic listening, where this level of listening and the subsequent inquiry that follows facilitate an organizational leader to understand the organization as an evolving, transforming, social construction, malleable to human choice (Barrett and Srivastva, 1991). The resulting and emerging recommended change strategies bear characteristics of being multidimensional, multi-level, qualitative and discontinuous, incorporating complete paradigmatic shifts (French and Bell, 1995). However, while the literature is evolving, implementation of recommended strategies is slow in application, which leads to a growing criticism of traditional theoretical frameworks for investigating and changing human action and interaction.

13.2.3   Revisiting investigation modes

The investigative methods and change strategies organizations utilize, which are typically grounded in orthodox scientific methods, often exclude subjects from all choice about the subject matter of the investigation and the resulting change strategies (Reason, 1988). If organizations are to effectively change, paradigms for investigating and intervening must also change.

Discourse analysis allows concepts such as trust to emerge and provides ways for investigating them. Unlike traditional research methodologies, it focuses on individual and group behaviours, with their beliefs and fears, motivation and resistance to change, social relationships made of trust, conflict, power... Because they go far beyond simple assumptions on organizational life, considering it as complex, multiple, diversified and embedded in social networks and structures (Granovetter, 1985), qualitative inquiries in general and interpretative approaches in particular offer wide possibilities for analysing change processes and human behaviours in uncertain environments. Although very demanding in time for collecting, analysing and presenting data, qualitative investigations are worth the effort, and illustrate the willingness to clarify and manage organizational complexity.

13.3 Collecting and analysing individuals and professional groups discourses

13.3.1 The case study

The sociological specification of professional organization (Mintzberg, 1982) has important effects on management, particularly because the link between activity and resources remains unknown, due to the fact that professionals do not specify it themselves. Hospitals' common characteristics explain the difficulties managers have in controlling those organizations, the power of professional groups and why change and managerial innovation are so crucial.

French public hospitals are organized around a powerful medical structure. The traditional responsibility centre is the medical service or department, the person in charge is the departmental head and the main activity is health care production (for clinical departments). The 'quest' for autonomy and responsibility remains problematic mainly because of the status of the medical department head, who is appointed by the prime minister and does not have a hierarchical link with the director of the hospital. Therefore, the consequences of not reaching objectives and not enforcing contracts are very limited. At the medical level, there is no individual sanction (that usually serves as an efficient control device) for bad management or inefficient use of financial resources. But this counterpart is quite fundamental since it validates the relevance of management structures. Actually, as Bouquin (1994, p. 20) states, the delegation of authority calls for individual responsibility and the acceptance of being evaluated on our own results.

Several dispositions have been undertaken to allow a more efficient monitoring of activities. First, the reform of 1991 aimed at promoting the decentralization of care management, through the implementation of a hospital strategic project (Claveranne, 1996). Second, the introduction of several information systems and the structuring of medical and accounting information around activities show a major evolution in the way to consider the medical output. It opens the way for activity-based management and process analysis, then making it possible to identify cost drivers linked to efficiency (Cauvin, 1999).

Another point is the complexity to evaluate the medical product: is it the patient, the hospitalization journeys, the patient's stay, the surgeries, the number of consultation hours? This inability to strictly define medical output limits the representation of health care activity and the implementation of appropriate management tools. Today, a new definition of medical output, focusing on homogeneous disease groups

(GHMs), is introduced to allow, for each group, a more efficient cost allocation than the previous one based on 'day-pricing'. Then, a cleavage between the medical profession and hospital administration exists, which partly explains why there is some retention of information. This phenomenon known as asymmetry of information exists between state administration and the hospital, and between the administration of the hospital and the medical services. Both adverse selection and moral hazard exist and trap the hospital in a game of local social forces, which limits the efficiency of control mechanisms.

In this context, Moisdon and Tonneau (1999, p. 252) consider that preserving fuzzy areas inside the organization is a necessary condition for system equilibrium. Thus, control in hospital must not only consist in developing mechanisms to monitor activities, but also to make individuals stick to organizational goals. Motivating the medical profession and other members of the medical department cannot be achieved by forcing congruence. By enhancing cooperation between departments, relationships and coordination between services are improved, resulting in an increase in efficiency and in quality of patient care.

13.3.1.1   *The merger: Georges Pompidou European Hospital*

The Georges Pompidou European Hospital (HEGP) is the materialization of one of the largest hospital mergers ever conducted in France. It gathered together people from three hospitals: Broussais, Boucicaut and Laennec. This new hospital aimed to be both a local hospital for the needs of nearby populations and a very specialized hospital with medical poles of excellence. A 'patient-centred organization' has been designed to favour a patient global quality care process. This was presented as a new concept for HEGP. The hospital structure was originally decentralized into seven poles of activity, associating medical, nursing, managerial, technical and hospitality competencies coupled with a network organization. Poles also operate as an innovative decentralized management structure in which decisions are made closer to operational problems and are based on internal contracting. The poles, as managerial tools, encourage the coordination of complementary medical activities and create a local decision level for budgetary control. They also facilitate procedures setting and performance evaluation processes in order to transfer responsibility and autonomy to medical services.

Finally, management information systems were implemented. They represent major and innovative tools that integrate multiple dimensions: physical (the buildings), care production, medical responsibility and operational management. One of the main objectives was to clarify department functionality and bring information on medical activities. They constitute major power stakes, around which groups of actors inside and outside the hospital develop strategies to favour or to limit their implementation.

13.3.2 The methodology

The quest for meaning of organizational behaviours guided the choice of a qualitative case study that allows understanding of a given situation, and gives the ability to propose a representation of it. This research strategy is centred on the understanding of social dynamics that exist in specific contexts (Eisenhardt, 1989). To evaluate the representations of organizational control, the managerial, behavioural and cultural impacts of the merger and the success of the change process, we focused on individuals, groups and organizational levels, utilizing content analysis of data, which resulted from detailed qualitative interviewing.

The investigation strategy started with an initial immersion in the field to become familiar with situations, places, people and habits. The geographical, historical, cultural and social context of the hospital and of the situations observed was of great importance for further interpretation of the data. Four months spent in the Department of Management Control and Finance of HEGP, as a non-participant observer, developed familiarity with people and with their work, a necessary step to be able to understand the relationships between different groups, to learn the specific medical and technical terms, and to be introduced to the members of the organization. Information, reports, journals and every document that seemed potentially useful for the research, were collected. Then 89 interviews were conducted in and around the hospital to access specific situations limited in time and space (Burgess, 1984, p. 102). This process database posed a considerable challenge, as Langley (1999) explains, due to the volume of information gathered, and its varied nature, complexity and ambiguity.

The complexity of the situations observed and the will to understand control relationships lead to the adoption of an adductive process that moves back and forth from theoretical perspectives to field data, making it possible to produce intelligible interpretations of observations. Discourse was integrated both as a methodology utilized to analyse qualitative data collected through interviews and conversations, and as an epistemology sound in human behaviours and narratives, that offers refreshing opportunities for management research and organizational understanding (Easley and Alvarez-Pompilius, 2003, 2004). The depth and breadth of the data collected in research provided valuable information for identifying the patterns which can impact on organizational change and an ability to successfully manage the organization (Alvarez, 2002). Discourse then operates as 'communicative action that is constructive of social and organizational reality' (Heracleous and Hendry, 2000).

Discourse analysis required a critical vigilance attitude fundamental to the social science researcher, always confronted with an impression of familiarity with its research object, which necessitates the use of breaking-off techniques (Bardin, 2001, p. 16). The 'theoretical sensibility' of the researcher, which refers to his/her personal qualities, reveals a consciousness of data meaning subtleties (Strauss and Corbin, 1990, p. 41). Robert and Bouillaguet (1997, p. 124) consider that content analysis, as every technical device used with mastery and discernment, can set free interpretive inventiveness. We tried to avoid 'climb[ing] the discursive ladder in organizational research and to ascribe to discourse determining capacities' (Alvesson and Karreman, 2000) by considering all empirical material before deciding what it can be used for. Attention was paid to the 'situated meaning' of the elements of discourse obtained through interviews.

This qualitative process preserved the meaning actors gave to culture, change and control, and allowed the identification of five major dimensions: the perceptions of management control, information, communication, interpersonal relations and trust. Although closely linked, it was possible to identify differences in the meaning actors gave to each of these dimensions. The constant challenge was to reduce the amount of information collected while preserving the content and meaning of that information. To allow the presentation of large quantities of information in relatively little space, we followed a 'visual mapping strategy' (Langley, 1999) using graphical forms (Huberman and Miles, 1991), aimed at representing a large number of dimensions, and that constitute useful tools for the development of theoretical ideas.

13.4 Alter, Ego and trust – or the conditions of an efficient information exchange process

13.4.1 Discourses on organizational control

Once data was collected in the form of discourse patterns, we analytically deconstructed discourse in order to reconstruct representations and meaning at different levels.[4] The process went from individual level to group level and collective meaning. The first result was the identification of five major dimensions of change and social relationships: control, information, communication, interpersonal relationships and trust. They represent an important result of the research since they indicate the way control relationships must be seen and analysed and reveal a complexity that goes far beyond the way some theories consider organizational processes. Although it seemed interesting to fully understand the way each actor combined those dimensions, we had to stick to the objective of the research which consisted in understanding the collective dynamics of control relationships and of the change process. This explains why a further step had to be taken in order to compare the way different actors perceived a particular dimension.

Creating relational ties appeared to be a key success factor for control purposes. Individuals favoured the development of relationships, whose structure varied from a simple role of intermediary to the construction of a personal network that favoured trust, and facilitates the flow of information. The analysis reveals that the question and the specific nature of trust are closely linked to the group of actors it concerns. The detailed analysis of two groups is presented here: the local financial controllers and the medical staff.

This last step of the qualitative discourse analysis process focused on *intra-group analysis*. Matrixes were built for each group of actors, indicating: the five dimensions of the control relationship, the different logics associated with each dimension, and the meaning of individuals' discourse. It remains difficult to bridge the gap between individual discourses and group discourse, but the possibility of transporting the results beyond the local context remains, since Langley (1999) and Eisenhardt (1989) open the way for building theory from process data and case study research. Context is in this case the cement that preserves homogeneity in this regrouping process.

Trust was itself analysed depending on its five dimensions (competencies/experience; intentions/morality; reputation; rules and procedures; organizational). Signs (+) and (−) indicated respectively trust or distrust. Symbols materialized the meaning individuals gave to the logic to which their discourse was referring. The matrixes resulted in the identification of *collective representations of control and change*. The relationships observed influenced attitudes toward the

Table 13.1　HEGP controllers' discourse

Theme	Logic	CG 902[a]	CG 903	CG 904	CG 905	CG 906	CG 907	CG 908	CG 909
Control	Formalization	■			♦	♦	♦	■	■
	Dialogue		●	●					
Information	Acquisition	■						■	■
	Driver				♦	♦	♦		
	Service		●	●					
Communication	Avoidance	■						■	■
	Encounter		●	●	♦	♦	♦		
Relations	Constraint	■						■	■
	Capital		●	●	♦	♦	♦		
Trust (+) or	Intentions		+	+	+		+?	−?	
mistrust (−)	Competencies	+					+?		
	Rules/ procedures					+			+?

[a] CG stands for management controller; each of them has a personal number to protect anonymity.

merger and HEGP project team, toward the new control devices that were implemented, or more generally toward change. The matrix in Table 13.1 is relative to HEGP controllers and shows the way discourse was categorized in order to identify patterns of control relationships and to associate them with a specific meaning.

Three types of relationships emerged from the analysis of HEGP controllers' discourse and relational patterns:

1. A relationship based on **'formalization'** (■) in which *control* is viewed as 'formalization', *information* is collected in a logic of 'acquisition', *communication* is expressed in a logic of 'avoidance', *relations* are considered as 'constraint' and no homogeneity was found for the *trust* dimension.
2. A relationship with **'mix'** or **hybrid** (♦) conceptions in which *control* is viewed as 'formalization', *information* is collected in a logic of 'information driver', *communication* is lived in a logic of 'encounter', *relations* is considered as 'capital' and *trust* is represented mainly though personal attributes.
3. A **'personalized'** (●) relationship in which *control* is viewed as 'dialogue', *information* is collected in a logic of 'service', *communication* is lived in a logic of 'encounter', *relations* is considered as 'capital' and *trust* is based on 'intentions'.

The matrixes in Tables 13.2 and 13.3 concern the medical staff.

The medical profession is a group in which positions on the different dimensions are very settled since their discourse is homogeneous. It was easier to derive interpretations and to identify groups' representations.

Table 13.2   The medical staff discourse (a)

Theme	Logic	MED[a] 201	MED 202	MED 203	MED 204	MED 301	MED 302	MED 303	MED 304
Control	Constraint	■	■						■
	Order			♦		♦			
	Resource provider				●		●	●	
Information	Manipulation	■	■				■		■
	Argumentation							♦	
	Sharing			●	●		●		
Communication	Avoidance		■			■	■		■
	Clarification	●		●	●			●	
Relations	Exclusion	■					■		
	Inclusion		●	●	●	●		●	●
Trust (+) or mistrust (−)	Intentions	+		+	+	+	−		
	Competencies		+					−	
	Reputation								−

[a] MED stands for medical doctors; each of them has a personal number to protect anonymity. MED 101 is a medical doctor who works in hospital number 1. MED 202 is a medical doctor who works in hospital number 2.

Table 13.3   The medical staff discourse (b)

Theme	Logic	MED 101	MED 102	MED 103	MED 104	MED 105	MED 106	MED 107
Control	Constraint			■	■	■	■	
	Order							
	Resource provider	●	●					●
Information	Manipulation					■	■	
	Argumentation		♦	♦	♦			
	Sharing	●						●
Communication	Avoidance				■	■	■	
	Clarification	●	●	●				●
Relations	Exclusion			■	■	■	■	
	Inclusion	●	●					●
Trust (+) or mistrust (−)	Intentions	+	−	+	−	−	−	+

Two types of control relationships clearly emerged, one 'open' and one 'closed':

1. In **'open'** (●) relationships, *control* is viewed in a logic of 'resources', *information* is expressed in a logic of 'sharing', *communication* aims at 'clarifying' situations, *relations* are lived in a dynamics of 'inclusion' and *trust* is based on 'intentions'.
2. In **'closed'** (■) relationships, *control* is viewed in a logic of 'constraint', *information* is expressed in a logic of 'manipulation', *communication* is lived in a logic of 'avoidance', *relations* are lived in a dynamic of 'exclusion', and there is mistrust linked to 'intentions'. In the two cases (MED103 and MED201) where trust was found whereas the actors belong to 'closed' control relationships, context analysis revealed that this 'trust' towards administration was in fact 'confidence' resulting from the possession of particularly reliable information.

13.4.2 Trust as a foundation for control relationships

When comparing the structure and content of relationships, and applying it to organizational control, we can broadly draw two tendencies. In the 'formalized control' tendency, the idea of control is lived as constraining, information is collected for the individual's own purpose or considered as being manipulated and not very reliable. That is why communication with other groups is avoided. This leads to distrust between groups or trust for which a collective homogeneity cannot be found. In the 'informal control' tendency, the focus is on dialogue and information sharing, which favours the reliability of information, the desire to meet other groups of actors and to develop communication situations. Trust exists and is based on the good intentions assigned to others.

The discourse analysis process provided the opportunity to evaluate the pertinence of the typology of trust built at the beginning of the study, as a pre-analysis grid. It showed that each of trust foundations (intentions/morality, competencies/experience, reputation, rules/procedures, and institution) found an echo in actors' discourse. If the more specific question of intentions is emphasized in the literature,[5] the field reveals that it does not constitute the only potential explanation of the existence or absence of trust. The effects of reputation, rules or competencies on control representations have been mentioned by the actors. In particular, competence-based trust appears as the dominant configuration for financial headquarters.

Although the question of trust is often associated with the relationship between doctors and their nurse team, half of the medical profession expressed trust in controllers, while the other half corresponded to the traditional cliché, by having relationships of mistrust with them. Analysis revealed that trust towards administration and controllers was based on intentions, morality or honesty, which relates to a main foundation of trust typology. The questions of data reliability and of information feedback are particularly important in this case. Trust towards medical staff relies on its competencies, experience or length of service, which concern the second basis of trust identified in the typology. Trust towards peers (other doctors) is based on respect of the rules. Symmetry with mistrust cases is observed. Therefore, trust and mistrust are not the prerogatives of one specific group of actors. Both controllers and medical doctors have experienced it. Whatever their position on what appears to be a complex relationship (trust or mistrust), its main and most common foundation relies on the perception of others' intentions.

13.4.3 Trust and information: when Ego interprets Alter's intentions ...

This study shows that each of trust foundations found an echo in actors' discourse. Nevertheless, intentions-based trust remains the central feature for both the controllers and the medical profession. This constitutes an important result of the research at two levels. First, although those groups are traditionally presented as opposite in the context of management, in each of them some actors are positioned toward trust. The controllers who believe in a 'personalized' or 'mix' approach of control situations express an intentions-based trust, which is legitimated by the personal relationships they have with doctors. We find the same configuration for the medical profession. Those who keep an 'open' attitude towards control situations, do not doubt the controllers' intentions and allow trust relationships to emerge. The doctors who remain 'closed' to control situations question controllers' intentions and express distrust towards control members, control tools, and control situations. Intention thus justifies both trust and distrust relationships. Second, this results challenge the various typologies of trust foundations, dimensions or characteristics that do not identify one particular element as being a strong trust driver.

It was shown that the actor's intention was an important foundation in the creation and working of trust relationships. The nature of the relationship between the persons exchanging what we have called 'information' influences information itself. We believe that when an individual trusts the issuer (source) of a message, the information received tends to be interpreted in a favourable manner. When an individual distrusts the issuer (source) of a message, he tends to interpret in an unfavourable way the information received or the request.

More precisely, trust as expressed in the actor's discourse or that emerges from its analysis, influences information exchange in control situations. We observe that when the individual trusts the person, the institution or the information source, he relies on the 'objective' information, namely 'data'. When the individual does not trust the person, the institution or the source of information, he does not consider the 'objective' information, but tries to interpret this information and derives a message. The notion of 'message' is thus extremely contingent and depends on the representation we make of the other individual, of his intentions and competencies. In the case of mistrust the 'objective' data gives way to a more subjective interpretation, possibly far from the original meaning, of the one that the issuer was willing to transmit. March and Simon (1958, p. 176) indicate that individuals' perceptions that clash with the original framework are filtered before reaching consciousness, or are reinterpreted or rationalized in order to set aside discord. Thus, the way the situation is defined represents a simplified outline of the objective situation, since every data entering the decision process is filtered. We thus promote the following propositions:

1. When trust exists between two actors, data-information supports control relationships;
2. When trust is not established between two actors, message-information supports control relationships.

As a consequence, technical aspects of management tool implementation cannot be dissociated from the psycho-sociological and cognitive aspects that guide individuals in their choices and actions. Organizations are interpretation systems (Daft and Weick, 1984) in which actors must evolve from simple agents to interpreters, thus compelled to assume, in addition to the traditional operating risk, a cognitive risk (Lorino, 1995, p. 280). We believe that trust reduces the cognitive risk, that is to say the risk of making wrong interpretations.

13.5 Conclusion

The different representations groups of actors have of organizational relationships are consequences of their struggle for information, since control and change modify the power equilibrium. The introduction of management tools brings new information into control situations, thus confronting actors with a 'symbolic violence'. This leads to resistance to the implementation of those control systems. The study also reveals that if we want to overcome that resistance, we must work on the actors' representation of control relationships, making them closer to each other. Hardy et al. (2000) showed that it was possible for individuals to engage in discursive activity and to access different discourses to generate new meanings that help – or hinder – the enactment of particular strategies. In a similar manner, as the study reveals that information exchange constitutes the base of control relationships, we argue that it is necessary to concentrate on this exchange to efficiently impact on the change process. In other words, it is the context in which the relationship operates (the interaction) that influences the meaning that individuals give to information transmitted to and received by others. Information does not carry any meaning by itself, but only in relation to an interactional context.

The question then becomes how to influence in a favourable way the exchange of information. We assume that the nature of the relationship determines the bases of information exchange. We show that trust relationships that exist between two or more actors, influence in a favourable way the actor's interpretation of the information received. When trust exists, the exchange will be based on the 'objective data' transmitted between the issuer and the receiver in the communication process. When the relationship is based on distrust, the exchange will depend on the 'subjective message' interpreted by the receiver of the information in the communication process. By focusing on a very particular aspect of social networks and human dynamics, the study specifies and illustrates the importance of *sense-making* (Weick, 1979, 1995) in organizational analysis.

Understanding how sense-making is co-produced in interactions (Alvarez and Oriot, 2007), how meaning and discourse are embedded (Alvarez, 2006), are crucial for a critical perspective on managerial change in organizations.

Notes

1. The notion of 'control relationship' refers, in the chapter, to the formal and informal relationships that emerge between individuals and groups, relative to a specific management device. Control relationships are embedded in a network of other interpersonal relationships (such as power, influence, trust...) and organizational communication processes.

2. For a detailed presentation of the discourse analysis process, see Alvarez (2002).
3. Breton and Wintrobe (1982) explain that individuals choose to be efficient or inefficient in their relations with their superior. The latter has to 'pay' the subordinates for their efficiency. What is exchanged in those informal networks are services (perquisites, etc.). The networks rely on trust relationships, as a means of coordination. This aspect has been developed in the case of interfirm networks.
4. For a more detailed analysis of the process of deconstruction and reconstruction, see Easley and Alvarez-Pompilius (2004).
5. The agency theory, which constitutes a strong reference in management control research, gives an important place to individuals' opportunism. This opportunism can be understood as a lack of trust in the intentions of the agent, which is considered as always attempting to cheat the principal.

References

Alvarez, F. (2002) 'Building typologies from discourse: a study of control relationships in a French public hospital', *5th International Conference on Organizational Discourse*, July, London.

Alvarez, F. (2006) 'Production de discours managérial et changement organisationnel', *Revue Entreprise et Histoire*, no. 42, April, 84–104.

Alvarez, F. and F. Oriot (2007) 'L'interaction chercheur–sujets organisationnels: du discours au sens', in A.C. Martinet (ed.) *Sciences du Management. Epistémique, pragmatique et éthique* (Coll. Fnege: Editions Vuibert), 139–64.

Alvesson, M. and D. Karreman (2000) 'Varieties of discourse: On the study of organizations through discourse analysis', *Human Relations*, 53 (9), 1125–49.

Bardin, L. (2001) *L'analyse de contenu*, 10th edn (Paris: PUF).

Barrett, F. and S. Srivastva (1991) 'History as a mode of inquiry in organizational life: a role for human cosmogony', *Human Relations*, 44, 236–44.

Berry, M. (1983) 'Une technologie invisible. L'impact des instruments de gestion sur l'évolution des systèmes humains', *Cahier du CRG (Centre de Recherche en Gestion)*, Paris, no. 1133, June.

Bouquin, H. (1994) *Les fondements du contrôle de gestion* (Paris: PUF).

Breton, A. and R. Wintrobe (1982) *The Logic of Bureaucratic Conduct, an Economic Analysis of Competition, Exchange, and Efficiency in Private and Public Organizations* (Cambridge University Press).

Burgess, R.G. (1984) *In the Field. An Introduction to Field Research* (London: Unwin Hyman Ltd).

Cauvin, C. (1999) 'Les habits neufs du contrôle de gestion', in *Questions de contrôle*, sous la direction de Lionel Collins (Paris: PUF).

Chia, R. (2000) 'Discourse analysis as organizational analysis', *Organization*, 7(3), 513–18.

Claveranne, J. P. (1996) 'Le management par projet à l'hôpital', *Revue Française de gestion*, 109.

Daft, R.L. and K.E. Weick (1984) 'Towards a model of organizations as interpretation systems', *Academy of Management Review*, 9.

Easley, C.A. and F. Alvarez-Pompilius (2003) 'Qualitative investigations: Evoking change and egalitarianism in a knowledge-based world', *Academy of Management*, August, 6–11.

Easley, C.A. and F. Alvarez-Pompilius (2004) 'A new paradigm for qualitative investigations: Towards an integrative model for evoking change', *Organization Development Journal*, 22 (3).

Eisenhardt, K.M. (1989) 'Building theory from case study research', *Academy of Management Review*, 14 (4), 532–50.

Flamholtz, E.G. (1996) 'Effective organizational control: a framework, applications and implications', *European Management Journal*, 14(6), 596–611.

French, W. L. and Bell, C. H. (1995) *Organization Development* (Englewood Cliffs, NJ: Prentice-Hall, Inc.).

Giddens, A. (1984) *La constitution de la société. Eléments de la théorie de la structuration* (Paris: PUF).

Granovetter, M. (1985) 'Economic action and social structure: the problem of embeddedness', *American Journal of Sociology*, 91 (3), 481–510.

Granovetter, M. (1992) 'Problems of explanation in economic sociology' in N. Nohria and R.G. Eccles (eds) *Networks and Organizations: Structure, Form and Action* (Boston: Harvard Business School Press), 25–56.

Ghidina, M. (1993) 'Organizational control and informal relations: the paradoxical position of middle-status workers', *Research in the Sociology of Organizations*, 11, 33–53.

Hardy, C., I. Palmer and N. Phillips (2000) 'Discourse as strategic resource', *Human Relations*, 53 (9), 1227–48.

Heracleous, L. and J. Hendry (2000) 'Discourse and the study of organization: Toward a structurational perspective', *Human Relations*, 53 (10), 1251–86.

Hofstede, G. (1978) 'The poverty of management control philosophy', *Academy of Management Review*, 3 (3), 450–61.

Huberman, A.M. and M.B. Miles (1991) *Analyse des données qualitatives, Recueil de nouvelles méthodes* (Brussels: De Boeck Université).

Langley, A. (1999) 'Strategies for theorizing from process data', *Academy of Management Review*, 24 (4), 691–710.

Lewis, J. D. and A. Weigert (1985) 'Trust as a social reality', *Social Forces*, 63 (4), 967–85.

Lorino, P. (1995) *Comptes et récits de la performance. Essai sur le pilotage de l'entreprise* (Paris: Editions d'Organisation).

Luhmann, N. (1988) 'Familiarity, confidence, trust: Problems and alternatives' in D. Gambetta (ed.) *Trust, Making and Breaking Cooperative Relations* (Basil Blackwell).

March, J. G. and H.A. Simon (1958) *Les organisations, problèmes psychosociologiques*, 2nd edn (Paris: Dunod), French translation, 1991.

Mintzberg, H. (1982) *Structures et dynamique des organisations* (Paris: Les Editions d'Organisation).

Moisdon, J. C. and D. Tonneau (1999) *La démarche gestionnaire à l'hôpital. 1- Recherches sur la gestion interne* (Paris: Editions Seli Arslan).

Reason, P. (1988) *Human Inquiry in Action, Developments in New Paradigm Research* (Newbury Park, Calif.: Sage Publications).

Robert, A.D. and A. Bouillaguet (1997) *L'analyse de contenu* (Paris: PUF).

Servet, J.M. (1994) 'Paroles données: le lien de confiance', *Revue du MAUSS: À qui se fier? Confiance, interaction et théorie des jeux*, 4, 37–56.

Strauss, A. and J. Corbin (1990) *Basics of Qualitative Research. Grounded Theory Procedures and Techniques* (London: Sage Publications).

Weick, K.E. (1979) *The Social Psychology of Organizing*, 2nd edn (New York: McGraw-Hill, Inc.).

Weick, K.E. (1995) *Sensemaking in Organizations* (London: Sage Publications).

White, H. C. (1991) 'Agency as control', in W. Pratt and R.J. Zeckhauser (eds) *Principals and Agents: the Structure of Business*, 2nd edn (Boston: Harvard Business School Press), 187–212.

Williamson, O. E. (1993) 'Calculativeness, trust and economic organization', *Journal of Law and Economics*, 36, 453–86.

Zucker, L. G. (1986) 'Production of trust: Institutional sources of economic structures, 1840–1920', *Research in Organizational Behavior*, 8, 53–111.

14
Technological Objects through Discourse: a Case Study from the Field of Telemedicine

Attila Bruni
Research Unit on Communication, Organizational Learning and Aesthetics,
Department of Sociology and Social Research, University of Trento, Italy

and

Laura Lucia Parolin
Department of Sociology and Social Research, University of Milan-Bicocca, Italy

Introduction

Contrary to the doctrine that technology and language are distinct domains and that reality articulates itself around the human/artefact dichotomy, for a number of years the view has been put forward that discourse and technology are intimately bound up with each other, and that one of the distinctive features of the contemporary world is the erosion of the boundaries between the human and the artificial (Knorr Cetina, 1997). Thus, more and more studies go beyond the analysis of human contexts and interactions to examine places characterized by complex and technologically dense practices (Law and Mol, 2002); places in which human actors and technological objects work 'together' (Heath and Luff, 2000); or virtual spaces in which human interaction is made possible by technologies (Hine, 2000).

 Besides their problematization of the boundaries that separate the natural from the artificial, shared by these studies is a common interest in technologies and discourses as social practices, or as collective accomplishments (Garfinkel, 1967) of particular forms of order and action. 'They are accomplishments readily achieved by, and routinely to be expected of members acting together, but they nonetheless have to be generated on every occasion, by agents concerned all the time to retain coordination and alignment with each other in order to bring them about' (Barnes, 2001, p. 25).

On the view that technology and discourse are social practices, in this work we will present a case study from the field of telemedicine, a setting where subjects located in different places discuss by means of different technologies, and concentrate on the discursive and technological practices mobilized by the diverse actors participating in the service. In particular, the study will focus on a telecardiology centre, where 60 cardiologists examine electrocardiograms transmitted telephonically by general practitioners: tracks are read on a PC's monitor, they are interpreted and reported by cardiologists, discussed with the doctors, and then sent back by fax to them.

Our analysis will focus on discursive practices as a call into action of the different elements of a heterogeneous network, showing the discursive construction of a new technological object (the telematic ECG) and its alignment with previous elements (patient, previous examinations and so on). We shall show in particular how actors discursively ensure the stability of relations among the various components that make up the reporting of the electronic ECG, as well as the discursive practices deployed in particularly ambiguous and/or problematic situations.

The first section of the contribution sets out the theoretical assumptions behind our analysis.

14.1   Technology and discourse as social practices

After the 'linguistic turn' that dissolved every 'thing' into a form of language and/or cultural representation (Barad, 2003), a 'practice turn' (Schatzki et al., 2001) is now marking a watershed in contemporary debate.

The concept of practice has been variously interpreted by authors, and with reference to diverse disciplinary fields (philosophy, linguistics, sociology), but its origins reside principally in Marxist praxis, in the speech act theory of the later Wittgenstein and of Austin, and in the being-in-the-world of phenomenology (Nicolini et al., 2003). According to this point of view, therefore, an interest in practice means focusing on specific features of the historical–social context and on the activities that construct it, understanding language as a form of action that constructs the surrounding reality, and analysing the interactive processes and volatile equilibria that underpin particular states of the world.

A survey of the diverse traditions and currents of study that gravitate around the concept of practice would be beyond the scope of this work. More modestly it will put forward an interpretation of technologies and discourses as social practices based on a number of cases reported in the literature.

14.1.1 Technology-in-practice

Considering technology as technology-in-practice requires one to accept the idea that technologies are inseparable from their use, that their use is always connected to other tools and practices (Suchman et al., 1999), and that there is an intimate relation between the work setting and the structuring of activities, as Lucy Suchman (1997) observes with regard to 'coordination centres'. For Suchman, coordination centres are typified by air traffic control rooms, places in which technology (telephone lines, radio frequencies, monitors, and so on) is indispensable for the personnel to do their work. She observes the everyday work of flight controllers: how they handle emergency situations, how they communicate with each other and coordinate their work, how they use technologies, and how they act in critical situations. She finds that technologies and objects have predefined roles, but their use is always contextual according to their importance for the actors in particular situations. At the same time, however, whenever people use a technology they leave a trace behind for future action, and with time actors come to view technological objects as more or less relevant or contextual, negotiable or resistant.

The case of infrastructure is emblematic. Typically, infrastructure is taken for granted: when we turn on a tap because we need water, we rarely think of the vast infrastructure necessary for us to be able to perform that action. The question becomes more complex, however, when we begin to interest ourselves in the situation of those who cannot take the existence of a particular infrastructure for granted: for an engineer designing and building a railway line, the rails are not part of the infrastructure but constitute one of the objectives of his/her work. Hence, objects and technologies that are simply part of the background for some are a matter for discussion for others. Infrastructure is consequently a relational concept (Star, 1999) which is defined relative to specific organizational practices.

Take for example the technical evolution of hospital beds (Strauss et al., 1985, p. 102). Initially, the beds were fixed, and helping an immobilized patient to change position was part of the nurse's 'comfort work', while s/he also ensured that the patient had assumed the correct posture for his/her condition. Since the mechanization of hospital beds, patients have been able to change position simply by pressing some buttons, but this is not sufficient to ensure their comfort. In fact, the autonomy of movement by (the beds of) patients has led to indifference among the nursing staff towards the posture of the patient, whose comfort is thus subject to further problems caused by this neglect. The use of new machinery/technology therefore modifies not only what from a distance appears to be simply an 'infrastructure' but also the 'autonomy' of patients, and especially the more general trajectories of action and organization of work involved therein (Strauss et al., 1985, p. 67).

Analysis of technology-in-practice therefore requires one to focus on how technological objects are constitutive of organizing. There are contexts in which humans and non-humans do not constitute a dichotomy but rather 'an ecology of representations' (Gibson, 1979): persons, symbols and machines operate jointly to structure and renew understanding of a social and organizational situation. The process that is able to give (relative) spatio-temporal stability to the organization of objects (and therefore technology-in-practice) is what John Law (1994, p. 2) has called the heterogeneous engineering of discourses, bodies, texts, machines and architectures, all symmetrically[1] involved in the social and its performance.

14.1.2   Discourse as practice

Just as considering technology as a social practice means going beyond the technical content of technologies to look at the heterogeneous engineering of their realization, so considering discourse in its practical dimension means going beyond the content of language to conceive discourse as an activity able to impose order and meaning on words, actions and material objects (Foucault, 1976; Laclau and Mouffe, 1985), as well as being an occasion to perform the meanings of words, actions and material objects (Garfinkel, 1967). An emblematic example of what is meant by discourse as a practice is provided by the ethnomethodologist Melvin Pollner's (1987) discussion of the mundane nature of scientific reasoning. The Azande tribe use the 'infallible poison oracle' to foretell the future and to solve problems. They ritually prepare a poisonous substance (*benge*) and feed it to a chicken. They then ask their question and wait for the answer from the *benge*: if the chicken lives the verdict is positive; if the chicken dies, it is negative. But now the Azende seek confirmation of the verdict and repeat the ritual, giving the poison to another chicken. This time, however, for the previous verdict to be confirmed the poison must have the opposite effect (if the first chicken has lived, the second must die, and vice versa). Almost always the two chickens suffer the same fate, the oracle delivers an ambiguous answer, and (one would expect) its 'infallibility' is disproved. Yet for the Azande this is not so, because from their point of view there may be good reasons why the oracle has failed to work: the poisonous potion has been prepared badly; a taboo has been violated; supernatural forces have intervened; the spirits are angry; the question was wrong; the oracle wanted to say something else; and so on.

Fundamentally, therefore, it is 'normal' for an Azande that the second verdict should not coincide with the first one. But one has to look at discourse as practice in order to understand how this normality is produced. Independently of the veracity of the justifications adduced by the Azande, it was discursive practice that ensured the stability of the relations among the various elements in the situation (the question, the poison, the chicken, the oracle, the second chicken, and the final verdict) and simultaneously performed a reality founded on ambiguity and the existence of supernatural forces. As practice, therefore, the Azande's discourse involved the assumptions on which their community's knowledge was founded, and through discursive practices this knowledge was transmitted and translated into appropriate forms of action.

This, moreover, is a point widely endorsed today by studies of knowledge-in-practice (Nicolini et al., 2003). Its philosophical origins reside in Wittgenstein's language games and their development in social terms by the literature on situated learning and communities of practice (Lave and Wenger, 1991).

Significant in this regard is the case of the Xerox technicians studied by Orr (1996). When technicians went to a customer to repair a photocopier, they frequently found on inspecting the machine that they were unable to understand the reason for its malfunctioning. At this point, the technicians would 'interview' the users of the photocopier, knowing that events other than a technical fault were probably the cause of the problem: tea or coffee spilt on the machine; the photocopier was malfunctioning and someone had tried to repair it; the users had not followed the instructions for switching it on and off; and so on. This knowledge sprang from the discursive practices of the community of technicians, who were accustomed to swapping 'war stories' (Orr, 1996) about the most significant episodes encountered in their work. Comprised in these stories were the memory and knowledge of the community, so that it was possible to find in the discursive practice of their narration the forms of action deemed valid by the members of the community. As stated, it is not so much in the content of discourses that the practical dimension resides; rather, it is in the discursive practices that one appreciates the performativity of language and its ability to hold together the heterogeneous elements deployed in organizational action (Bruni and Gherardi, 2001).

14.1.3   Medical practice as the alignment of heterogeneous elements

To provide an example of what is meant by regarding technologies and discourses as social and organizational practices (and to introduce the empirical case that we describe later), we refer to a body of literature that has developed at the intersection of disciplines which, though diverse, share a common interest in contemporary clinical settings. For some years, in fact, increasing numbers of sociologists have set about opening the 'black box' of medical practice and knowledge in order to examine the interweaving between organizational practices and technologies, scientific and mundane knowledge (Elston, 1997; Berg, 1997). Medical practice has therefore been thematized as a process of alignment and mobilization of heterogeneous elements (data, laboratory tests, doctors, patients, health facilities, political decisions, and so on) in which 'patients' bodies, lives and subjectivities become entrenched within networks of technologies, medical personnel and institutional arrangements' (Casper and Berg, 1995, p. 402).

Drawing on the insights of ethnomethodology (Garfinkel, 1967; Sudnow, 1967), the majority of these authors have concentrated on the processes of standardization and alignment of the various elements that combine to transform the 'problem of the patient' into a problem that can be handled by organizational routines. Berg (1997) uses the expression 'heterogeneous management of the patient's trajectories' to highlight that the outcome of medical action does not necessarily depend on a pre-established and coherent sequence of decisions, but is instead the emergent effect of the encounter among diverse materials and performances that takes place within a network. The solution of the 'patient problem' is therefore the result of a translation process (Callon, 1986), a 'result-in-course' (Lynch, 1985), to which the status of a decision is attributed only a posteriori, and internally to which the original problem is redefined.

Various authors have examined how the reciprocal influence between everyday organizational practices and work instruments enables medical practice to be translated into an ordered and enduring series of actions and interventions (Law and Mol, 2002). Medical protocols and guidelines are thus viewed as 'technoscientific scripts which crystallize multiple trajectories' (Timmermans and Berg, 1997, p. 275), as well as actors in organizational spaces (Bruni, 2005). The purpose is to emphasize how the coherence and universality of medicine are constructed into an amalgam of knowledge, routines and assembly techniques, a heterogeneous mix of bodies, machines, images, estimates, interactive and discursive practices (Berg and Mol, 1998). Within this amalgam, technology is meaningful inasmuch as it is technology-in-practice – that is, constantly standing in relation to other technologies, practices, actors and forms of professional knowledge (Timmermans and Berg, 2003), just as discursive practices comprise the forms of knowledge and action that substantiate medical activity. Alignment among these elements is not a natural phenomenon, and for this reason how it is accomplished is of interest from the organizational point of view.

14.2 Studying medical technologies through discursive practices

In order to analyse the technologies and practices that give material form to clinical activity, authors employ mainly ethnographic methods and historical analysis of the medical literature (Berg, 1997; Berg and Mol, 1998). In our case, however, it will be the discursive practices enacted by/among various specialists (in general medicine and cardiology) that will show how a network of heterogeneous elements is deployed in the treatment of an individual patient. We would stress that we are aware of the fact that sociologists have widely analysed medical discourse using the techniques of conversational analysis (Atkinson, 1995; Silverman, 1987; Cicourel, 1986, 1999), and that so-called 'cooperative supported communicative work' and/or workplace studies (Heath and Luff, 2000) have furnished interesting insights into micro-interactions in work settings.

However, it will be precisely our reference to a different tradition that will enable us to interpret discourse as the alignment of different social–material elements (Bruni and Gherardi, 2001) and to show how it is possible to construe conversation as a performative act that produces and ensures the relations among a network of elements that do not naturally go together (Bruni et al., 2007).

14.2.1　The empirical case: a brief overview

The data presented is part of a broader research project on knowledge and organizational learning in virtual work settings. The research focused on a number of case studies from the field of telemedicine, a setting where subjects, with different levels of *expertise* and located in different places, discuss by means of different technologies, producing the encounter of a plurality of organizational and professional appurtenances.

The setting for our analysis is a telecardiology centre in North Italy – the Health Telematic Network (HTN) – created in 1998 and which was at the time of the research the most advanced telecardiological call centre in Italy. The centre uses the services of cardiologists distributed over several locations in the country who take turns to examine electrocardiograms sent (telephonically) by general practitioners (henceforth GPs) in various regions. The GP records the patient's ECG with a portable apparatus. The recordings can be made in the doctor's surgery or in the patient's home, because the apparatus can store ten or so ECG traces so that they can be sent at a later time.

A call centre coordinates the consultation process, putting GPs into contact with cardiologists and handling the transmission of the ECGs. The traces are sent by the GP, they are received by the call centre by means of a specific software program and distributed among the cardiologists in service, who see them displayed on their PC screens. The traces are discussed via telephone with the GP and then sent back via fax with the report attached.

The data analysed in what follows was collected by listening to all the telephone calls made to the centre in one month (November 2002) for a total of just over 1000 calls. Given the large volume of data, the first phase of the research involved constructing a form which could be used to describe the general features of the service schematically. The form was tested on 30 phone calls (which was the average number made in a day) and then validated by comparing its compilation by two researchers listening to the same phone calls, who thereafter listened to different phone calls.

This preliminary filing work yielded the background data on the service. The form was designed to enable classification of the most general events and to understand the various uses made of the service. In particular, it was evident that the telecardiology service was almost always used to handle routine events (like checks on known cardiopathic patients and the compiling of certificates of 'robust constitution'). Indeed, only 6 per cent of contacts were prompted by urgent or critical situations, and only 7 per cent of calls led to the patient's emergency hospitalization.

The calls were distributed more or less equally between the morning (52 per cent) and the afternoon (48 per cent) and were concentrated in the first five days of the week (90 per cent). The average duration of conversations was around two and a half minutes. The form of the interaction was highly standardized, both because of the protocols used in cardiology (which homogenize the data and criteria to which the two doctors refer) and because the cardiologists had to compile a patient card for each ECG consultancy, and therefore asked the GPs standard questions, almost always in the same order. However, as we shall see, it is not so much the content of the questions and/or answers that characterizes a teleconsultation as the discursive practices used by the actors.

14.3 Discursive practices as the alignment of a heterogeneous network

The most striking feature of the telephone calls was their invariant structure: the cardiologist opened the conversation; the GP explained the reason for the call and described the case; the cardiologist asked for further information; and the GP replied (see Table 14.1).

As shown by the transcript, the conversation is also influenced by the fact that usually when the consultation begins the cardiologist has not yet received the ECG (which takes around 50 seconds to transmit/receive). While s/he is waiting he asks the GP about the patient and then interrupts (more or less brusquely) when he has received the trace. The activity of interpretation seems to be aproblematic, and the telephone call lasts as long as is necessary to close the conversation. Consequently, the presence of a telematic ECG (and the wait for it) gives the two doctors a chance to 'teleconsult', and the ECG is an active element which is read but also has its own 'voice' in the interaction. However, although the ECG is indeed an important element, it is not the only object present in the consultation.

14.3.1 Aligning the elements

The discourse of the two doctors calls into play and activates a network of elements (objective assessments, references to other examinations, risk factors, pharmacological therapy), the alignment of which

Table 14.1   Typical conversational structure of telecardiological calls

Feature of phone call	Conversation	Times
Opening	C: Hallo? GP: Ciao, this is… C: This is…, ciao, tell me	5 sec
Patient description	GP: I've done this electrocardiogram mostly as a control. This male patient has just been with me…I found an initial hypertension…he's dyspneic…dyspneic, slightly, especially…when stressed…he's overweight and a heavy smoker. It's a check more than anything else…	5–23 sec
Request for further information	C: Is he on medication, this man? GP: No, no. C: Wait till I get the rest of the trace, so tell me…have you put him on something for the pressure, or…	23–38 sec
GP's reply with further information	GP:…no, no, it's a check now, because I've done…I've started,…I've also had him take haemotochemical tests…to see whether, you know, whether there are…	38–53 sec
Interruption when ECG is received	C:…I understand. Listen, he's got a sinus rhythm, arterioventricular delivery within the norm. He's got an incomplete right branch block. The rest of the trace is perfectly normal. There's nothing else as far as I can see.	53 sec to 1 min 24 sec
Closure	GP: I agree C: I'll send you the trace, then…ciao GP: Right…yes..yes, thanks…ciao	1 min 24 to 1 min 34 sec

contributed to the patient's trajectory. This is particularly visible in those (frequent) situations where there is no automatic correspondence between the patient's state of health as shown by clinical assessment and the ECG trace, which obliges the two doctors to construct a discourse able to follow other paths and, by involving other objects, redefine the meaning of the situation:

(Greetings)

GP: I've had this ECG done on a patient already affected with chronic ischemic cardiopathy because he felt ill while he was eating, he felt faint and a weight on his stomach (…)

C: Mah...the trace doesn't seem...how is he now?

GP: He's lying down now...he feels weak...he hasn't got dyspnoea, absolutely not...he still feels this weight...I think it's indigestion, I mean, he needs to vomit...but, you know...I preferred to do the ECG...

C: I'd say...there aren't any evident alterations...of course, then you have to look at the clinical [assessment]...because these things, sometimes...these things are a bit tricky...For the moment I'd keep an eye on him...there's a left axial deviation...(...) there's...some ventricular extrasystole...(...) Is he taking Cardioaspirin?

GP: No, in fact I wanted to give it to him...

C: ...but he has a history of ischemic cardiopathy but he hasn't had acute episodes?

GP: No, no. Perhaps...five years ago, there was something...when the chronic ischemia diagnosis was made...

C: ...I'd wait a bit longer...how old is he?

GP: 85.

C: The risks are clearly there, if the thing doesn't sort itself out, I'd have him looked at, just to be on the safe side...(...) but, at the moment the trace doesn't show anything...

GP: ...out of the ordinary...

C: ...although traces can sometimes be negative...(...)

GP: ...right.. in fact...that's true, you can't always rely on the trace...

C: ...no, no there's a good percentage of heart attacks with normal traces...except that this...well...I mean...at 80 years old, of course, some problem always comes out!

GP: Yes, I'll give him an antacid and then we'll see...

(Salutations)

This telephone call shows that when the ECG and the patient do not intersect (the ECG is normal but the patient feels ill), various elements are discursively mobilized, and the trace moves into the background, losing its status as a privileged object. To paraphrase Latour (2002), it as if the trace has become a 'labyrinth' through which the two doctors must find their way. Thus, previous ECGs, reports on other examinations, medications, family histories, become elements that must be discursively activated and aligned in order to restore meaning to the situation. The cardiologist and the GP seem almost to suggest interpretations to each other, as in a dance where two actors must lean on each other to find a point of balance which allows the movement of their bodies. The action of the cardiologist and the GP, in fact, does not take place in an empty space, but internally to a broader medical practice. It is consequently to the latter that they turn their attention in the absence of points of contact between patient and ECG.

In the above transcript, for example, the doctors collaborate to discredit, discursively, the predictive capacity and reliability of an ECG, mobilizing elements which though contrasting are meaningful in everyday medical practice. The cardiologist deploys a discursive practice typical of medicine (Cicourel, 1986), showing that there is a scientific basis for his disparagement of the value of the trace ('there's a good percentage of heart attacks with normal traces...') and then substantiates his assertion with a common-sense observation ('at 80 years old, of course, some problem always comes out!'). The GP, for his part, adheres to the same practice, agreeing that an ECG (on its own) is unable to ensure the stability of the elements ('that's true, you can't always rely on the trace...') and identifying a common-sense remedy (an antacid) as able (momentarily) to 'align' the patient's case.

14.3.2 Framing and postscripting

During the teleconsultation, therefore, it is essential for the doctors to deploy discourses that make the trace and the patient compatible. For this to occur, it may happen (as in the case just seen) that GP and cardiologist align themselves around a discourse whose task is to belittle the significance of the ECG in order to foreground everyday medical practice. But the reverse may happen as well: the doctors instead discredit the patient's symptoms, activating from the first exchange onwards (as in the following case) complicity on the latter's unreliability:

(Greetings)

GP: Ciao, she's a girl who's always got these pains here... she's already been examined by a cardiologist but... (laughs)

C: ... (laughing) there's nothing you can do... she's convinced she's going to die tomorrow...

GP: ... right... but I can't die for her...

(they laugh)

C: It seems that everything's fine here, a sinusal rhythm, normal atrioventricular delivery... there's a slight delay in right branch conduction. There's an incomplete right branch block... that's almost normal, especially in women, and anyway there's no ischemic alteration, and there are no significant alterations in the repolarization

GP: OK...

C: ... I'd say that everything's fine...

GP: ... at least we've made her happy...

C: ... we've made her happy... I don't think so... according to me, she'd be happier if we told her she had something...

GP: All right, so let's tell her...

(Salutations with laughter)

As he begins to describe the patient, the GP already introduces elements that point to a non-problematic reading of the trace. At first, the GP does not describe the patient's pain but gives a generic interpretation, suggesting that the nature of the pain is almost a characteristic of the patient ('she's a girl who's always got these pains here...'), to the point that other specialists have not been able to resolve her 'problem' ('she's already been examined by a cardiologist but...'). The ECG is therefore invoked as an element of accountability (Garfinkel, 1967; Timmermans and Berg, 1997), which furnishes the GP with 'objective' and 'scientific' arguments for transforming the patient's problem into a problem manageable in terms of everyday routines ('I can't die for her...'). Moreover, that it is the performance of the consultation itself (regardless of the outcome of the reading of the trace) that resolves the patient's problem is made explicit by the final exchange, when the cardiologist's ironic suggestion ('according to me, she'd be happier if we told her she had something...') is promptly taken up by the GP ('All right, so let's tell her...').

But it is above all the initial framing activity that produces the discursive alignment of the actors. Pollner and McDonald-Wikler (1985) use the terms 'framing' and 'postcripting' to denote those situations in which the actors establish a set, before or after the action, in which the same action is then interpreted. As in the case just seen, therefore, characteristics of the situation (the unreliability of the patient) activated before the event occurs (the referral of the ECG) then return within the event itself and, indeed, delineate its meaning boundaries (so that an 'incomplete right branch block' may become 'almost normal'). That the entire consultation is marked by a framing activity is once again evident in the final moves of the conversation, when the cardiologist shares and reinforces the GP's framing by suggesting to him a response coherent more with the set than with the ECG trace.

Thus, while framing is used *ex ante* to generate a 'space' of signification for the (subsequent) action, postscripting corresponds to 'commanding the already done' (Pollner and McDonald-Wikler, 1985, p. 245) and therefore to the retrospective reproduction of meaning for the event. Examples of this activation mechanism are easily found in cases (like the one that follows) where, although the ECG does not signal any problems, the patient's symptoms acquire meaning in relation to its importance within the medical practice:

(Greetings)

GP: the patient was born in '62 ... a couple of hours ago he had a lipothymic episode accompanied by sweating, now he's got sternocostal pain but in correspondence with the joints ... irradiates when palpating ... he has a pain in the right subscapular region ...

C: ... but is he cardiopathic?

GP: No ... this episode lasted 5 minutes I think ...

C: ... he's not cardiopathic? did he lose consciousness?

GP: Yes, he had this lipthymic episode and was attended to, then he recovered.

C: But did he lose consciousness?

GP: Yes, for 5 minutes.

C: So he had a syncope ...?

GP: ... a syncopal event, sure ...

C: Mah, here the trace is normal ... but someone who's had a syncope should be kept under observation ...

GP: Right, so the trace is normal ...

C: ... the trace is fine ... but does he suffer from any disease?

GP: No, now he's only overweight ... he doesn't take medication ...

C: Do you think he should be hospitalized?

GP: Yes, I reckon so ... what do you advise?

C: Syncope is by definition something rather important ...

GP: Right, so I'll have the checks made ... thanks.

(Salutations)

In this case, the cardiologist and the GP find it difficult to construct a meaningful context for the event, to the point that for a moment they exchange roles, with the cardiologist asking the GP for advice on what should be done ('Do you think he should be hospitalized?'). The way out therefore results from a postscripting practice: the cardiologist responds to the GP's 'advice' by shifting the attention from the meaning of the

ECG to the meaning of a syncope within medical practice and therefore, 'by definition', offers a solution to the problem.

14.3.3 Footing

Framing and postscripting are often accompanied by another discursive practice: footing (Goffman, 1974, 1980), or the dialectic that enables people to align themselves within a predetermined frame and disrupt its coordinates, because once 'in step with it' they are able to disturb its rhythm and deviate its path:

(Greetings)

GP: The girl's always been in good condition, her grandmother's recently died...she has a familiarity with quite severe diabetes (...) and her father's had a stroke. She said that she's had night-time episodes when she felt her heart racing...and that it was missing beats. I advised her to have some thyroid tests...but there shouldn't be anything serious.

C: The trace is absolutely normal...

GP: ...right!

C: Exactly, the electrocardiogram is absolutely normal...there are no tachycardias, there are no extrasystoles...also because she's young, this woman...

GP: ...but in fact it was she who asked me for it...I realized she was going through a particular time...(...) and I did what she wanted...but I reckon it was more to do with the thyroid than a cardiac problem...

C: ...also because a woman of this age...thinking about a cardio-pathy...

GP: ...I would never have thought of it, it was she who asked me (laughs)...

C: ...exactly...

GP: ...more at the psychological level...to reassure her...

C: ...so reassure her...

(Salutations)

In this conversation, the discursive alignment between the GP and the cardiologist seems to be the emergent result of the interaction itself between the two doctors. The cardiologist interjects in the GP's discourse by aligning himself on the normality of the trace, but he introduces a change of 'rhythm' by referring to the age of the patient, which should already have induced the GP to rule out cardiological problems ('the electrocardiogram is absolutely normal... also because she's young...'). At this point the GP has to tune in with the cardiologist's discourse; an operation performed through the distinction made by the GP between cardiological medical practices to which the specialist alludes and those of a GP who knows his patients and understands their needs ('I realized she was going through a particular time... and I did what she wanted'). This last change of rhythm in the conversation allows the GP again to deviate the course of the discourse, and the entire conversation between doctor and cardiologist thus reacquires meaning as a medical (discursive) practice intended to reassure the patient ('so reassure her').

14.3.4   Delegating: non-humans and medical practice

The final discursive practice deployed by the doctors in order to have coherence between traces and patients concerns the ability of the two actors to delegate the performance of the clinical practice to non-humans, which they construct as active subjects within the teleconsultation:

(Greetings)

> GP: The patient has already had two ECGs done with other doctors, but she says they couldn't read the V1. She's got to have surgery and she must have an ECG, let's try with mine...
>
> C: ...the trace is not very good, in fact, but the V1 is clear and it has an incomplete right branch block, it has low voltages in the precordials... is she robust?
>
> GP: No.
>
> C: This here is certainly due to the position of the electrodes...
>
> GP: ...eh...I know...except that...where shall I put them? I mean, if it put them...
>
> C: ...I don't know...
>
> GP: ...they probably go too low in the sense that...
>
> C: ...no no, it's certainly not that. The reason is this...probably... so, anyway the position is weird because this type of rotation with the...from V1 to V5 there's an extremely low R, and this you get with clockwise rotations, for example in a broncopneumopathy patient, if she isn't one, or if she's thin, perhaps with a drip-shaped heart, we should have a normal rotation. Here, probably it's either the position of the electrodes or she's so thin that you get a rib... and a rib is disastrous.
>
> GP: Ehm...that's what I suspect.

C: Yes, it sometimes happens, and it's probably the position of the electrodes... it's as if all the recordings were made from the front... it's probably either that the electrical axle is rotated askew or there's an adhesion problem with the electrodes. Anyway, from a practical point of view, the trace is compatible with the woman's young age... it has a frequency of 65 and an incomplete right branch block... (...) I report a slow progression of the R wave, but with no pathological significance...

GP: ... Right...

(Salutations)

That non-humans play an active role in medical practice, and more generally in organizational settings, is well established in the literature (Law, 1994; Berg, 1997; Knorr Cetina and Bruegger, 2002), and it was already apparent in the previous telephone calls, where (for example) medicines were sometimes attributed the capacity to substitute for and/or substantiate clinical action. The above transcript, however, shows a more radical delegation, and moreover one involving an object not typically part of medical practice, but without which teleconsultancy would certainly not be possible: the apparatus which records the ECG traces.

The framing work with which the GP depicts the patient as non-problematic (she needs the trace for surgery, not for cardiological problems) enables the cardiologist to recognize the anomalies in the trace as due, not to pathological factors but to errors in the positioning of the apparatus, which thus becomes the focus of the discourse. The two doctors discuss the height at which the apparatus should be placed, the adherence of the electrodes on the patient's body, her thin thorax, the interference caused by the ribs, the shape of the heart, as if all these things could influence the recording of the electrocardiogram. From a certain point of view, the doctors' discourse constructs the patient's body in parallel with the 'body' of the apparatus, in an endeavour to align human and non-human 'bits and pieces' (ribs, electrodes, heart, R wave, and so on). It is interesting that this parallel construction of 'bodies' manifests the blending of tacit and aesthetic knowledge which forms the background to medical practice (Polanyi, 1958; Strati, 2003). The patient's physique (thin/robust), the 'weird' rotation of the electrical axle, the ribs that are 'disastrous', the recording that seems to have been all 'made from the front': these are all expressions that do not impede the advancement of the conversation; indeed, they seem to facilitate it.

Constructing a narrative able to align all these various elements thus permits the cardiologist to conclude that the trace is 'compatible' with the patient's age, and to report to the GP in neutral and almost incidental tones (at the end of the conversation) a 'slow progression of the R wave, but with no pathological significance'. Bearing in mind that a slow progression of the R wave is usually associated with infarct, one realizes that the cardiologist's entire discourse makes sense as a discursive translation of the meaning possessed by the various elements and their relations 'from a practical point of view' (as the cardiologist emphasizes) – that is, from within professional medical knowledge and action. These latter no longer concern human bodies alone but technical apparatuses as well, and they no longer consist of material practices alone but of discursive ones as well.

14.4   Conclusions

By means of a description of the discursive practices enacted by the GP and the cardiologist we have shown how teleconsulting activity is constituted by the alignment of heterogeneous elements mobilized and interrelated in order to make the ECG trace and the patient's health mutually consistent. The processes enacted by the cardiologist and the GP to perform the alignment have been identified as framing and postscripting: that is, the concrete ways in which the actors construct an interpretation set which enables them to generate, a priori or a posteriori, a signification 'space' for action. Together with framing and postscripting, we have identified a further way to handle the alignment process, namely 'footing', which is the discursive practice that enables speakers to align a different frame to themselves through agreement, thereby effecting a change of rhythm. Finally, we have identified a strategy based on the delegation to non-humans of clinical practice, turning them into active subjects in the performance of medical practice. These processes constitute the concrete modes in which discursive practices operate, highlighting the capacity of discourse to hold together the heterogeneity of the elements mobilized in respect of forms of action deemed valid by the members of the community. The professional medical practice enacted in teleconsultation therefore rotates around the ability to deploy expert discursive practices. In other words, being able to manage the elements and align the network is knowledge constitutive of the professional practice of the doctor engaged in teleconsultancy. This analysis of discursive practices and expert competences highlights the influence that the introduction of information and communication technologies (even, as we have seen, a simple telephone) may have on work practices by generating new forms of expert knowledge and by translating the practice of this knowledge: from diagnosis of a present patient to interaction with a distant doctor, from material action to discursive practices.

Note

1. The notion of symmetry was first introduced in the sociology of science (Bloor, 1976) and was developed further by actor network theory (Latour, 1987; Law, 1992) in order to explore the creation of social, natural and technological phenomena without distinguishing a priori between human actors, on the one hand, and technical or natural objects on the other.

References

Atkinson, P. (1995) *Medical Talk and Medical Work* (London: Sage).

Barad, K. (2003) 'Posthumanist performativity: Toward an understanding of how matter comes to matter', *Signs*, 28 (3), 801–31.

Barnes, B. (2001) 'Practice as collective action' in T.R. Schatzki, K. Knorr Cetina and E. von Savigny (eds) *The Practice Turn in Contemporary Theory* (London: Routledge), 17–29.

Berg, M. (1997) *Rationalizing Medical Work* (Cambridge, Mass.: MIT Press).

Berg, M. and A. Mol (eds) (1998) *Differences in Medicine: Unraveling Practices, Techniques and Bodies* (Durham: Duke University Press).

Bloor, D. (1976) *Knowledge and Social Imagery* (London: Routledge and Kegan Paul).

Bruni, A. (2005) 'Shadowing software and clinical records: On the ethnography of non-humans and heterogeneous contexts', *Organization*, 12 (3), 357–78.

Bruni, A. and S. Gherardi (2001) 'Omega's story: the heterogeneous engineering of a gendered professional self' in S. Whitehead and M. Dent (eds) *Knowledge, Identity and the New Professional* (London: Routledge), 174–98.

Bruni, A., S. Gherardi and L. Parolin (2007) 'Knowing in a system of fragmented knowledge', *Mind, Culture and Activity*, 14, 1–20.

Callon, M. (1986) 'The sociology of an actor-network: the case of the electric vehicle' in M. Callon, J. Law and A. Rip (eds) *Mapping the Dynamic of Science and Technology* (London: Macmillan), 19–35.

Casper, M.J. and M. Berg (1995) 'Constructivistic perspectives on medical work: Medical practices and science and technology studies', *Science, Technology, and Human Values*, 20 (4), 395–407.

Cicourel, A.V. (1986) 'The reproduction of objective knowledge: Common sense reasoning in medical decision making' in G. Bohme and N. Stehr (eds) *The Knowledge Society. The Growing Impact of Scientific Knowledge on Social Relations* (Dordrecht and Boston: Reidel), 87–122.

Cicourel, A.V. (1999) 'The interaction of cognitive and cultural models in health care delivery' in S. Sarangi and S. Roberts (eds) *Talk, Work and Institutional Order.*

Discourse in Medical, Mediation and Management Settings (Berlin and New York: Walter de Gruyter), 183–224.

Elston, M.A. (1997) *The Sociology of Medical Science and Technology* (Oxford: Blackwell).

Foucault, M. (1976) *The Archaeology of Knowledge* (New York: Harper and Row).

Garfinkel, H. (1967) *Studies in Ethnomethodology* (Englewood Cliffs, NJ: Prentice Hall).

Gherardi, S. and A. Strati (eds) (2004) *Telemedicina. Tra tecnologia e organizzazione* (Rome: Carocci).

Gibson, J.G. (1979) *The Ecological Approach to Visual Perception* (Boston: Houghton-Mifflin).

Goffman, E. (1974) *Frame Analysis: an Essay on the Organization of Experience* (New York: Harper and Row).

Goffman, E. (1980) *Forms of Talk* (Oxford: Blackwell).

Heath, C. and P. Luff (2000) *Technology in Action* (Cambridge: Cambridge University Press).

Hine, C. (2000) *Virtual Ethnography* (London, Thousand Oaks, New Delhi: Sage).

Knorr Cetina, K. (1997) 'Sociality with objects', *Theory, Culture and Society,* 14 (4), 1–30.

Knorr Cetina, K. and U. Bruegger (2002) 'Traders' engagement with markets: a postsocial relationship', *Theory, Culture and Society,* 19 (5/6), 161–85.

Laclau, E. and C. Mouffe (1985) *Hegemony and Socialist Strategy* (London: Verso).

Latour, B. (1987) *Science in Action: How to Follow Scientists and Engineers through Society* (Cambridge, Mass.: Harvard University Press).

Latour, B. (2002) 'Morality and technology. The end of the means', *Theory, Culture and Society*, 19 (5/6), 247–60.

Lave, J. and E. Wenger (1991) *Situated Learning. Legitimate Peripheral Participation* (Cambridge, Mass.: Cambridge University Press).

Law, J. (1992) 'Notes on the theory of the actor-network: Ordering, strategy and heterogeneity', *System/Practice*, 5 (4), 379–93.

Law, J. (1994) *Organizing Modernity* (Oxford: Blackwell).

Law, J. and A. Mol (eds) (2002) *Complexities. Social Studies of Knowledge Practices* (Durham: Duke University Press).

Lynch, M. (1985) *Art and Artifact in Laboratory Science: a Study of Shop Work and Shop Talk in a Research Laboratory* (London: Routledge and Kegan Paul).

Nicolini, D., S. Gherardi and D. Yanow (eds) (2003) *Knowing in Organizations* (Armonk, NY, and London, UK: M.E. Sharpe).

Orr, J.E. (1996) *Talking about Machines. An Ethnography of a Modern Job* (Ithaca and London: IRL Press).

Polanyi, M. (1958) *Personal Knowledge. Towards a Post-Critical Philosophy* (London: Routledge and Kegan Paul).

Pollner, M. (1987) *Mundane Reason. Reality in Everyday and Sociological Discourse* (Cambridge: Cambridge University Press).

Pollner, M. and L. McDonald-Wikler (1985) 'The social construction of unreality: a case study of a family's attribution of competence to a severely retarded child', *Family Process*, 24 (2), 241–54.

Schatzki, T.R., K. Knorr Cetina and E. von Savigny (eds) (2001) *The Practice Turn in Contemporary Theory* (London: Routledge).

Silverman, D. (1987) *Communication in Medical Practice* (London: Sage).

Star, S.L. (1999) 'The ethnography of the infrastructure', *American Behavioral Scientist,* 43 (3), 377–91.

Strati, A. (2003) 'Knowing in practice: Aesthetic understanding and tacit knowledge' in D. Nicolini, S. Gherardi and D. Yanow (eds) *Knowing in Organizations* (Armonk, NY, and London, UK: M.E. Sharpe), 53–75.

Strauss, A., S. Fagerhaugh, B. Suczek and C. Wiener (1985) *The Social Organization of Medical Work* (Chicago: The University of Chicago Press).

Suchman, L. (1997) 'Centers of coordination. A case and some themes' in L. Resnik, L. Saljo, C. Pontecorvo and B. Burge (eds) *Discourse, Tools and Reasoning. Essays on Situated Cognition* (Berlin: Springer Verlag).

Suchman, L., J. Blomberg, J.E. Orr and R. Trigg (1999) 'Reconstructing technology as social practice', *American Behavioural Scientist,* 43 (3), 392–408.

Sudnow, D. (1967) *Passing On: the Social Organization of Dying* (Englewood Cliffs: Prentice-Hall).

Timmermans, S. and M. Berg (1997) 'Standardization in action: Achieving local universality through medical protocols', *Social Studies of Science,* 27 (2), 273–305.

Timmermans, S. and M. Berg (2003) 'The practice of medical technology', *Sociology of Health and Illness,* 25, 97–114.

15
Chunks in Meetings

Leila Barbara[1] *and Tony Berber Sardinha*[1]
Pontifícia Universidade Católica de São Paulo, Brazil

15.1 Introduction

Meetings are a routine form of interaction in business. Most companies, regardless of their size, hold meetings for a number of purposes. They are so part of the business culture that it is almost impossible to envisage a company where no meetings take place, either site-based or virtually. Some are more casual assemblies, while others are more regulated forms of interaction.

Unlike other forms of specialized business communication, there is scarcely any specific training for meetings. This seems to be because few people would have trouble knowing what a meeting is, and being able to perform at a meeting with considerable confidence.

Nevertheless, meetings attract a lot of criticism in the work-place. There is a general feeling in most organizations that meetings are ineffective, tedious, long-drawn-out forms of interaction. One would be hard-pressed indeed to find a colleague who is truly enthusiastic about going to a meeting!

This negative image of meetings is what fuels a large number of consultancy firms that propose all sorts of training and expert advice on how to improve meetings. One of these offering their services on the web (http://www.openthis.com/market.htm) argues that according to a poll, senior and middle managers believe only 56 per cent of meetings are productive. Further, 'they added that a phone call or a memo could have replaced over 25% of the meetings they attend'.

In another of these services (http://www.effectivemeetings.com), there is mention of typical characters in meetings identified as 'meeting saboteurs', such as 'the two-faced meeting monster' and 'the swindling scribe', all of whom conspire against fair-minded individuals at meetings. In view of such fear-inspiring characters, the same site provides 'tips for mitigating meeting sabotage', which include 'keeping one's cool', 'speaking up' and 'sharing your end goal'.

Despite the different approaches followed by such consultancies, one aspect that seems to bind them all together is that their advice and solutions seem idealized. There is little, if any, mention of actual research into the very substance of meetings: the language used in verbal interaction at meetings.

Research into the discourse of meetings is absolutely essential if one wants to attain an understanding of what people do, what they talk about, how they talk, how their discourse is organized, what kinds of ideational, interpersonal and textual meanings are construed and shared in these events, and so on.

In the investigation presented here, we focus on meetings held in Brazil, in Portuguese among native speakers. Our aim is to look at recurrent lexical choices by speakers (in the form of fixed sequences of words) as means to grasping issues of role assignment and topic sequencing in meetings (see Berber Sardinha, 2003 for a similar study in business reports).

There have been several studies into a number of aspects of language of meetings. Schwartzman (1989) discusses meetings in a range of settings, from business to communities. Bargiela-Chiappini and Harris (1997) are a collection of papers focusing on meetings in corporations. As English becomes the dominant language in a globalized world, there has been an increased interest in meetings from an intercultural point of view. For example, Poncini (2002) investigates footing and frame relationships in meetings held in a Italian company with distributors from around the world. Bilbow (2002) looks at commissive speech acts (such as promises and statements of commitment) in meetings held in English between Hong Kong Chinese and English native-speaking participants at a large airline corporation. Collins and Scott (1997) focus on the lexical choices that give rise to 'landscapes' (networks of shared lexical choices) made by participants in Brazilian and British meetings. Finally, Yamada (1997) compares differing strategies for accomplishing goals employed by American and Japanese participants in meetings. In other related fields, such as foreign language teaching, there has also been a realization of the need to look at instances of authentic meetings in order to observe what meetings are really like. Williams (1988) compared the language used in meetings to that presented in language teaching textbooks preparing for meetings and found discrepancies that point to an idealization of what meetings should be like.

A problem facing anyone interested in looking at real meetings is the scarcity of data. There are several reasons for this. Firstly, and probably most important, most meetings are private, which restricts free access to the event. Secondly, meetings are spoken, and so they need recording of some sort; field notes are not enough to give account of the complexity of the discourse taking place. Thirdly, being spoken data, it needs transcribing to permit analysis; rendering speech in words is a very time-consuming job, especially for events where there are several participants, whose turns often overlap, and so on. Finally, most theories and methods for looking at oral interaction (e.g. conversation analysis), because of their emphasis on manual micro-analytical research (e.g. Bilbow, 2002), make it hard for anyone to approach more than one or at best a few meetings. All of these problems seem to preclude investigation of a larger body of data. Yet, if meetings are so pervasive and a part of business culture as we argued before, then we must find ways to collect more data and, more importantly, analyse such data in its entirety.

In the investigation presented here, we tackle both of these problems. With respect to the scarcity of data issue, we have gathered ten different meetings from as many different firms in Brazil. These are part of the corpus for DIRECT,[2] a business language project taking place in Brazil from the early 1990s, and of the project Discourse and Social Practice in Lusitanian and Brazilian Companies shared by the Catholic University of Rio de Janeiro and of São Paulo and the University of Lisbon.

In so far as the analysis of such data is concerned, we make use of corpus linguistics to help us deal with the language, both on theoretical and methodological grounds. Corpus linguistics is an area concerned with gathering and analysing electronic corpora, which are collections of naturally occurring data stored in computer-readable form. Corpus linguists also make use of specialized software to search the corpus and obtain all kinds of information. A great deal of corpus linguistics research is carried out with an interest in finding and describing patterns present in language. Patterns are systematic occurrences of words with other words or with grammatical structures, or functional and cultural characteristics. There is ample evidence in corpus-based research to suggest that patterns are not simply recurrent groupings of words; what is most striking about them is the fact that different patterns indicate different meanings. As a result, the way lexis collocates with other lexis is revealing of the kinds of meaning present in the language.

In addition to corpus linguistics, our theoretical foundation is systemic functional linguistics, a theory of language that states that meanings are made in language as a result of choices in a complex network of systems. Three major kinds of meaning are proposed in systemics: ideational (what is being talked about), interpersonal (who is involved), and textual (how language is organized). Systemics is founded on an understanding that the realization of meanings cuts across levels of linguistic expression. Thus, meanings made at the higher level of genre (culture-bound kinds of language events) are also present at the lower level of lexico-grammar (the specific choices of words and patterns). This theoretical underpinning allows us to focus on the lexico-grammatical patterns being used in the meetings without losing sight of the more general ways in which language is being used during the meetings to accomplish goals, talk about topics, position speakers in relation to each other, stage the talk in sequences, among other aspects.

From the brief account presented above, it should be clear that systemic functional linguistics and corpus linguistics have a clear connection with each other. In both of them, lexico-grammatical patterns are seen as an important resource to encode meaning in language.

There are several different kinds of pattern, such as collocation (the habitual co-occurrence of words near each other), colligation (the co-occurrence of lexis in grammatical categories), semantic prosody (the colouring of meaning across a whole pattern by virtue of the presence of a 'prosodically charged' word), textual colligation (the preference for patterns to occur in selected parts of a text) and lexical sets (the clusters of related words occurring with a certain item). These patterns may occur without positional restrictions or in groupings whose position allows little variation. The first are simply called collocations (Firth, 1957), whereas the latter have a larger array of names: n-grams (Brown et al., 1992), chains (Stubbs, 2002), bundles (Biber and Conrad, 1999), clusters (Scott, 1998), multi-word units (Cowie, 1992). Chunks is a general label used in the literature to refer to these fixed sequences of words (Lewis et al., 1996). We prefer this term to avoid connotations suggesting allegiance to any one particular theorist or method.

The relevance of chunks in language relates to at least the following reasons:

1. People do not communicate through isolated words. Thus, meanings are not made in interaction via words in isolation, but in larger clusters and structures, such as groups, patterns, clauses, and so on.

2. Words form patterns, which in turn evoke the kinds of meanings expressed by these words (Hunston and Francis, 2000). A word form such as 'bank' has totally different meanings, including those which refer to 'river', on the one hand, and to 'finance', on the other. The specific meaning intended by the user can be apprehended by looking at the patterns in which it appears, so that a pattern like 'river bank' immediately tells us that it is the 'river' meaning that is being evoked, whereas 'high street bank' signifies a financial institution. Hence, patterns are not simply bundles of co-occurring lexis, but they are closely tied to the meaning-making potential of language.

3. Chunks (as defined here in terms of fixed sequence patterns) are most revealing of the formulaic kinds of expression in language. Patterns formed by strings of words typically indicate the most stable and user-independent prefabricated expressions. As such, they are most representative of the idiom principle of language. These are particularly important in speech, where the cognitive load of processing ongoing communication has to be diminished by drawing on prefabricated units stored in the mental lexicon (Wray, 2002). These units are certainly multi-word, otherwise we would not be able to account for their frequent appearance in discourse.

4. Chunks are register-dependent. High-frequency fixed patterns can discriminate among registers (Biber and Conrad, 1999), so that academic registers typically make use of a different range of chunks than newspaper registers, for instance. We would argue that not only are they register-discriminant, but some of them, at least, are also genre-specific.

5. Chunks are markers of expert use. There is evidence in the literature on learner corpora to suggest that the presence of chunks seems to be a feature of expert and native speaker usage, as opposed to novice or beginner learners. We might extrapolate those findings to speculate that those users whose speech shows the presence of chunks may be more proficient users of the language needed in a particular meeting.

15.2   Analysis

15.2.1   Keywords in the meetings

One feature of chunks in language is their abundance. In order to help us zero in on the most revealing chunks, we employed a preparatory keywords analysis. Keywords are words whose frequencies are statistically higher than those found in a reference corpus. They are not to be mistaken with 'key words', which are words that are selected for their perceived importance to a document. Unlike key words, WordSmith Tools keywords are chosen on the basis of comparative frequency alone. Having said that, frequency has a major role to play in both corpus linguistics and systemic functional linguistics, which provide the theoretical underpinning for this work, as discussed above. Frequency reveals what are the most typical choices made by speakers, and as such has a fundamental role in defining which are the preferred ways of referring to the world, to other speakers, and so on. A linguistic approach or theory which takes into account frequency is therefore better equipped to make statements about typicality, use and systematicity (cf. Barlow and Kemmer, 2000; Bybee and Hopper, 2001).

Keywords have been found to indicate a number of features in texts, such as their topic, or what they are about, interactional devices, and genre-specific markers of different kinds, among others (Berber Sardinha, 1999, 2001; Lima-Lopes, 2001; Santos, 2002; Scott, 1997; Scott and Barbara, 1999). We extracted a keyword list from the corpus of meetings using WordSmith Tools, a PC package that offers concordancing and word-listing extraction and comparison facilities (Scott, 1998). The business meetings corpus used for the purposes of this work consists of 10 texts, of 125,176 tokens and 8433 types. The reference corpus is the Banco de Português, a large monitor corpus of Brazilian Portuguese, created and maintained at the Catholic University of São Paulo, by the members of the DIRECT project; it consists of 1822 files with 230,460,560 tokens and 607,392 types.

The top 25 keywords from our corpus are shown in Table 15.1, sorted by statistical significance, as per the log-likelihood score. A column indicating rough equivalents for each keyword is provided for ease of reference. Thus, the word 'eu' is the most 'key' in the corpus, since its log-likelihood statistic is the highest. Its importance may be seen by comparing its relative frequency, in percentage, in both corpora. While in the meetings corpus it corresponds to 1.81 per cent of the total running words, in the reference corpus its share of the total frequencies is much smaller: only 0.11 per cent of the total; this means it is over 16 times more frequent in the meetings than in the Portuguese language as a whole (as represented in the reference corpus).

What is immediately striking in the list is the absence of words indicating technical language. In fact, there are very few words that are not grammatical (functional) words, and these are 'gente', 'acho', 'coisa', 'fazer', 'entendeu' and 'vamos'. Among these, words such as 'gente' and 'vamos' are arguably non-lexical, as these are used as a pronoun and an auxiliary verb, respectively.

Table 15.1 Top keywords

	Word	Translation	Meetings No.	Meetings %	Reference No.	Reference %	Log-L	p
1	Eu	I	2,265	1.81	248,174	0.11	8,539.5	0.000000
2	Pra	For	1,351	1.08	48,410	0.02	7,972.6	0.000000
3	Gente	People/we	1,263	1.01	70,789	0.03	6,362.4	0.000000
4	Então	So/then	1,095	0.87	89,223	0.04	4,731.3	0.000000
5	Você	You (sing.)	1,068	0.85	130,921	0.06	3,793.7	0.000000
6	É	Is	3,554	2.84	1,971,886	0.86	3,606.6	0.000000
7	Aí	There	731	0.58	51,773	0.02	3,351.8	0.000000
8	Tem	Has	1,529	1.22	433,609	0.19	3,142.9	0.000000
9	Está	Is	1,465	1.17	419,868	0.18	2,984.6	0.000000
10	Que	That (conj.)	5,765	4.61	4,981,254	2.16	2,678.6	0.000000
11	Vai	Will (vb.)	1,153	0.92	280,363	0.12	2,671.3	0.000000
12	Isso	This	1,019	0.81	247,368	0.11	2,362.9	0.000000
13	Né	Isn't it	584	0.47	67,533	0.03	2,135.9	0.000000
14	Acho	Think	492	0.39	44,264	0.02	2,031.3	0.000000
15	Aqui	Here	569	0.45	75,829	0.03	1,931.1	0.000000
16	Nós	We	534	0.43	64,214	0.03	1,914.0	0.000000
17	Porque	Because	770	0.62	172,549	0.07	1,891.8	0.000000
18	Não	No	2,597	2.07	1,786,080	0.78	1,880.6	0.000000
19	Lá	There	542	0.43	70,894	0.03	1,858.0	0.000000
20	Coisa	Thing	504	0.40	64,845	0.03	1,743.0	0.000000
21	Vocês	You (pl.)	271	0.22	15,004	<0.01	1,369.5	0.000000
22	Ele	He	986	0.79	524,670	0.23	1,048.7	0.000000
23	Fazer	Do/make	542	0.43	170,570	0.07	1,016.6	0.000000
24	Entendeu	Understood	138	0.11	3,256	<0.01	924.6	0.000000
25	Vamos	Let's/will/go	271	0.22	38,543	0.02	886.7	0.000000

Technical and/or topic-specific words appear further down the list. The first such word is 'mostruário' ('display'), at rank 62. With a frequency of 37 tokens, this word represents only 0.03 per cent of the corpus. A list of the top 20 technical/topic-specific keywords appears in Table 15.2.

It can be seen that the most frequently occurring of these words has a frequency of only 0.08 per cent, which is in marked contrast with the top keywords, all of which occur at least 0.11 per cent. More importantly, the top keywords have a mean frequency of 278, against 37 of the topical ones, which means that the top keywords on average occur 7.5 times more frequently than the topical ones. Hence, there is evidence here to suggest that not only are top keywords non-technical, but they are also far more frequent. As such, they seem to deserve a better look, which will be presented in the next section.

15.3 Chunks around keywords

The analysis so far indicates that the keywords in the meetings consist basically of the following types of words:

- *Non-technical vocabulary*: Key words do not include words revealing the kinds of technical topics dealt with in the different meetings represented in the corpus, such as clothing, health insurance, computer networks, etc.
- *Pronouns*: These are abundant among the top keywords. These suggest a need to refer to the speakers, either oneself or the others. Particularly striking is the presence of 'eu' (I), as Portuguese is a pro-drop language, allowing for the pronoun to be omitted. The non-dropping of the first-person singular pronoun seems to be a feature of spoken Brazilian Portuguese (Barbara and Gouveia, 2001), in contrast to the European variety, where omission seems to be far more frequent.
- *Dummy/delexicalized verbs*: These are verbs whose meaning depends on their complement, such as 'have', 'make' and 'do'. The word forms 'tem' and 'fazer' are the two forms of such verbs.
- *Deictics*: These are words that express the position of the speaker in relative terms, and include 'aí', 'isso' and 'lá'.
- *Conjunctions*: These help the speaker indicate logical connections in their talk. The keywords in this category are 'que' and 'porque'.
- *General noun*: The only true noun on the list is 'coisa' (since 'gente' is part of the pronoun 'a gente', meaning 'we').
- *Other*: Preposition ('pra'), verb ('entendeu').

Table 15.2 List of the top 20 technical/topic-specific keywords and relative position in keyword list

	Word	Translation	Meetings		Reference		Log-L	p
			No.	%	No.	%		
62	mostruário	Display	37	0.03	136	<0.01	377.0	0.000000
67	fornecedor	Supplier	58	0.05	1,841	<0.01	355.3	0.000000
80	paritização	Parity	20	0.02	0	0	300.7	0.000000
84	manutenção	Maintenance	94	0.08	15,837	<0.01	278.4	0.000000
86	operador	Operator	50	0.04	2,255	<0.01	272.3	0.000000
98	paritizada	Parity	16	0.01	0	0	240.6	0.000000
105	formulário	Form	41	0.03	1,911	<0.01	220.7	0.000000
117	telegrama	Telegram	30	0.02	706	<0.01	201.1	0.000000
118	cm	Cm	53	0.04	5,836	<0.01	198.5	0.000000
122	tecido	Fabric	43	0.03	3,528	<0.01	184.9	0.000000
124	cento	Cent	40	0.03	2,829	<0.01	183.3	0.000000
126	cronograma	Schedule	40	0.03	3,074	<0.01	177.0	0.000000
127	cliente	Client	74	0.06	17,417	<0.01	175.1	0.000000
129	logística	Logistics	28	0.02	877	<0.01	172.2	0.000000
131	promotoras	Reps	20	0.02	191	<0.01	168.7	0.000000
134	insight	Insight	18	0.01	116	<0.01	165.1	0.000000
155	CRECI	(acronym)	21	0.02	522	<0.01	138.6	0.000000
157	subestação	Substation	20	0.02	430	<0.01	137.6	0.000000
168	despachante	*	19	0.02	452	<0.01	127.0	0.000000
175	Logístico	Logistical	17	0.01	327	<0.01	120.6	0.000000

*Someone whose job it is to obtain documents from government offices.

In the remainder of the chapter, we will look at how keywords falling within the category of pronoun express meanings in the meetings, what these meanings are and what they tell us about the interaction that went on in the workplace. We will do this through the analysis of the chunks that include the keywords. Our choice of pronouns is based on three factors. Firstly, the topmost keywords are pronouns; three out of the five most distinctive keywords are pronouns. Secondly, most of the keywords relate to the interpersonal metafunction, in which pronouns play a central role. Finally, a number of (if not most) of the non-pronoun keywords seem to colligate naturally with the pronouns, forming patterns such as pronoun + verb. As a result, if we start off with pronouns, we may be able to incorporate other keywords in the process, as these will fit together in larger patterns.

15.3.1 Chunk extraction

In this section, we give details of how the chunks were extracted from the corpus and how they were matched against the keyword list.

Chunks were extracted using WordSmith Tools, a PC package that includes a concordancer, a word-lister and a keyword extractor, among other utilities. Chunks are obtained through WordList with the 'clusters' option activated. In our case, we set the length of each cluster to 2. There is no limit to the length for chunks, but chunks become rarer as they grow longer. Hence, chunks of length equal to 2 are the most frequent of all. They can also be more fragmentary, since larger identifiable patterns get broken down by the chunking mechanism. In our case this did not present a major issue, since we used chunks as a starting point for the investigation, and not as an end. Chunks deemed to be worth a closer look were investigated in larger context through concordances. Once the chunks had been identified, a statistic for assessing the strength of association between the words in each pair was computed. The statistic used in our case is Mutual Information, which measures the probability of two words occurring next to each other in view of their separate frequencies and the size of the corpus in which they occur. Mutual Information was computed with the aid of a Perl package named 'ngram statistics package' (Pedersen et al., 2003) available on the web at http://sourceforge.net.

15.3.2 Pronoun chunks

Below we look more closely at this class of chunks. We will concentrate on these for the following reasons:

1. Pronoun chunks are the most frequent grouping of chunks.[3]
2. They aggregate some of the other chunks. For instance, keyword chunks such as those formed with 'tem', 'está', 'vamos' and 'isso' all appear alongside the main pronoun chunks.
3. These chunks play an important part in the way interactants talk about themselves and others, and how roles are construed for participants at the meetings and outside.
4. They are closely tied to the way meetings are construed as social events, in which people engage with each other through talk.
5. They provide a means for understanding the processes whereby speakers establish individuality and group membership.
6. They relate more readily to the interpersonal metafunction in systemic functional linguistics, as these words fulfil the role of subject and process (and/or finite), which means they may allow us to see how participants build relationships with one another.

15.3.2.1 *Eu*

The top ten chunks formed with the keyword 'eu' appear in Table 15.3, each together with its Mutual Information (MI) score. Out of these ten, eight appear in the pattern 'eu + verb'. The meanings expressed by these chunks seem to be:

- Relational transitivity: 'Eu tenho', 'eu estou' (I have/I am)
- Verbal transitivity: 'Eu falei' (I said/told you)
- Futurity: 'Eu vou' (I'm going to)
- Modality: 'Eu acho', 'eu posso', (I think that/I am capable of)
- Modulation: 'Eu quero', 'eu queria', 'deixa eu', 'eu tenho (que)' (I want/ed/would like; let me/I have (to))

Table 15.3 Chunks with 'eu' = I

Frequency	Chunk		MI
158	Eu	acho	5.4604
62	Eu	tenho	5.5972
62	Eu	estou	5.6386
151	Eu	vou	5.2757
31	Eu	posso	5.8015
20	mas	eu	3.4449
15	Eu	quero	5.6339
15	Eu	queria	4.9924
14	Eu	falei	5.3709
14	deixa	eu	5.7188

In general, the meanings associated with the 'eu' chunks have to do with expressing opinions, possibilities, likelihood and desire. These are some of the ways in which speakers have expressed their individuality. This does not imply, though, that by asserting one's individual thinking, speakers are in disagreement or in conflict with other speakers. The excerpt below illustrates this point:

<J> *Eu acho* que essa é a questão mais importante, eu acho que isso é o mais importante.

<F> *Eu acho* que essa é a questão mais complicada. Ele vai responder lá as atividades da primeira semana, você vai ter que responder.

<V> Mas *eu acho* ...

<F> *Eu acho* que a tendência é essa mesmo, é um curso ...

One can see in the above excerpt from an extramural course-planning meeting a rapid succession of 'eu acho' chunks. These are used to assert each speaker's point of view with respect to the importance of the points raised. But note that each speaker's point of view is expressed in cooperation with the previous one's. There is no clear break in cooperation, except with respect to 'mas eu acho', which is left unfinished, as speaker V is interrupted. The chunks with 'ter' (have) and 'estar' (be) are realized mostly with the relational meaning but they also occur as modulation and auxiliary to a lesser extent.

Finally, 'eu acho' is a doubly 'key' chunk, as it incorporates two keywords. A typical role construed for individuals speaking in the meetings, then, is that of having an opinion. As such, though, as noted above, these opinions are not expressed necessarily as a means of showing dissent or disagreement, but rather as a contribution to an ongoing process of interaction.

15.3.2.2 *Gente*

The top ten chunks incorporating 'gente' are shown in Table 15.4. The most frequent chunk ('a gente') is simply the pronoun meaning 'we' used either inclusively or exclusively. In all the other chunks above, there is 'a' in front of 'gente'. The basic pattern is therefore 'a gente + verb', which is analogous to that found for 'eu'. The verbs coming into the pattern in turn express:

- Material transitivity: 'faz', 'fez' (do/make; did/made)
- Mental transitivity: 'viu' (saw)
- Modality: 'pode', 'podia' (can/could)
- Modulation: 'precisa' (have to)

Table 15.4 Chunks with 'gente' = people

Frequency	Chunk		MI
588	A	gente	4.8005
67	gente	vai	3.4268
29	gente	pode	4.0582
16	gente	faz	4.0152
12	gente	fez	4.2676
11	muita	gente	5.3715
7	gente	precisa	4.0229
6	gente	podia	5.6546
6	gente	viu	5.3550
6	gente	chama	4.8956

As with 'eu', the choices for 'a gente' seem to emphasize possibility and necessity, but they also include other types of processes that are not prominent with respect to the first person singular, mainly the forms of 'fazer' ('do/make'), a material process. In addition, the counterpart for 'acho' is missing from among the top chunks (although it does occur, it appeared only twice, as in 'a gente acha', with an MI of 3.8632).

These choices seem to indicate a somewhat different role being construed for the collective group. When speakers talked about themselves as 'a gente', they typically seemed to indicate suggestions for action and actions, as in the following concordance lines:

Concordance 1 A gente (we)

01	ilton: =é só pegar uma universidade, a	gente	faz isso (vai ficar tudo) junto
02	interação também, né? A gente teve, a	gente	faz isso porque é. Hoje é sab
03	nhando em cima dos teus desenhos, a	gente	faz já algumas peças do teu
04	mos ... (*) P2 - Aquela 'Almenati', que a	gente	fez aquele negócio de ....,
05	as: não, claro. deixa eu falar. porque a	gente	fez essa coisa pô, e isso tem
06	ra que está vendendo e quer desistir a	gente	pode alegar isso bom eu de
07	do uma vez o curso, dão (.) H - E daí a	gente	pode contar com as férias to
08	é que dá pra implementar, o que que a	gente	pode fazer com as outras ár
09	ais, mais né? . Não,não é, mas a	gente	pode fazer uma lavagem lega
10	il que é enviado prá pessoas chaves. A	gente	pode fazer uma rotina que e

Two features seem to stand out in the concordance to complement the analysis of 'a gente' presented above (some of which are not shown above for reasons of space). The first is the co-occurrence of 'vague' words such as 'isso' ('this'), 'lá' ('there'), 'uma' ('a'), 'essa coisa' ('this thing'), 'aquele negócio' ('that thing') with the forms of the verb 'fazer', on lines 1–8 of the concordance. The second is the wide range of verbs forming a pattern with 'pode' and 'podia', although 'fazer' predominates (it occurs nine times in all with the patterns discussed here). The third is the fact that five of the eight main chunks with 'a gente' are used with modals, one with the auxiliary for future, and two others have also got a vague relation to truth ('viu', 'chama'). These three findings together suggest that the actions that are signalled as possibilities (through 'pode/podia') are far more specific than those expressed as actually having been carried out (with 'faz/fez') and some of these are to some extent evaluative.

15.3.2.3 Nós

The top ten chunks where 'nós' ('we') participates are given in Table 15.5. As in the chunks seen so far, the basic pattern for the 'nós' chunks is 'nós + verb', and the verbs fall into the following categories:

- Material transitivity: 'fizemos', 'fazemos' (did/made)
- Modulation: 'precisamos', 'deveríamos', 'temos', 'tivemos' (have to/ had to/would have to)
- Relational transitivity: 'estamos' (are), 'temos', 'tivemos' (have, be)
- Future: 'vamos' (are going to)

Unlike the previous chunks, here most processes are of the material kind, where speakers invoke actions that are being or have been performed. The second largest grouping is made up of verbs indicating

Table 15.5 Chunks with 'nós' = we

Frequency	Chunk		MI
34	nós	vamos	6.1819
33	nós	temos	7.1874
14	nós	estamos	7.1402
8	nós	tivemos	7.1629
8	nós	já	3.2348
6	nós	precisamos	7.9178
4	olha	nós	4.6604
4	nós	fizemos	7.7479
4	nós	fazemos	7.1629
4	nós	deveríamos	8.3328

necessity and obligation. The concordance below illustrates the extended phraseologies of the chunks under analysis:

Concordance 2 Nós (we)

01	! (*) P- É horrível.(*) D- E o que	nós	fazemos aqui é ruído. Então vamos b
02	atividade profissional tranqüilo.	nós	fazemos o back office, nós organiza
03	ou- ou- Milton: um plano qualquer.	nós	temos dois construídos, que é o de
04	uinte: nós temos muitas anomalias,	nós	temos muitos problemas. A logística
05	disse o seguinte olha gente, eh::	Nós	temos que encontrar um grupo coeso,
06	que ir embora. Agora, o que é que	nós	temos que fazer sempre quando as co
07	prazo –399— a longo prazo	nós	temos um tipo de trabalho diferenci
08	sa entrar nos nossos padrões. Hoje	nós	temos uma centralização que está em
09	lto, profissionais, somos empresa,	nós	temos uma relação profissional, que
10	aso do W., a verdade é bem outra,	nós	tivemos que nos violentar, pra fech

The lexical choices in patterns of 'nós' followed by 'fizemos/ fazemos/temos/tivemos/precisamos/deveríamos' are less vague than those for 'a gente', as in, for example, 'cinqüenta lugares' ('50 places'), 'back office', 'período' ('term'), 'centralização' ('centralization'), 'meta' ('goal'), 'reunião' ('meeting'). There are also choices indicating 'large unknown quantities', with 'muitas/muitos'. Overall, the choices for 'nós' seem to indicate a different referent than that for 'a gente'. Here, there is evidence that seems to suggest that 'nós' stands for the company, or the company staff, whereas 'a gente' appears to be associated with the people at the meeting. This would be in accordance with the predominance of modulation being expressed here. It seems as though speakers reserve the 'nós' form to talk about those tasks that the company needs to do, while reserving 'a gente' for those actions that the actual people attending the meeting could do.

15.3.2.4 *Você*

The top ten chunks for 'você' are given in Table 15.6. The basic pattern, again, is 'você + verb'. The verbs in the pattern are distributed across the following categories:

- Material transitivity: 'fez', 'faz' (did, does)
- Relational transitivity: 'tem' (have, are)
- Mental transitivity: 'sabe' (know)
- Verbal transitivity: 'falou' (said)
- Modulation: 'tem', 'quiser' (have to, would like)
- Modality: 'pode' (can)

Table 15.6 Chunks with 'você' = you (sing.)

Frequency	Chunk		MI
71	você	tem	3.3024
59	se	você	3.7076
19	Você	pode	3.6604
15	Quando	você	4.2893
13	Você	fez	4.5953
13	Você	faz	3.9279
10	Você	quiser	5.8448
10	Você	Se	4.2168
7	você	sabe	3.4321
7	você	falou	5.1458

In addition, there are three other non-verbal categories which provide elements for the chunks:

- Condition: 'se', 'quando' se (+ você) (if you)
- Time: 'quando' (when)
- False reflexive: se (você + se)

The chunks for 'você' include, like all the previous ones, material processes and modulation. The lexical items that co-occur with these verbs indicate a degree of explicitness that is higher than for 'eu' and 'a gente', indicated by words such as 'parte' ('part'), 'curso' ('course'), 'pesquisa' ('research'), 'comentar' ('comment'), 'comprar' ('buy'), 'empresas' ('companies'), 'mostrar' ('show'), 'pagar' ('pay'), and so on (some of which are not depicted in the concordance for reasons of space). However, 'você' in a large number of these cases seems to be generic, like the English 'you' when it means 'one' including the speaker. This indefinitely specified person is most clearly noticed in the pattern 'você tem + noun', as concordance 5 illustrates:

Concordance 3 Você (you)

1	na home page do evento, por exemplo,	você	tem é:: o acesso de pessoas do
2	xatamente. eles não conseguem. depois	você	tem é:: universidades por exem
3	casa Milton: o problema é o seguinte:	você	tem hoje em dia Flávio: sendo
4	a Flávio: sendo consultores = Milton: =	você	tem hoje em dia- o fato é que
5	— se você sai 10 vezes por mês	você	tem mais chance do que se sair
6	contece? o resultado desse downsizing	você	tem milhões de pessoas espalha
7	uer dizer você, .digitar o CPR SINES .	você	tem não sei quantos mil . M [
8	coisa que eu tava falando aqui, agora	você	tem o CEP, chamado pra pequeno
9	você tem o esquema de fechamento	você	tem o compromisso de compra e
10	undo- Flávio: uma pousada ( ) Milton:	você	tem pousadas em- em Portugal h

It is interesting to note that 'Se' is another important element that forms chunks with você – and it is not a top cluster with any other pronoun; although 'se você' and 'você se' are both top clusters, the former, with the meaning of 'if', is much more frequent than the latter, which is an expletive pronoun.

Also, 'voce tem' is the third doubly key word occurring in the corpus.

15.4   Discussion

In this section, we would like to summarize and comment on the analysis presented so far.

Table 15.7 summarizes the range of choices of pronominal chunks signalled in the meetings. 'Eu' chunks tend to be concerned mostly with asserting one's individuality through desires, capabilities and action. Notice that the 'eu' is the only one that forms a chunk with *achar*; although *achar* is being used as a grammatical metaphor of modalization it also preserves its cognitive basis as a mental process as *pensar* (to think); in Portuguese *achar* can form a grammatical metaphor whereas *pensar* cannot. 'A gente' chunks represented inclusive membership mostly through suggesting possible courses of action but exclusive when referring to past actions. This was in contrast to the 'nós' chunks, which seemed to be employed to refer to the speaker or the company they represent with specific past actions, and including the hearer in future actions. Finally, 'você' chunks seemed to make reference to a generic being, instead of the local participants, and it was also used in relation to specific actions. In all, there is some evidence to suggest a

Table 15.7   Chunks with pronouns

	eu	*a gente*	*nós*	*você*
Material transitivity	fiz	faz/fez	fizemos, fazemos	fez, faz
Relational transitivity	tenho	–	estamos/temos/tivemos	tem
Futurity	vou	–	vamos	–
Verbal transitivity	falei	–	–	falou
Behavioural transitivity	–	–	–	–
Mental transitivity	–	viu	–	sabe
Modulation	quero/queria/tenho	precisa	precisamos/deveriamos/temos/tivemos	tem/quiser
Modalization	acho/posso	pode/podia	–	pode

major division between these two groups of pronoun chunks. While 'eu' and 'a gente' seem to attribute roles to local participants in terms of possible future action, 'nós' and 'você' might be characterized in the opposite direction, as they were often used to ascribe specific actions to abstract entities, respectively 'the company' and 'the people'.

With respect to the different meanings attributed to 'a gente' and 'nós', previous research in other contexts also found an analogous distinction in reference. Bilbow (2002) suggests that, in his MAW ('Meetings at Work') corpus of meetings, 'we' could either refer to the people at the meeting or to the company, and, more importantly, that this difference seemed to correspond to cultural differences. Chinese speakers at the meetings tended to use 'we' to refer locally to the group, whereas Westerner English-speaking participants typically used it to refer to the company. We did not find any evidence of systematic differences across users with respect to a choice for reference in our corpus, not least because there are no major culturally demarcated groups of speakers at our meetings. Nevertheless, we find it striking that each of the two pronouns in Portuguese often take on separate meanings.

15.5   Closing remarks

The analysis of our meetings suggests, above all, that speakers make use of chunks in meetings for a range of purposes, such as assigning roles to oneself and others, associating oneself with the local group context or with the outside world, proposing tentative or more assertive action, and initiating or shifting topics.

This may be taken to mean that devices commonly associated with an expert performance in a meeting, such as the skilful packaging of content, technical vocabulary and jargon may actually have a lesser role in the goings-on of the meetings than is actually thought. This is not to say, of course, that using high-content, specialized vocabulary is not relevant, which it is, but rather that discourse in meetings happens between people, and as such, those linguistic devices needed to allow one to interact, and keep the dialogue going, are essential.

Notes

1. The authors wish to thank CNPq (Brasília, Brazil) for its financial support.
2. Today, the DIRECT corpus comprises over 5 million words of business Portuguese, both written and spoken, from a variety of genres. In addition, the project also hosts the largest general language corpus of Portuguese, the Bank of Portuguese, with over 230 million words.

3. We are taking into account only *chunks with explicit pronouns* as the omission of subject pronouns is not as frequent in Brazilian Portuguese as its presence. Just to illustrate, there are, in the corpus under study, 1167 occurrences of explicit 'eu' in subject position in the top chunks studied, whereas occurrences of the same processes with 'eu' omitted were 450.

References

Barbara, L. and C. Gouveia (2001) 'It is not there, but [it] is cohesive: the case of pronominal ellipsis of subject in Portuguese', *DIRECT Papers*, 46 (http://lael.pucsp.br/direct/direct*papers.htm*).

Bargiela-Chiappini, F. and S.J. Harris (eds) (1997) *Managing Language. The Discourse of Corporate Meetings* (Amsterdam/Philadelphia, Pa: John Benjamins).

Barlow, M. and S. Kemmer (eds) (2000) *Usage-Based Models of Language* (Stanford: CSLI).

Berber Sardinha, A.P. (1999) 'Word sets, keywords, and text contents: an investigation of text topic on the computer', *Delta*, 15, 41–149.

Berber Sardinha, A.P. (2001) 'Comparing corpora with WordSmith keywords', *The ESPecialist*, 22, 87–99.

Berber Sardinha, A.P. (2003) 'Chunks as markers of topical segmentation in business reports'. Unpublished manuscript.

Biber, D. and S. Conrad (1999) 'Lexical bundles in conversation and academic prose' in H. Hasselgard and S. Oksefjell (eds) *Out of Corpora. Studies in Honour of Stig Johansson* (Amsterdam/Atlanta, Ga: Rodopi).

Bilbow, G.T. (2002) 'Commissive speech act use in intercultural business meetings', *Iral*, 40, 287–303.

Brown, P.F., V.J. Della Pietra, P.V. de Souza, J.C. Lai and R.L. Mercer (1992) 'Class-based n-gram models of natural language', *Computational Linguistics*, 18, 467–79.

Bybee, J.L. and P. Hopper (2001) 'Introduction to frequency and the emergence of linguistic structure' in J.L. Bybee and P. Hopper (eds) *Frequency and the Emergence of Linguistic Structure* (Amsterdam/Atlanta, Ga: John Benjamins), 1–26.

Collins, H. and M. Scott (1997) 'Lexical landscaping in business meetings' in F. Bargiela-Chiappini and S. Harris (eds) *The Languages of Business. An International Perspective* (Edinburgh: Edinburgh University Press), 183–210.

Cowie, A.P. (1992) 'Multi-word units and communicative language teaching' in P. Arnaud and H. Bejoint (eds) *Vocabulary and Applied Linguistics* (London: Macmillan), 1–12.

Firth, J.R. (1957) *Papers in Linguistics. 1934–1951* (Oxford: Oxford University Press).

Hunston, S. and G. Francis (2000) *Pattern Grammar. A Corpus-Driven Approach to the Lexical Grammar of English* (Amsterdam/ Philadelphia: John Benjamins).

Lewis, M., M. McCarthy and N. Schmitt (1996) 'Vocabulary as lexical chunks: Descriptive psycholinguistic and pedagogical perspectives', Colloquium, 30th TESOL Annual Convention, Chicago, Ill., 27 March.

Lima-Lopes, R.E. (2001) 'Estudos de transitividade em língua portuguesa: o perfil do gênero cartas de venda'. Unpublished MA thesis, LAEL, PUC/SP, São Paulo.

Pedersen, T., S. Banerjee and A. Purandare (2003) *N-gram statistics package*. Perl package available online at http://sourceforge.net).

Poncini, G. (2002) 'Investigating discourse at business meetings with multicultural participation', *Iral*, 40, 345–73.

Santos, V.B.M.P. dos (2002) 'O perfil das comunicações internas escritas de uma empresa brasileira: um estudo de caso sobre o contexto de produção e as realizações discursivas em locais de trabalho'. Unpublished PhD thesis, LAEL, PUC/SP, São Paulo.

Schwartzman, H.B. (1989) *The Meeting: Gatherings in Organizations and Communities* (New York/London: Plenum Press).

Scott, M. (1997) 'PC Analysis of key words, and key key words', *System*, 25, 233–45.

Scott, M. (1998) *WordSmith Tools Version 3* (Oxford: Oxford University Press).

Scott, M. and L. Barbara (1999) 'Homing in on a genre: Invitations for bids' in F. Bargiela-Chiapini and C. Nickerson (eds) *Writing Business: Genres, Media and Discourse* (New York: Longman), 227–54.

Stubbs, M. (2002) 'Two quantitative methods of studying phraseology in English', *International Journal of Corpus Linguistics*, 7 (2), 215–44.

Williams, M. (1988) 'Language taught for meetings and language used in meetings: Is there anything in common?', *Applied Linguistics*, 9, 45–58.

Wray, A. (2002) *Formulaic Language and the Lexicon* (Cambridge: Cambridge University Press).

Yamada, H. (1997) 'Organisation in American and Japanese meetings: Task versus relationship' in F. Bargiela-Chiappini and S. Harris (eds) *The Languages of Business* (Edinburgh: Edinburgh University Press).

16
Gesture and the (Workplace) Imagination: What Gesture Reveals about Management's Attitudes in Post-Apartheid South Africa

Beverly A. Sauer
Johns Hopkins University, USA

16.1 Introduction

While much of the official literature on workplace discourse in pre-1994 South Africa focused on 'black workers' attitudes' (cf. Marais and Van der Kooy, 1979; Pheta, 1982), researchers also attempted to understand the complexity of white people's attitudes to black people, the effect of historical prejudice on racialist attitudes (MacCrone, 1937), and the role of the Afrikaner myth as 'a justification of social discrimination and ... a defense mechanism against feelings of social insecurity' (Crijns, 1959, p. 47). More recently, the findings of the Truth and Reconciliation Commission forced Afrikaans writers to wrestle with their own role in the oppression of black people and their responsibility for creating economic and political justice in the new South Africa (Krog, 2000; Malan, 1990; Godwin, 1997). The problem is particularly difficult in the workplace, where differences in race were invisibly inscribed in policies of job reservation and a heavy reliance on transitory labour. Today, industry needs trained workers, but the new government is dependent on industry to educate the so-called 'lost generation' of black workers who were denied education under apartheid. The problem of illiteracy directly affects safety and training in coal mines (Leon et al., 1994), which have some of the highest accident rates in the world.

The present project draws upon data collected in 1997 at the Kloppersbos Training Centre near Pretoria, South Africa, investigating the role of gesture in workplace training in a particularly difficult cross-cultural context.[1] The present project analyses the gestures of one Afrikaans-speaking trainer (P) in pre-training interviews in order to disambiguate his beliefs about his notions of audience and his strategies in training.

Analysis of P's gestures shows how he manages two contradictory notions of social transformation within the same gestural space. Trainer P constructs a gestural space that crudely locates miners, management and trainers within a segregated and orderly workspace. P's gestures depict two competing processes of transformation: one, grounded in regulation and control, moves individuals step by step into the domain of expertise by applying proper procedure within a tightly controlled and well-defined bureaucratic system; the other, grounded in notions of drawing out and building up, borrows images from explosions in a controlled space. It is easy to interpret the meaning of these opposing frameworks in light of past and existing racial tensions inscribed in the institutional and material workspace.

But racial identity is not a sufficient explanation for the tensions in P's gestural workspace. In hazardous environments, risk decision makers – regardless of race – must learn to balance the tension between regulation and uncertainty in environments where safety depends upon workers' ability to identify and communicate hazards. The inherited legacy of apartheid has had a profound effect on safety training and adult education. But Trainer P's gestural workspace also reflects more general differences in the ways that individuals experience risk and hazard within institutions and material environments that were engineered – literally and figuratively – by laws designed to create separate spheres of development for black and white people. Communication practices are learned and reinforced within institutions where 'skills in communication' and 'literacy in English' are often equated with managerial competence (Barton, 1994).

This contribution argues that the analysis of gestural space can reveal patterns of behaviour invisible to participants that continue to 'minoritize' workers in the new South Africa (cf. Gumperz, 1992). The clearly inscribed racial and ethical boundaries that still persist in post-apartheid South Africa allow us to see more clearly the relationships between identity, authority, risk management and social regulation as they are mapped onto existing regulatory frameworks that continue to affect safety and identity in the workspace. At the same time, however, we must resist abandoning the notion of regulation entirely in workspaces where regulations have been designed to protect workers.

16.2   The present project

The present project analyses the construction of gestural space in order to understand how notions of identity are embodied in gesture in the regulatory frameworks that individuals apply to manage risk in the workplace. The term *regulatory framework* takes into account that hazardous worksites are complex decision environments where safety depends upon effective communication at the local and systems level. The term thus includes conventional notions of regulation in real space (emphasizing the importance of proper procedures, warnings, hazard identification, instructions and regulations) as well as the social and institutional practices that regulate the behaviour of individuals within large systems (in the construction of social difference and the application of disciplinary standards across diverse and often very different worksites).

The present analysis brings together two complementary frameworks – psycholinguistic analysis of gesture (focusing on an individual's co-production of speech and gesture and the relationship between gesture, language and thought) and cultural analysis (focusing on the underlying contexts that give meaning to gestures within specific cultures) – in order to understand how individuals locate themselves within cultural and institutional space. Section 16.3 ('The rules of the game') describes the social and cultural dimensions of identity and transformation in South African coal mines. In Section 16.4, analysis of P's gestural space shows how one individual locates himself in relation to larger cultural narratives of race, authority, regulation and identity.

As the following discussion suggests, any analysis of work and space in South Africa is necessarily loaded with meanings inherited from apartheid. But training is also intended to alter relations within the workspace. The present analysis of speech and gesture is intended to understand how individuals manage culturally constructed notions of identity, authority, control and uncertainty within the more general regulatory frameworks that guide safe practice in the workspace. Future projects will investigate whether these gestural forms are typical within particular language groups and contexts.

16.3   The 'rules of the game'

Under apartheid, the 'rules of the game' were clearly marked in the spatial and economic separation of the races (Cobley, 1997, p. 3; cf. Popke, 2003). In coal mines, black workers were positioned (literally and economically) under white bosses. Although they occupied the most dangerous positions and assumed the greatest risk, their pay reflected the inequalities they suffered under apartheid. After 1994, mines could no longer reserve jobs for white people only, but lack of training and education still prevented many black people from moving into positions formerly held by white people.

Moodie and Ndatshe (1994, ˙p. 69) describe how the 'typical white miner [under apartheid]...frequently gave orders without giving reasons, forgetting that blacks did the work most of the time without them'. In many cases, the white miner's presence was 'counterproductive', because it broke the 'cooperative rhythm' of black work teams and actually aroused resentment (Moodie and Ndatshe, 1994, p. 69). Regulation, surveillance and regimen were critical to mine efficiency (Moodie and Ndatshe, 1994, p. 11); these practices were inscribed in the geography of the mine compound and the formal and informal rules and regulations that structured the sexual, social, economic and institutional lives of black miners (Moodie and Ndatshe, 1994). Regulations were enforced by mine police, inspectors, white 'native overseers', local authorities (*induna*), and (black) 'boss boys' (Moodie and Ndatshe, 1994, p. 46), who all knew their place within the hierarchical mine structure.

The 1994 elections did not entirely disrupt existing social and geographic divisions (Lester et al., 2000). Attitudes acquired under apartheid (often as children) have slowly evolved into more subtle forms of 'symbolic racism', a blend of anti-black prejudice and traditional conservative values whose effects exceed the effects of either prejudice or conservative traditions separately (Sears and Henry, 2003). The narrative of apartheid re-emerges as a narrative of expertise within institutions whose structures still privilege those who benefited most under apartheid (Dubow, 1989). Regulations governing workplace safety invisibly encode assumptions about the status of individuals within institutions and environments that locate individuals differently in relation to risk (Sauer, 2003). The social engineering of apartheid still intersects with the institutional structures of (capitalist) mines under apartheid (Dubow, 1989). Yet we cannot therefore dismiss the need for expertise and regulation in hazardous environments where miners' unions have been most active in the pursuit of regulation and safety.

The stakes are high. Black South Africans need more than competency in English to move into supervisory positions where they can achieve economic parity and develop more effective means of protecting the health and safety of colleagues. Illiteracy 'hinders the development of effective safety training and education and communication, and undoubtedly contributes to [South Africa's] poor safety record' (Leon et al., 1994, p. 38), but literacy alone will not help miners develop the understanding they need to become effective risk decision-makers. Despite declines in accident and injury rates, the number of injuries and deaths is among the highest in the world, and middle management remains largely white (Chief Inspector of Mines, 2001, p. 1).

As South Africans struggle to create a more democratic distribution of wealth and power, government and industry are struggling to renegotiate notions of expertise and authority without sacrificing safety (Kraak, 2002; South African Dept. of Education, 1997; Mangena, 2001). Training must be made transportable and referenced to national norms so that workers can receive credit for prior learning and experience (McCarthy, 1997). Although South Africa's Language in Education Policy (1996) guarantees South Africans the right to be instructed in their language of choice where practical and reasonable, the government lacks funding and must depend upon private industry to educate workers (South African Dept. of Education, 1997, 2001). The problem of workplace transformation is particularly difficult because Afrikaans-speaking trainers who benefited most under apartheid are now on the front lines of transformation without a clear road map for how that transformation will take place.

Dubow (1992, p. 235) argues that the power of the apartheid narrative was 'related to the ability of its adherents to hold together contradictory ideas, while maintaining an overall appearance of consistency'. Adherents of apartheid described the potential equality of the races under apartheid even as they created separate homelands, separate educational systems and separate 'spheres of development'. They celebrated mother-tongue-language education that denied black people access to education in English (cf. Franz et al., 1955). Sharp (2001, p. 67) concludes: 'No one can mistake the rhetoric of apartheid – its fulsome claim to being based on the principle of respect of cultural difference – for the real thing.' Space is critical to this narrative.

Prior to 1994, Europeans in Africa defined themselves by attempting to control and define racial and geographic boundaries (Popke, 2003). In Natal, 'the progress of History was explicitly spatialized... to justify white privilege' (Popke, 203, p. 263). After 1994, white Afrikaners could no longer call upon a unified ethnic narrative (Hyslop, 2000). On the one hand, they feared the loss of their own ethnic identity; but they also confronted the negative associations that resulted from the link between white Afrikaner identity and the policies of apartheid (Korf and Malan, 2002).[2] Afrikaners suddenly faced high uncertainty as they attempted to maintain their economic status and preserve their identity within a non-racial culture (Motsemme, 2002, p. 662).

The present contribution investigates what gesture can reveal about the intersection of cultural and individual identity within contemporary discourses of workplace transformation.

16.4 Gestures of the workspace

The following analysis of gestural space draws on videotaped interviews with miners, management and safety officials in an explosives training course at the Kloppersbos training facility near Pretoria, South Africa, in the summer of 1997. Because trainers play a critical role in economic and institutional transformation, the present project focuses on data from a video- and audio-taped interview with an Afrikaans-speaking trainer (Trainer P) prior to the training course. This interview was designed to understand the trainer's conception of training, his training strategies, his understanding of his audience, and his own training and prior experience. The interview also included three questions relating to roof bolting, a method for supporting mine roofs. These additional technical questions served as a baseline for interviews with all research subjects.

The explosives training course had been set up by the Council on Scientific and Industrial Relations (CSIR) in Auckland Park, South Africa, for the purpose of evaluating training. All interviews were video- and audio-taped and transcribed and translated (where necessary) by Hector Tshablala in Cape Town, who also kept a running protocol of difficult terms and concepts that might create confusion. The interview with Trainer P was conducted in English (not his mother tongue).

Following the training session, we recommended changes in practice based on our analysis of audio-taped interviews with miners and trainers and observation of the training sessions (Sauer and Lawrence, 1997). The present project revisits Trainer P's pre-training interview in order to focus on gesture.

Using methods derived from McNeill (1992) and Sauer (1999), we identified nine primary gestural forms across 23 topics encompassing approximately 3100 words (approximately 700 clausal units). We digitalized 196 gestures in JPEG format, categorized these gestures according to their primary form, and examined the conceptual meaning of the gesture and its location in gestural space. These gestures are identified in parentheses in the text according to disk location (e.g. 3G) and position in relationship to numbered clausal units in the transcript (e.g. 43). Table 16.1 describes these nine primary gestural forms.

Table 16.1 Description of primary gestural forms and meanings

Regulatory framework	Gestural form	No.	Description of the gesture
Institutional space	Control	16	BH [both hands] approx 1 foot apart, hands cupped, fingers down and slightly splayed
	Space	20	BH parallel, thumbs up, 4–6 inches apart, shape space in centre of body
	Rules	59	BH parallel, 2 inches apart, cut space in slices or (var.) wedges
Educational space	Illustrate1	38	BH flat and perpendicular to arms, which generally rest on the table in front of the speaker; thumbs up. In variants: one hand moves forward in direction of audience
	Illustrate2	17	BH rounded as if holding a larger globe, fingers slightly rounded and splayed, thumbs up
	Draw out	3	LH [left hand] stationary. RH [right hand] moves away from LH towards right, as if drawing out from a fixed position
Disciplinary space	Visualize	7	RH at eye level, thumb and index finger touching in a rounded, slightly pointed O-shape. Hand moves away from eye in direction of audience
	Model	26	One or both hands form C shape to represent objects that are the focus of discussion; LH may point to RH to direct reader's attention to object
	Scale	10	BH (wide) measure distance in front of speaker. This gesture is similar to space gesture with more movement

Figure 16.1 shows the number of repetitions (and close variants) for these nine forms, which were named first on the basis of shape (e.g. 'parallel wedge') and then on their relation to the semantic context of speech ('regulation space'). With the exception of the category 'model space', which includes a range of iconic gestures relating to the

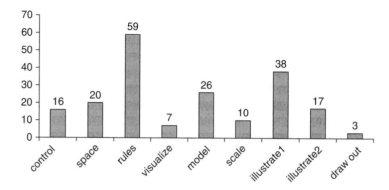

Figure 16.1 Number of occurrences of each gestural form

operation of a coal mine, these nine gestural forms represent easily recognized, well-formed gestures. These gestures constitute P's regulatory framework.

The limited number of gestures may reflect the quality of the interview questions, the metadiscursive character of the interview, or a set of scripted responses that produce a limited repertoire of gestural forms (cf. Chawla and Krauss, 1994). More recently, Brookes (2000) shows that there is a large repertoire of quotable gestures in use among black urban South Africans across all nine African language groups. Brookes (2004) suggests that black urban South Africans value information conveyed in gesture and show facility in understanding changes in gestural meaning (Brookes, 2004). White South Africans, by contrast, use few conventionalized gestures that illustrate meaning and few quotable gestures (Brookes, 2004).

16.5   Constructing a regulatory framework

Following Levinson (1996), researchers in gesture have described many different frameworks for categorizing gestural space: concrete and referential (McNeill and Pedelty, 1995); real space, surrogate space and token space in American sign language (Liddell, 1995); topographic and referential (Emmorey, 1995).

Analysis of gestural space (Figure 16.2) reveals how P (1) locates educated and uneducated workers in separate gestural spaces; (2) applies the notion of 'proper procedure' to safety systems, as one might expect, but also to issues of worker–management disagreement over issues of safety; and (3) assumes that workers will immediately see the relation

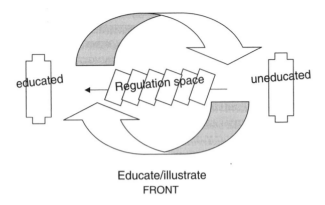

Educate/illustrate
FRONT

Figure 16.2   The location of gestures in P's regulatory framework

between a simple Plexiglas model of the mine and their own experiences underground – a difference of perspective grounded in the unarticulated relationship between disciplinary knowledge (model space) and miners' embodied experience underground (haulage space). Control-space gestures exert top-down control by locating and manipulating individuals in gestural space; in these gestures, both hands are cupped downward, like a carnival operator moving cups on a gaming table.

Gestures associated with training and education 'build up' (draw out) across gestural space. P conceives his work as 'building up' miners and 'drawing out' his audience. The training itself uses a clearly ordered sequence of demonstrations that are represented in gestural space as a series of evenly spaced, controlled steps (regulation space). Education occurs at the front of P's gestural space (illustration space); proper procedure, regulation and scientific principles are represented as simple steps that segment both institutional and gestural space.

P applies this framework to many different semantic topics. These extensions reveal the tensions in P's regulatory framework: 'Illustrations' (physical demonstrations of the explosive features of methane and coal dust) become increasingly larger ('build up'). Their increasing scale gradually anticipates the final, massive explosion, but these illustrations take place in the controlled space of a plasticene model or at a safe distance. The illustrations presented in training necessarily distance miners from real disaster. Danger is controlled in experiments that do not really reflect the uncertainty of mine regulation in an underground coal mine (see Sauer, 2003).

Disciplinary assumptions are also embodied in P's construction of gestural workspace. Illustrations (we would call them 'demonstrations') are intended to build up miners from their current state of misunderstanding to an expanded understanding of the rationale for safety practice in the workplace. P expects miners to draw on experience to 'visionalize' (see) in their heads the connection between model and mine. But P never explicitly articulates the principles of gas mechanics illustrated in the model that provide the rationale for safety practices – either in the interviews or later in training, even though these principles are fundamental to the systems perspective that miners must acquire to manage large regulatory systems. Ultimately, P's gestures construct a tightly structured regulatory framework (institutional space) (1) whose rules and procedures (he believes) can be understood 'immediately' through a series of demonstrations that build up from a simple model to a (final) massive explosion (disciplinary space) and (2) whose structures can be extended to all aspects of social and institutional governance (educational space). For P, the system works as long as everyone follows proper procedure.

16.6 Description of gestures

16.6.1 Institutional space

Institutional space comprises the physical environment (haulage space) and the institutional regulations that govern activity in the workspace (control space and regulation space). In theory, individuals are located in institutional space within hierarchies regulated by notions of competence, expertise and education.

16.6.1.1 *Haulage-space gestures*

Haulage-space gestures depict 'haulageways' (passages) underground. These gestures are common in mining contexts. For working miners, who do not ordinarily reference idealized models when they talk about their work, haulage-space gestures help miners reconstruct a portable and economic three-dimensional visual representation without the limitations of two-dimensional maps and static visual representations (cf. Sauer, 2003). The ability to assume an analytic perspective is fundamental to effective risk management and assessment, and the flexibility to assume new perspectives *rhetorically* must be learned as part of a larger systems perspective (Sauer, 2003).

In contrast to working miners, P's haulage-space gestures depict a *model* of a mine. P's understanding of space is thus at a second level of abstraction (gestures of a model of 'real space') from the workspace experience of the Zulu-speaking miners he instructs. It is thus not

surprising that P believes that miners will immediately see the relationship between the model and their experience underground, despite the
difference between the neat configuration of space in the model and
the uncertain messiness of a working coal mine. For P, model and mine
converge in institutional workspace.

16.6.1.2   Control space

The notion of control embodied in control space is fundamental to
training. Because mines cannot ethically expose miners to real hazards
during training, training must provide a controlled space where miners
can visualize danger in a controlled environment. P applies the notion
of control space more generally to configure the institutional locations
of miners, management and safety representatives. When he talks about
the composition of his audience, he uses the control-space gesture to
locate 'educated' and 'uneducated' miners on opposite sides of gestural control space (17/1). Control is an important feature of his training
'because a lot of times there are educated people among the uneducated
people, so you have to try and give them enough information to keep
them both satisfied' (ll. 80–3).[3]

P uses the control-space gesture to describe his own role within the
social–institutional structure of the mine. When he describes his previous experience, he obliquely refers to policies of job reservation which
required 'persons with my qualifications' (600/10I) and 'a job for that
person' (598/7I) to inspect and supervise black miners.

16.6.1.3   Regulation-space gestures

Regulation-space gestures subdivide the gestural workspace into uniform
segments as his hands move across gestural space from a fixed point of
origin or resting point. In their most literal sense, regulation-space gestures depict the stone dust barriers that prevent mine explosions from
propagating through the mine. P extends this meaning to depict science
as an orderly process that can be made visible through an increasing
sequence of step-by-step demonstrations.

Like control space, regulation-space gestures depict the unspoken
agreements that constrain what researchers can tell miners about
management's liability for safety. Because the trainers are primarily
researchers, the safety training programmes are a 'once-a-month visits
from the mines that's a privilege' (1D/262). Regulation-space gestures
also depict the fine line that separates fear from reasonable caution.
P must present enough information so that miners understand risk
('just to scare them enough' 451/12G), but not enough information

'to scare the pants off them' (451/11G). Ultimately, regulation space defines the 'fine line' trainers must walk between management and worker (11H/12H/546-7) because 'a lot of mining companies, they don't enjoy it when I try... [to talk about management liability]' (13H/548). Because he has been on the mines, P understands the structure and the 'red tape' and 'all that kind of stuff'. P sees his role (literally) as explaining 'why the different precautions are there' (199) so that miners 'can look after those precautions' (200). He does not rock the boat: 'I just try and explain (7H/519-20) what is there and why the regulations on the mine are there' (8H/521; 10H/522). Despite his insistence that 'You work easier with a person if he understands what the job is about', P simply explains the rules: 'I tell them this is the way to go and this is how it works on the mine' (4I/575; 5I/577; 6I, 578).

While it is easy to read the term 'barriers' metaphorically, P's extension of procedure-space gestures to all aspects of social and institution regulation suggest the natural transparency, for him, of rule-based procedures that govern both social and material practice and the fine line he himself walks between miners and management as he works to shift inherited authority relations within a tightly regulated industry.

16.6.2   Educational-space gestures

Educational-space gestures embody P's notion that 'training works better with illustrations [demonstrations] than just talking about it' (61-62/8). P uses two different gestural forms to represent his notion of education. Both gestural forms express the cliché that showing works better than telling. In P's regulatory framework, miners' indigenous knowledge provides a ground for understanding, but P must build them up to achieve workplace transformation. This analysis shows the effects of training dependent upon private industry to educate workers.

16.6.2.1   *Illustrate-space 1 gestures*

Illustrate-space 1 gestures define the boundary of gestural space at the interface of speaker and audience. The gesture locates P and his audience on opposite sides of an invisible institutional line defined by notions of expertise and education. P can open the boundary to determine 'what [his audience's] needs are' (14a/77-8), but the gesture can also limit miners' access to P's (expert) gestural space. The gesture iconically imitates the stone-dust barrier or flaps in the model which can open and close to regulate ventilation in the system.

16.6.2.2   *Illustrate-space 2 gestures*

Illustrate-space 2 gestures imitate the rolling motion of the final big explosion ('the big one' 134/21B) in the gestural space between speaker and audience. This gesture thus depicts what happens if miners do not follow the safety instructions presented in the seminar within a controlled environment. P explains: 'You can't have a explosion underground and have a person there to try and show them' (1C/145). 'Now they see it in a controlled environment' (168), and they can 'imagine it to themself [*sic*]' how it would be if they were present (2C/170-71).

P uses this gesture to contrast his own training methods with the former trainer's static notions of education (7/1-58 and 10/1, 59) which consisted mostly of talking. P explains that his illustrations are 'very learning' (124) 'because now they can see' (15B/125) how explosions happen.

P's illustrate-space gestures work together to assert the value of experience on two levels. First, they embody the notion that miners can apply their experience to understand the scientific demonstrations in the training session. Second, the notion of experience as a ground for education enables P to argue that his own workspace experience provides a better basis for training than the academic format of previous training sessions. This insistence on experience as the ground for understanding is not value-free, however. P does not assert a radical third conclusion that valorizes miners' experience in the workspace. Illustrate-space gestures depict the movement of information from trainer to miner at the front of P's gestural space, where knowledge is 'given', 'shown' and 'illustrated' to miners in a one-way notion of training.

P's illustrate-space gestures show how social and institutional relations grounded in apartheid continue to be embodied in notions of training that were 'always there' (227). Given the linguistic complexity of South African mines, the limitations of Fanakalo (a pidgin used on the mine) as a medium of communication, and his own experience underground, it is not surprising that P might conclude, 'it's easier to, er, show a person (229/3D) what to do than just to tell him' (229–231). Ultimately, however, training must 'build up' miners so that they are no longer dependent on others' showing and telling.

16.6.2.3   *Build-up space gestures*

Build-up space gestures depict notions of growth and expansion. P first uses the gesture to depict the 'feedback' (12A and 13A/76) he hopes to extract from his audience in training. P depicts education as a process that 'builds them up' (197/18C) so they can 'look after those precautions' (200). Otherwise, 'uneducated' miners will carelessly destroy safety barriers they do not understand (203–207). For P, 'build-up' gestures do not depict a radical change in attitude. Like other aspects of P's regulatory framework, build-up gestures depict the increasing complexity of P's illustrations that 'build up small and small and we carry on...' (1H/472).

16.6.3 Disciplinary space

Disciplinary space represents the link between the systems perspective represented in the model and their experience underground. Because he has worked underground, P easily moves between disciplinary perspectives. When miners have difficulty envisioning the scale of the model and the role of ventilation in a methane explosion, P blames their lack of education and the limits of a single training session. He does not examine (reflexively) his own assumptions about the transparency of scientific knowledge and its relation to material experience.

16.6.3.1 *Model-space gestures*

Model-space gestures depict the model of the mine used in training. Model space is co-present with mine space when P describes what interviewers would see 'as soon as [they] walk[ed] in' to the model (6E/314). This shift in gestural viewpoint from an observer viewpoint (outside and above the model) to a character viewpoint (within the model) confused interviewers, who believed that the model would be 'the size of the office' – the same size as a mine haulageway underground.

16.6.3.2 *Visualize-space gestures*

Visualize-space gestures depict the immediate processes of apprehending meaning embodied in the model (24F/388; 23F/389). In the visualize-space gesture, the hand moves forward from the eye in the direction of the audience. The gesture depicts P's assertion that miners will look at the model and immediately 'visionalize in their head' (12E) how events happened underground. When they see the model, he believes, 'immediately they realize' (11B/116) the rationale for safety practices underground. P tells interviewers that the model was originally built 'to show [lawyers and judges] visually what happened' (10D/280) because they lacked mining experience and could not visualize events like miners. Trainers decided to reuse the model to help miners visualize the role of methane in a disaster.

Although different in form, the visualize-see gesture is similar in semantic content to Brookes' 'clever gesture' (Brookes, 2000). Brookes (2000) describes how the 'clever gesture' indicates 'seeing' (as a core concept) as well as a person's insider/outsider status within township communities. Glossed in the sense of streetwise or 'city slick', the gesture can be extended to mean: *You are streetwise, Look, Wake up, Be alert, Watch out, I want to see you, He's observing* or *I see you* (as a greeting). Brookes (2004) argues that quotable South African gestures like the 'clever ges-ture' reflect 'key ideological concerns' in black South African townships that can be more effectively or safely expressed in gesture. Although P's gestural form suggests a more literal notion of 'seeing', his gesture also expresses ideological assumptions about the immediacy of scientific understanding. This notion of 'seeing' validates P's authority as one who apprehends the relation of the scientific model to workplace experience.

16.6.3.3   Scale-space gestures

Scale-space gestures depict the mathematical relationship between model space and haulage space: 1 metre on the model (BH wide paral-lel) equals 47–50 metres underground (13B). P believes that miners will 'immediately... get the distance and the size of the model' (123/14B) when he tells them that the scale is 1 : 47 (119). P tells interviewers that the model's designer 'built it to precise as possible' (302). The designer decided on a scale (22D) 'to make it not too big (308/24D) and not too small' (308/1E) and he 'even built the machines to that scale' (301/5E). P's explanation confuses interviewers who cannot enter the imaginary workspace P constructs in his gestures: 'As soon as you walk in and I tell you: "Listen, this is 1 meter here and it's 47 meters underground (8E)", if you work underground, you immediately (12D) can visionalize (11D, *sic*) it in the back of your head' (314–319). Not surprisingly, miners are also confused about the 1 : 47 scale model and its relation to problems of ventilation and dust control in the actual training session.

16.7   Transforming the workspace imagination

The complexity of individual motivations complicates any attempt to generalize about training and education in pre- and post-apartheid South Africa. Trainers' assumptions about miners influenced how they interpreted miners' questions. But liberal assumptions about literacy and education can also produce misinterpretations of miners' responses. It was not always possible to disambiguate these two positions in practice.

In speech, Trainer P's assumptions seem to acknowledge the realities of the inherited legacy of apartheid and the constraints of on-site training sessions that cannot educate miners in gas mechanics and engineering safety in two hours. In South Africa, these 'realities' were institutionalized in a large body of industrial relations and educational research that attempted to describe black South Africans' attitudes to work, health and safety issues. Not surprisingly, published accounts of black aptitudes and attitudes reflect racialist ideologies that depict black workers as children or naifs who hold absurd and primitive beliefs about material reality (e.g. Franz et al., 1955). Neutral or race-blind accounts (e.g. Tustin, 1994), on the other hand, fail to consider the continuing legacy of apartheid on the shop floor. The assumptions that motivate Trainer P's instructional strategies may thus reflect deep-seated prejudices (including assumptions about black literacy) even in the context of training that attempts to 'build up' workers' competence to prevent disaster.

The rhetorical situations in which experts communicate risk can also affect workplace training. Trainers must convince individuals to act safely, for example, but training sites may not allow the kinds of individualized instruction tailored to particular workers' needs. Trainers who work through translators may not be able to control the meaning and persuasiveness of language in new and different cultural and rhetorical contexts. When trainers speak to large groups (in some cases as many as 100–150 workers), they must develop arguments that will persuade audiences with diverse education, experience and understanding. When trainers address these large groups, they must address individuals with political agendas, language differences, and racial and ethnic backgrounds that create resistance and hostility. This resistance may be visible, when labour leaders deliberately use group sessions as a forum for communicating their own agendas, or silent, when translators misinterpret or misrepresent critical details to protect individual mineworkers or management. Many problems occur, however, because trainers have no training in pedagogy and often engage in no prior planning.

The present analysis suggests that analysis of gesture can provide insight into the processes of thinking for speaking that trainers apply in the workplace (cf. Slobin, 2003), but it does not suggest that technical expertise necessarily produces rhetorical competence or a reflective mastery of gestural production. More important, this analysis cautions us that experts may embody ideological frameworks in their gestures that reflect the dark side of 'mastery' in a racially stratified workplace (cf. Haviland, 2003), particularly when subjects lack regulatory power to transform existing practices (Bollens, 2002, p. 35). Unlike previous studies that have attempted to understand gesture as a function of race and culture or a more generalizable human capacity for imagistic thought, the present project demonstrates the interplay between an individual's construction of identity *in* gestural space and the larger regulatory frameworks that govern safe (good) behaviour in the workplace.[4] These frameworks can then be negotiated to achieve a more general workplace transformation.

On a theoretical level, this analysis suggests that gesture may reflect social and institutional norms of appropriateness, tone and style – in the same way that individuals apply verbal and stylistic norms of appropriateness and tone across diverse social situations (cf. Kendon, 1996). It suggests that within-culture differences in gesture may reflect differences in occupation and experience (Efron 1941/1972, p. 145; Sauer, 2003), and it provides the ground for further *cross-cultural* comparisons to determine (a) whether 'specific domains' (such as instructions) might produce quotable gestures regardless of culture; (b) whether similar forms might convey different meanings in different cultures; and (c) whether gestures relate to other processes of language acquisition in specific cultures (Johnson et al., 1981). Similarly, this study begins to fill gaps in previous studies which have not articulated the 'conditioning background' of gestural interactions (Poyatos, 1981, p. 397), differentiated within-culture differences between urban and rural speakers, or used native speakers to articulate the paralinguistic aspects of gesture (Poyatos, 1981, p. 382). We intend to pursue this line of inquiry in future research.

Notes

1. The present work was funded by NSF Grant no. 9812059. I am grateful to Rachelle Hollander for her continuing support and to Heather Brookes of the HSRC for her comments and collaboration. I am grateful to Carnegie Mellon graduate students Susan Lawrence, Terri Palmer and Angela Meyer, and undergraduates Anne Garibaldi, Laura Martin and Amy Cyphert for their assistance in this project.
2. The terms 'white' and Afrikaner are not redundant. Traditional 'white' Afrikaners have ambiguous and complicated relationships with so-called Bruin Afrikaners, black, and mixed race mother-tongue speakers of Afrikaans (Motsemme, 2002, p. 660).
3. Moodie and Ndatshe (1994) describe the often conflicting tensions that mine inspectors faced under apartheid. On the one hand, they were conscious of their duty to enforce an increasing array of rationalized mine regulations. But they could also be bribed or persuaded to overlook safety infractions that

might interfere with production. Under apartheid, policies of job reservation encouraged mines to develop job titles like Inspector I and Inspector II when qualified whites were not available to fill certain required jobs on the mine. White miners often supervised from a distance (Moodie and Ndatshe, 1994).

4. Kendon (1996) and Roth (2002) provide useful reviews of research in gesture.

References

Barton, D. (1994) 'Globalisation and diversification: Two opposing influences on local literacies' in D. Barton (ed.) *Sustaining Local Literacies* (Clevedon: Education for Development), 3–8.

Bollens, S.A. (2002) 'Urban planning and intergroup conflict: Confronting a fractured public interest', *Journal of the American Planning Association*, 68 (1), 22–42.

Brookes, H.J. (2000) 'O clever. 'He's streetwise': When gestures become quotable: the case of the clever gesture', *Gesture* 1(2), 167–84.

Chawla, P. and R.M. Krauss (1994) 'Gesture and speech in spontaneous and rehearsed narrative', *Journal of Experimental Psychology*, 30, 580–601.

Chief Inspector of Mines (2001) *Chief Inspector of Mines Annual Report Calendar Year 2000*. 26 February. http://www.gov.za/documents/combsubmr.htm, date accessed 30 January 2008.

Cobley, A.G. (1997) *The Rules of the Game: Struggles in Black Recreation and Social Welfare Policy in South Africa* (Westport, Conn. and London: Greenwood Press).

Crijns, A.G.J. (1959) *Race Relations and Race Attitudes in South Africa: a Socio-Psychological Study of Human Relationships in a Multi-Racial Society* (Nijmegen: Drukkerij Gebr. Janssen).

Dubow, S. (1989) *Racial Segregation and the Origins of Apartheid in South Africa, 1919–1936* (New York: St. Martin's Press).

Dubow, S. (1992) 'Afrikaner nationalism, apartheid, and the conceptualization of "race" ', *Journal of African History*, 33, 209–37.

Efron, D. (1941/1972) *Gesture, Race and Culture: a Tentative Study of the Spatio-temporal and 'Linguistic' Aspects of the Gestural Behavior of Eastern Jews and Southern Italians in New York City, Living under Similar as well as Different Environmental Conditions* (The Hague: Mouton).

Emmorey, K., D. Corina and U. Bellugi (1995) 'Differential processing of topographic and referential functions of space' in K. Emmorey and J.S. Reilly (eds) *Language, Gesture, and Space* (Hillsdale, NJ: Erlbaum), 43–62.

Franz, G.H., T.S. van Rooyen, E.F. Potgieter, B.S. van As and W.E. Barker (1955) *Bantu Education: Oppression or Opportunity?* (Stellenbosch: South African Bureau of Racial Affairs).

Godwin, P. (1997) *Mukiwa: a White Boy in Africa* (New York: HarperPerennial).

Gumperz, J.J. (1992) 'Interviewing in intercultural situations' in P. Drew and J. Heritage (eds) *Talk at Work: Interaction in Institutional Settings* (Cambridge: Cambridge UP), 302–27.

Hanks, W.F. (1992) 'The indexical ground of deictic reference' in A. Duranti and C. Goodwin (eds) *Rethinking Context: Language as an Interactive Phenomenon* (Cambridge: Cambridge UP), 43–76.

Haviland, J.B. (2003) 'Master speakers, master gesturers' (Conference paper) Fest in Honor of David McNeill (Chicago, Ill.: University of Chicago).

Hyslop, J. (2000) 'The imperial working class makes itself white: White labourers in Britain, Australia, and South Africa before the first world war', *Journal of Historical Sociology*, 12(4), 398–421.

Johnson, H.G., P. Ekman and W.V. Friesen (1981) 'Communicative body movements: American emblems' in A. Kendon (ed.) *Nonverbal Communication, Interaction and Gesture*. Selections from Semiotica (Approaches to Semiotics, 41) (The Hague: Mouton), 401–19.

Kendon, A. (1996) 'An agenda for gesture studies', *Semiotic Review of Books*, 7(3) http://www.univie.ac.at/Wissenschaftstheorie/srb/srb/gesture.html, date accessed 30 January 2008.

Korf, L. and J. Malan (2002) 'Threat to ethnic identity: the experience of white Afrikaans-speaking participants in postapartheid South Africa', *Journal of Social Psychology*, 142(2), 149–69.

Kraak, A. (2002) 'Competing education and training policies: a "systematic" versus "unit standards" approach'. HSRC Occasional papers. http://www.hsrc.ac.za/papers/pp6.html, date accessed 31 January 2008.

Krog, A. (2000) *Country of My Skull: Guilt, Sorrow and the Limits of Forgiveness in the New South Africa* (New York: Three Rivers Press).

Leon, R.N., Q.W. Davies, M.D.G. Salamon and J.C.A. Davies (1994). *Report of the Commission of Inquiry into Safety and Health in the Mining Industry*, vol. 1 (Braamfontein: Commission of Inquiry into Safety and Health in the Mining Industry).

Lester, A., E. Nel and T. Binns (2000) 'South Africa's current transition in temporal and spatial context', *Antipode*, 32(2), 135–51.

Levinson, S.C. (1996) 'Language and space', *Annual Review of Anthropology*, 25, 353–82.

Liddell, S. (1995) 'Real, surrogate, and token space: Grammatical consequences in ASL' in K. Emmorey and J. S. Reilly (eds) *Language, Gesture, and Space* (Hillsdale, NJ: Lawrence Erlbaum Associates), 19–42.

McCarthy, S. (1997) 'Personal interview, SA Chamber of Mines', Johannesburg, August.

MacCrone, I.D. (1937) *Race Attitudes in South Africa: Historical, Experimental and Psychological Studies* (Johannesburg: University of the Witwatersrand).

McNeill, D. (1992) *Hand and Mind: What Gestures Reveal about Thought* (Chicago: University of Chicago).

McNeill, D. and L.L. Pedelty (1995) 'Right brain and gesture' in K. Emmorey and J.S. Reilly (eds) *Language, Gesture, and Space* (Hillsdale, NJ: Erlbaum), 63–86.

Malan, R. (1990) *My Traitor's Heart: a South African Exile Returns to Face his Country, his Tribe, and his Conscience* (New York: Grove Press).

Mangena, M. (2001) 'Address by the Deputy Minister of Education, Mr. Mosibudi Mangena at the launch of the Maths and Science Campaign, June 25, 2001'. http://education.pwv.gov.za/Media/Mangena/June01/Maths%20Science%20Tech.htm, date accessed 31 January 2008.

Marais, G. and R. van der Kooy (eds) (1979) *South Africa's Urban Blacks: Problems and Challenges* (Pretoria: Centre for Management Studies).

Moodie, T.D. and V. Ndatshe (1994) *Men, Mines, and Migration* (Berkeley: University of California Press).

Motsemme, N. (2002) 'Gendered experiences of blackness in post-apartheid South Africa', *Social Identities*, 8(4), 647–73.

Pheta, R.T. (1982) 'Claimed proficiency of black mine employees in various languages'. (Research Report no. 5/83. Project no. GHQ01, November) (Johannesburg: Chamber of Mines).

Popke, E.J. (2003) 'Managing colonial alterity: Narratives of race, space, and labor in Durban, 1870–1920', *Journal of Historical Geography*, 29 (2), 248–67.

Poyatos, F. (1981) 'Gesture inventories: Fieldwork methodology and problems' in T.A. Seboek and J. Umiker-Seboek (eds) *Nonverbal Communication, Interaction, and Gesture* (The Hague: Mouton Publishers), 373–99.

Roth, W.M. (2002) 'Gestures: Their role in teaching and learning', *Review of Educational Literature*, 27(3), 365–92.

Sauer, B. (1999) 'Embodied experience: Representing risk in speech and gesture', *Discourse Studies*, 1(3), 321–54.

Sauer, B. (2003) *The Rhetoric of Risk: Technical Documentation in Hazardous Environments* (Mahwah, NJ: Lawrence Erlbaum Associates).

Sauer, B. and S. Lawrence (1997) *Kloppersbos Training Session Evaluation: Explosion and Rock Dusting. July 31, 1997* (Technical Report no. CSIR-1-1997) (Johannesburg: Council for Scientific and Industrial Research).

Sears, D.O. and P.J. Henry (2003) 'The origins of symbolic racism', *Journal of Personality and Social Psychology*, 85(2), 259–75.

Sharp, J. (2001) 'The questions of cultural difference: Anthropological perspectives in South Africa', *South African Journal of Ethnology*, 24(3), 67–74.

Slobin, D.I. (2003) 'Language and thought online: Cognitive consequences of linguistic relativity' in D. Gentner and S. Golding-Meadow (eds) *Language in Mind: Advances in the Study of Language and Thought* (Cambridge: MIT), 157–92.

South African Dept. of Education (1997) *General Policy for Technikon Instructional Programmes* (Report 150, January 1997) (Pretoria: Dept. of Education).

South African Dept. of Education (2001) *Policy Document on Adult Basic Education and Training*. http://education.pwv.gov.za/DoESites/ABET/ABETPolicy.htm, date accessed 31 January 2008.

Tustin, C. (1994) *Industrial Relations: a Psychological Approach* (Cape Town: Southern Book Publishers).

Index